BULBS

Four Seasons of Beautiful Blooms

LEWIS & NANCY HILL

A Garden Way Publishing Book

STOREY

STOREY COMMUNICATIONS, INC.

The mission of Storey Communications is to serve our customer by publishing practical information that encourages personal independencein harmony with the environment.

Edited by Liz Stell and Gwen W. Steege
Cover design by Greg Imhoff
Front cover photograph by David Cavagnaro
Back cover floral photograph by Richard Brown, author photograph by Martha Storey
Text design and production by Cindy McFarland
Production assistance by Susan Bernier
Line drawings by Elayne Sears
Indexed by Northwind Editorial Services
Photographs courtesy of the Netherlands Flower Bulb Information Center, unless otherwise noted

Garden Way Publishing was founded in 1973 as part of the Garden Way Incorporated Group of Companies, dedicated to bringing gardening information and equipment to as many people as possible. Today the name "Garden Way Publishing" is licensed to Storey Communications, Inc., in Pownal, Vermont. For a complete list of Garden Way Publishing titles call 1-800-827-8673. Garden Way Incorporated manufactures products in Troy, New York, under the Troy-Bilt® brand including garden tillers, chipper/shredders, mulching mowers, sicklebar mowers, and tractors. For information on any Garden Way Incorporated product, please call 1-800-345-4454.

Printed in the Canada by Interglobe Inc.

10 9 8 7 6 5 4 3 2

Library of Congress Cataloging-in-Publication Data

Hill, Lewis, 1924-
   Bulbs : four seasons of beautiful blooms / Lewis and Nancy Hill.
            p.   cm.
      "A Garden Way Publishing book."
      Includes index.
      ISBN 0-88266-878-1 (hc) — ISBN 0-88266-877-3 (pbk.)
      1. Bulbs. I. Hill, Nancy. II. Title.
SB425.H54   1994
635.9'44—dc20   94-14240
                                 CIP

Contents

Acknowledgments

We are grateful to all our bulb-growing friends for sharing their experiences with us,
and to the Netherlands Flower Bulb Information Center,
Dr. Leonard Perry, Brent and Becky Heath of the Daffodil Mart,
Elisabeth Delaney, Pat Hall, Tom and Beryl Smith, and Jane Johns.
Special thanks to our editor, Gwen Steege, for her unfailing patience and inspiration.

The Miracle of Bulbs

EACH FALL WHEN WE DIG HOLES in the soil and kneel to plant our plump brown tulip and daffodil bulbs, and scilla the size of small marbles, we realize that once again we're taking part in a miracle. Like the mythological Greek maiden Persephone, who disappeared underground for the winter months, these plain brown packets stay alive in the frozen earth and emerge in the spring transformed into beautiful red, gold, pink, blue, and multicolored blossoms of every shape and size imaginable.

The bulbs of summer, fall, and winter withdraw into themselves for a dormant period at some time during the year, too. We're always delighted when their first green shoots appear, whether they emerge from an amaryllis on our living room windowsill or poke through the soil from a lily bulb in the garden.

Growing bulbs isn't a complicated procedure and, unlike many other projects, you can be assured of success on your first attempt. But to get them to bloom successfully year after year, it is important to know how to treat them properly. In our nursery business we frequently received calls about bulbous plants:

When should we plant our bulbs? How deep? In sun or shade? In dry or wet soil? Should we cut them after flowering? How do we divide them, store the tender ones, and force spring bulbs indoors during the winter? We forgot to plant our tulips last fall — what should we do with them now? Which bulbs naturalize easily?

In this book we hope to answer those questions and many more, to help you enjoy the bulbs you have, to introduce you to new exciting ones from all over the world, to spend your dollars wisely, and to clear up any mysteries about bulbs. Except, of course, the wonder of it all — no one can give a logical explanation of a miracle.

1

Becoming Acquainted
with Bulbs

WHEN WE STROLL AROUND our gardens in the springtime, we feel lucky to be able to enjoy beautiful bulbs that grow so well with so little work and expense. During the famous tulip craze in Holland in the early seventeenth century bulbs sold for thousands of dollars each. Imagine how much the far lovelier ones we grow now would be worth at those prices!

We are gardening at a time in history when in our own modest gardens we can grow extraordinary bulbs that only a few decades ago were not available. To see their ancestors in the last century we would have had to climb Himalayan mountaintops or travel to the jungles of Africa. Fortunately, horticulturists not only have collected wild species from all over the world, but they have hybridized common plants into fantastic new colors and forms. At a country wedding last summer we were surrounded with enormous bouquets of exquisite scented pink and red lilies that a Turkish sultan would have given half his harem to possess.

The wide diversity of bulbous plants available often surprises even experienced gardeners. The blooms come in an amazing number of colors, shapes, forms, and sizes; the plants range from tiny 2-inch-tall wild hyacinths on stony hillsides in Turkey to vigorous 7-foot-tall Bellingham Hybrid lilies in our backyards.

People who don't garden at all may not be aware that so many of the common flowers they see blooming throughout the different seasons arise from bulbous roots. Dainty white snowdrops (*Galanthus*), the true harbingers of spring, sometimes push through the snow before it has completely melted in late winter, beginning a succession of welcome spring bulbs. Spring snowflakes (*Leucojum vernum*) also appear early,

3

along with blue and white squills (*Scilla*), glory-of-the-snow (*Chionodoxa*), and the common crocuses that delight us all with masses of yellow, purple, and white blooms. Narcissus, tulips, and hyacinths are not far behind, and meanwhile native spring bulbs carpet the woodland floors with lush green wild garlic, yellow trout lilies; pink and white spring beauties; and red, white, and painted trilliums.

Dwarf iris begin to bloom later, along with lily-of-the-valley, ushering in the warmer weather. It is time then to set out the tender bulbous plants: dahlias, gladioli, cannas, and tuberous begonias. Before they begin to flower, a succession of hardy bulbs brighten the summer garden with blooms, including the lilies, alliums, and irises — Siberian, bearded, and Japanese.

As summer days become shorter, buds form on the montbretia (*Crocosmia*), and the lycoris and autumn crocuses suddenly pop up and bloom. After snow falls and winter takes over outdoors, bulbous houseplants including amaryllis, calla lilies, gloxinias, and cyclamens brighten our living rooms. When the days gradually begin to lengthen again, we bring in for forcing the potted narcissus, tulips, and hyacinths stored in the cellar since October. Finally the last bloom fades, and our thoughts turn to outdoors and the first snowdrops. The bulbs and the gardening seasons have come full circle.

Each bulbous plant we cultivate originated from a wild species that was well adapted to its own unique climate somewhere in the world. Both its hardiness and the conditions it needs in the garden depend upon where it came from. Many of our hardy bulbs are natives of the cold, mountainous regions of Turkey, Iran, Russia, China, and Japan and of the northeastern United States and Canada. Most of them don't mind being frozen and covered with snow for several months, nor are they bothered by warm summers that are either unusually wet or dry during their dormant season. But there are exceptions. Certain bulbs, such as those native to the area between the Sierras and Rocky Mountains, can withstand cold snowy winters but thrive only in the dry summers of the West or Midwest.

Those from southern Europe, central Asia, the Far East, the tip of South Africa, and other areas with mild climates and wet winters are hardy in similar climates. They are considered tender bulbs in the northern United States and northern Europe, as are those from spots with cool winters but rainy, warm summers, including southern Chile and Argentina, and the South African mountains. Although some of these plants have adapted to the temperate climate, others, such as gladioli, dahlias, and tuberous begonias, must be grown as tender perennials and taken indoors and stored for the winter.

Bulbs in History

Not surprisingly, people have cultivated bulbs since the beginning of recorded time. Although our primitive ancestors no doubt first valued them for their food and medicinal value, they eventually began to appreciate their cheery colors and beautiful shapes.

We know that Minoans on the island of Crete grew and treasured crocuses before Greece became the center of the civilized world, that ancient Egyptians and Syrians prized irises, and that Sumerians cherished lilies. The Babylonians, too, cultivated various bulbs, probably in their famous hanging gardens, one of the seven wonders of the ancient world.

A variety of lilies, irises, and other bulbous plants have bloomed for many centuries in the great gardens of China and Japan. The Chinese have long used certain lilies medicinally and even ground them into a starchy flour for cooking.

The predecessors of most of the lovely lilies we now grow were transported to Europe from the Far East, first by early silk, tea, and spice traders and then later by missionaries and horticulturists.

While bulbs are dormant they are easier to carry around than many other plants, and they went with ease wherever people traveled. Among the many bulbs that reached Europe from other areas were tulips, imported from Turkey by an ambassador in the mid-1500s. They flourished in the cool, humid conditions of Holland, Britain, and Belgium, and quickly became the most popular flowers in Europe. They were even used as currency. The narcissus, which originated in southern Europe, quickly became beloved in Britain and northern Europe where gardeners collected and planted their seeds, developing — mostly by accident — larger and more showy kinds.

The Dutch took their tulip bulbs with them when they emigrated to New Amsterdam, soon after they bought Manhattan Island at a bargain price in 1623. The English and French pioneers packed easy-to-handle narcissus bulbs along with their necessities soon after they began settlements in North America. Women frequently traded with each other the few kinds that were available. As the continent was explored, affluent settlers grew tulips and hyacinths on their large estates, but most people chose to plant the longer-lived, easier-to-care-for narcissus. The tough, golden yellow, double-flowering ones commonly called daffodils were the most popular, but the fragrant, single white narcissus with bright red edges on their tiny cups were also prized. Some of both are still blooming after two centuries.

We like to explore abandoned farm sites scattered through the back hills of Vermont, where often the only evidence of former habitation is a nearly filled-in cellar hole, stone walls, or rotted wooden fence rails. Plants provide living reminders that there were once people around, however: a few decrepit fruit trees, a lilac bush, a rhubarb plant, and a clump of rugged yellow daffodils bloom bravely among encroaching conifers.

Although it might seem that the world has been thoroughly explored, botanists even now continue to find new plants and to add more species to the family of bulbs. Some of the most obscure specimens have characteristics that may fit into the hybridizing program of horticulturists, perhaps by adding a new color, scent, or vigor to the bulbs we already grow.

True Bulbs, and their Relatives

The term *bulb* is frequently used loosely. When we owned a daylily nursery, nearly every day at least one customer asked about buying our daylily "bulbs." Because daylilies (*Hemerocallis*) have fleshy fibrous roots, it is easy to confuse them and many other plants that have lilylike flowers with the true lilies (*Lilium*) that grow from bulbs.

Even in this book we use the term *bulb* freely; the plants described all have bulbous underground stems that store nutrients during a dormant season, but technically not all are true bulbs. Many grow instead from corms, rhizomes, tubers, or tuber-corms.

Onions, lilies, and tulips are classic examples of **true bulbs.** All grow from enlarged buds surrounded by modified leaves called scales, although on onions and tulips these may not look like scales because they are densely packed together. Lily bulbs, on the other hand, have loose and conspicuous scales that you can easily pick off one by one and, if you want, can use to start new plants. True bulbs always have pointed tops and divide naturally each year.

Tunicate bulbs, such as tulips, are enclosed within a papery outer cover described as a tunic, and the embryonic flower is fully formed inside it. While the bulb grows, new bulbs form inside it, and as they grow they emerge and finally split from the parent. They are called bulblets, and the larger ones often bloom the following year.

True bulbs

Corms resemble bulbs, and it isn't always easy to tell the difference. Gladioli, crocuses, and freesias all grow from corms, which are actually solid stems. Like a bulb, a corm has a terminal bud at the top that grows to form the stalk, leaves, and flower buds, but unlike a true bulb, each summer a new corm forms on top of the old one. The old corm disappears and the roots at the base of the new corm pull it downward into the hole left by the decayed corm. Small corms, called cormels, grow around the base of the new bulb.

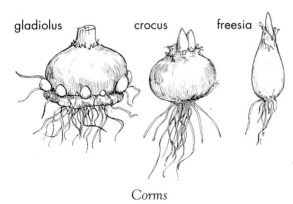

Corms

Rhizomes are also modified stems, sometimes called stem tubers. Unlike corms, which grow upwards, they spread horizontally under-ground or on the surface of the ground. Roots grow from their undersides, and sprouts emerge from the upper sections to become stems, leaves, and flowers. Rhizomes reproduce from these spreading layers, sometimes very rapidly, as in the case of invasive weeds such as quackgrass and bindweed. Bearded irises and cannas both grow from rhizomes but behave much better. In plants such as these, the rhizomes lie either on or just below the soil surface. Plants like quackgrass, however, can grow and reproduce at depths of over 2 feet, a devastating characteristic that makes them the bane of any gardener's existence.

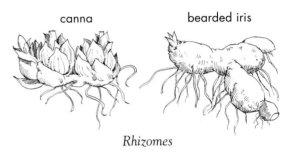

Rhizomes

Dahlias and caladiums (as well as potatoes and Jerusalem artichokes) grow from **tubers,** which are swollen rhizomes (fat roots) of various shapes. Tubers usually grow just below the soil surface and, like bulbs, store food for the plant. Buds on the tubers grow into the stems, leaves, and flowers, and a cluster of roots forms at the base. Tubers multiply by division, and as they divide, the old tuber deteriorates.

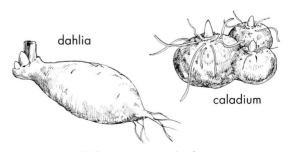

Tuberous root and tuber

Tuberous begonias, ranunculuses, cyclamens, and certain anemones grow in a slightly different manner, from **tuber-corms** that are flat disks, each shaped somewhat like a top. One or more buds emerge from the top, and fibrous roots grow from the bottom. Unlike corms that decay at the end of the growing season, tuber-corms grow larger with age.

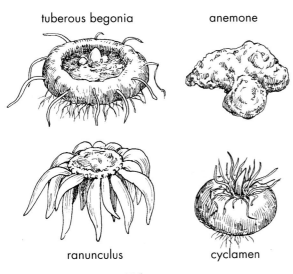

tuberous begonia

anemone

ranunculus

cyclamen

Tuber-corms

Whether bulbous plants grow from a true bulb, corm, tuber, or rhizome, their ability to store nutrients makes them special. Not only can they often endure harsh climatic conditions during dormancy, like camels without water in the desert, but they also require amazingly little maintenance once they are planted. They grow and bloom quickly because they get a jump start from their self-contained storehouse of nutrients.

A Bulb by Any Other Name

Although "guinea-hen flower" is certainly a more colorful name than *Fritillaria*, we use the latter and other botanical names for plants throughout this text. Common names are usually more fun, but scientific, botanical nomenclature is more precise. Botanical names are standardized throughout the world, whereas common names vary widely from place to place. *Narcissus* is the botanical name for the genus that includes the daffodils and jonquils, for instance, but many people use the terms interchangeably when referring to these spring bulbs. Another reason to use the scientific name is that the common name may refer to many different plants. We've heard people use the term "Turk's Cap Lily" for "Tiger Lily" (*Lilium lancifolium*), for Bellingham Hybrid lilies, for *L. superbum*, and even for certain daylilies.

Although botanical names may seem well standardized, we can't be sure that even they will always stay the same, since plant classifications change from time to time. You will find some plant names have another name listed beside them. The tiger lily is not only *L. lancifolium*, but also *L. tigrinum*, the name it went by until recently. The names change because botanists discover more information about a plant or the nomenclature may have been in dispute. *Hortus Third* (Macmillan, 1976) is the standard reference text for most of the plant industry in the United States, and the one we use. European botanists, as well as some Americans, use the Royal Horticultural Society classification. The two sources are not always in agreement, another indication that in this world there are few absolutes.

Each family of bulbous plants, like all other plants, has botanical subdivisions — genera, species, varieties, and named cultivars that are usually hybrids of different species within the same genus. Crocus, for instance, belongs to the Iris Family (*Iridaceae*). The *Crocus* genus has seventy-five to eighty different species, including some fall bloomers and the spring-flowering *C. vernus* from which most of our garden crocus have been developed. Within most species

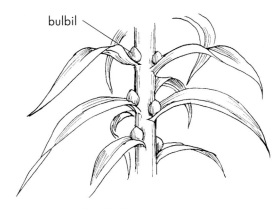

bulbil

Bulbils are small bulblike structures on the flowering stems of some bulbous plants.

there are also varieties, which are closely related natural variations of the species. Var. argenteus, for example, indicates a variety of C. *biflorus*, the Scotch crocus. Named cultivars such as 'Peter Pan' are enclosed in single quotation marks.

The world of bulbs has its own lingo, like any specialty. *Bulblets*, as we noted, are small bulbs that form underground at the edge of a larger bulb. Similar structures that grow on corms are called *cormels*. *Bulbils* are small bulblike structures that emerge among the flowers or leaves on the flowering stems of certain bulbous plants. *Scales* are modified leaves that may cover a bud and in a true bulb they form the base. The *tunic*, as we mentioned, is the thin, paperlike layer that covers certain bulbs. For other terms that may be unfamiliar, see the glossary in the appendix.

Of course, all of us know super gardeners who don't know a scale from a cormel, and their gardens flourish. But gardening is always more enjoyable when you are aware of what is happening underground as well as above and are able to communicate in the language of bulbs with other growers.

Fitting Bulbs into Your Landscape

MANY YEARS AGO when we were driving home from a wholesale nursery with a load of plants, we stopped to buy gasoline at a small store in rural New England. The elderly woman who pumped the gas asked what kind of tomato plants we were hauling. When we told her, she remarked, "You mean they're flowers! What do you use 'em for? You can't eat 'em, can you?"

We had to admit we couldn't, and knew better than to try to convince a practical Yankee that, as Emerson pointed out, "Beauty is its own excuse for being."

She probably would not approve of the many bulbs we have scattered around our hilly landscape, although if she could see them in bloom, we hope she might understand. In times past, certain bulbous plants have provided food for human consumption, and in eastern Mediterranean regions today a staple cereal called salep is made from orchid tubers. In North America, however, we grow bulbs only because they look nice.

Some of the most beautiful displays of spring bulbs to be found anywhere are at botanical gardens, among them Longwood Gardens in the Brandywine Valley of Pennsylvania, once the country home of Pierre du Pont. Each spring tens of thousands of daffodils border garden paths, surround pools, and cover fields in golden yellow waves. Masses of tulips, grouped according to color, also provide feasts for the eye and soul. The beds are visually exciting particularly because colorful underplantings and borders accent the blooms. Carpets of light blue forget-me-nots contrast with yellow and white narcissus, vivid peach violas complement creamy peach tulips, and bright primulas and tiny pink English daisies provide similar foils for other bulbs.

Bulbs in Home Landscapes

How can a gardener at home use bulbs as effectively? The experts at botanical gardens have obvious advantages. At Longwood we noticed teams of workers moving unobtrusively among the visitors, doing their digging, fertilizing, clipping, and weeding. They have greenhouses for forcing and beds that have been skillfully designed. With their large budgets and large staffs they can afford to remove every tulip and hyacinth bulb after its blooming season and replant the beautiful large beds with other blossoming plants. Furthermore, because the grounds are so well manicured, very few weed seeds blow in from surrounding unmowed pastures and vacant lots, as they do in many country gardens.

Even though we don't have all the advantages of a large arboretum, home gardeners can have impressive plantings even on a small lot. The horticulturists at Longwood must work within limitations of space, climate, time, and budget, just as the rest of us do. Fortunately, unless we choose the newest cultivars, bulbous plants are inexpensive. Most spread naturally, too, and don't need a lot of maintenance once they are established.

Bulbs can fit into many different spots in a home landscape; where you put them may depend upon their vigor, longevity, and invasive habits, as well as their size, color, and blooming season. Consider some of the following plantings, which illustrate the wide range of traditional uses of bulbs.

Beds and Borders

"Bed" usually refers to a cultivated plot of any size, ordinarily planted with a single bulb type or cultivar. It can be a huge area filled with massive drifts of bloom or a simple, narrow strip alongside a path or road or around a garden structure such as a lamp post, sundial, or lawn ornament. "Border" usually refers to combinations of plants and can include herbaceous perennials, annuals, and sometimes shrubs as well as bulbs. You can choose delicate bulbs as well as vigorous bulbs for beds and borders since they need to be cultivated, mulched, and kept free from weeds and grass. For such spots, suitable bulb or bulblike plants might include some of the following:

Spring bloomers — hyacinths, narcissus, anemones, hybrid tulips
Summer bloomers — lilies, irises; tender kinds such as gladioli, dahlias, tuberous begonias
Fall bloomers — autumn crocuses, colchicums, cannas, late dahlias, lycoris

Cut Flower Gardens

Such gardens are usually planted in an out-of-the-way spot without much thought to their landscaping potential. Plant bulbs in rows for easy care. We reserve a few rows in our vegetable garden for this purpose. Good bulbs for cutting include these:

Spring bloomers — hyacinths, narcissus, tulips, anemones
Summer bloomers — dahlias, irises, gladioli, lilies, tuberous begonias
Fall bloomers — autumn crocuses, colchicums, dwarf cannas

Ground Covers & Naturalized Areas

Banks, slopes, or other places that are too steep or rocky to mow or too shady for grass to grow well are ideal spots for bulb ground covers. Vigorous types that perennialize easily and spread rapidly by seeds or offsets, or both, are best for this purpose.

Corners or edges of lawns, among trees and shrubs, around ponds, and semi-wild spots that get only occasional mowing are potential places for naturalizing. Vigorous, long-lasting, easy-care bulbs, especially the wild species, usually naturalize well.

Naturalized daffodils are the ideal solution for landscaping a rocky hillside.

Spring bloomers — *Crocus vernum*, grape hyacinths (*Muscari armeniacum*), snowdrops (*Galanthus nivalis*)

Summer bloomers — dwarf iris (*Iris reticulata*), lily-of-the-valley (*Convallaria*), ornamental onion (*Allium oreophilum*)

Fall bloomers — autumn crocus (*Colchicum autumnale*)

For more useful bulbs for ground covers and for naturalizing see chapter 6.

Rock Gardens

Naturally rocky areas make good homes for bulbs, as do specially constructed mounds of rocks and soil located on a gentle slope in a sunny spot with good drainage. The best bulbs

Group same-colored blossoms for best effect.

for such locations are vigorous, shallow-rooted, low-growing plants that need little care and do not require much moisture. Among them are the following:

Spring bloomers — *Anemone blanda, Bulbocodium vernum,* crocuses, *Muscari,* trout lilies, species tulips, miniature narcissus
Summer bloomers — certain *Alliums, Iris reticulata, Ranunculus amplexicaulis, Oxalis*
Fall bloomers — colchicums

The Idiosyncrasies of Bulbs

Before planting bulbs on your property, familiarize yourself with their special characteristics. Spring bulbs, for instance, unlike most herbaceous plants do not have interesting foliage to display when they are not in bloom. Narcissus and tulip leaves can be downright unattractive for a month or more after the flowers fade, especially in a cool, damp climate where the greenery lasts longer. Consequently, you may want either to set shallow-rooted bedding plants on top of deep-rooted bulbs or to tuck the bulbs into empty spots in a perennial border

A dependable stand of perennial phlox hides the dying foliage of spring-blooming narcissus.

RICHARD BROWN

These spring bulbs will be followed by a succession of perennial plants throughout summer.

Asiatic lilies provide a welcome splash of color in this shady garden with hosta and veronica.

where the growing foliage of nearby herbaceous perennials will hide the dying greenery.

Like herbaceous perennials, the blooming time of most bulbs is limited to only a few weeks, and the duration depends both on the kind and the weather conditions. In northern areas where winters last late, spring can sometimes be disappointingly short if warm weather suddenly terminates the blooming season of daffodils and tulips.

Most bulbs that are readily available grow over a wide spectrum of climates and soil types. Some are fussy about sun and shade require-

ments, however, and for these bulbs to thrive you must provide them with the conditions they prefer.

Spring bulbs, as a rule, have the same sun and shade requirements as many spring-blooming wildflowers. They need bright spring sunshine during their active growing and blooming time, but can tolerate summer shade. Consequently, some can thrive when planted under deciduous shrubs and trees that cast partial shade during their summer dormant season.

Few bulbs do well in deep shade although some native plants such as jack-in-the-pulpit

Gaily-colored lilies (front) combine well with (clockwise from top) purple loosestrife, meadowsweet, daylilies, and lady's-mantle in this old-fashioned perennial bed.

(*Arisaema*) and lily-of-the-valley (*Convallaria*), thrive in shady spots such as the north side of a building or beneath trees or tall shrubs.

Most summer-flowering bulbs need sun, but bloom best when they receive some light afternoon shade. For instance, when lilies are shielded from sun during the warmest part of the afternoon, the blooms last longer and don't fade as quickly. For these reasons you may want to plant certain bulbs in a spot where a tall hedge, solid fence, wall, or building provides shade in the afternoon but still lets bright skylight hit the bed. Tall herbaceous perennials, annuals, shrubs, or slender trees can also be used as sun-shields for part of the day, as long as their roots do not compete with the bulbs' roots.

The fall bloomers, such as autumn crocus, need spring and fall sunshine to flourish, but need no sunlight during their summer rest period.

For the requirements of the various bulbs see the individual listings in chapters 8 through 12.

Height and Color

Before you plant an unfamiliar bulb, find out how tall it will grow. You don't want the low-growing grape hyacinths (*Muscari*) to be hidden behind tall Darwin tulips, or the giant alliums to obscure the irises. Catalog descriptions and the individual bulb entries in this book will give you a fairly accurate idea of a bulb's height, but sometimes bulbs have their own agenda and become taller or shorter than you expect.

Group same-color plants, separated by areas of white or pale shades.

Fortunately, most can be moved easily when they are dormant. Good gardeners spend much of their time digging and moving plants to create the garden they envision.

Groupings of bulbs are more aesthetically pleasing in a border than individual bulbs spaced here and there or single, narrow rows, which belong in a vegetable garden rather than a flower border. When planting bulbs for naturalizing, many people simply toss them in the

Forcing bulbs in containers gives you a head start on spring.

air and plant them where they land for a "natural" effect, but as we explain in chapter 6 that is not our favorite method.

When you set groups of bulbs in a bed or border, it is more effective to plant the same cultivar and color in each group, keeping in mind the appearance of the entire area relating to color, height, and symmetry. In a small bed planted entirely with bulbs, you will also find it is better to use only one or two colors, plus a compatible underplanting if you wish.

In a mixed border, if you are using the large spring bulbs (narcissus, hyacinth, tulip), plant at least ten to twelve of the same cultivar and color in each grouping. The small spring bulbs (*Crocus, Chionodoxa, Muscari,* and similar ones) look best if you plant at least a dozen or more together. Summer bulbs also look nice in

groups, but since most of them produce plants that are larger than the spring-bloomers, three bulbs of the same type are fine in a small border, five or more in a larger one. Tall upright bloomers such as gladioli need from six to twelve in each group to be effective. See the descriptions of individual bulbs for the distance apart to space each type.

Mixed plantings can be fun and even interesting, as in a country cottage garden. But as a rule, a hodgepodge of color is less attractive with bulbs, as you can see if you study photos of various plantings.

Much has been written about color combinations in the garden, and while many gardeners feel that in nature anything is beautiful, a well-designed planting can give that thesis quite an argument. Gertrude Jekyll, the matriarch of

Bulbs are among the best cut flowers, providing long-lasting dramatic displays

British gardening, felt that color should be used in large masses she called "drifts," a technique she managed nicely with 300-foot-long borders that were 14 feet wide. Using the spectrum, Jekyll separated the bright primary colors with the paler shades or white, so they wouldn't clash with each other. Without her large staff of gardeners, most of us have to think in more modest terms, but we can use the same principles.

Handling Disappearing Bulbs

If you plant spring bulbs in a bed that contains herbaceous plants, ideally you should first make a long-term plan. As insurance, insert small stakes to indicate the bulb plantings. If you don't mark the spot, you are likely to dig into the bulbs after their foliage disappears unless you have a phenomenal memory. An ideal way to mark the space is to plant shallow-rooted annual bedding plants there as soon as the bulb foliage begins to die and the danger of frost is past. Some annuals that do well on top of deeper planted bulbs are alyssum, asters, calendula, dwarf marigolds, nasturtiums, petunias, salvia, dwarf zinnias, and foliage plants such as dusty miller. Avoid using deeper rooted plants for this purpose. Cleome, geraniums, and summer bulbs such as gladioli or dahlias have extensive root systems that may disturb the bulbs.

Some gardeners reserve a space for spring bulbs that is at least 2 feet wide or more across the front of a perennial border. By separating the bulbs from the rest of the planting it is easier to know where they are and much handier to divide or replace them when necessary. If you do a front-of-the-border planting, don't let aggressive perennials crowd forward into the empty spaces during the summer.

If you are patient, and willing to put up with dead foliage for a few weeks, you can have a no-maintenance bed of spring bulbs. Each spring visitors to a nearby town drive slowly by the home of an elderly friend of ours, so they can admire the beautiful display she has in her small front lawn. It consists of a large circular plot of narcissus surrounded with deep purple grape hyacinths (*Muscari*). Only after the foliage has died back completely does her husband mow the grass there, which by then is several inches high. After that the area becomes part of the lawn for the rest of the summer. She could, of course, plant annual flowers there if she wanted, but the way she manages it, no bulb garden could be simpler.

Two peculiar late-blooming bulbs — lycoris and colchicum (autumn crocus) — have foliage that appears early in the season. The leaves then disappear during the early summer months and only late in the summer do the flower stalks and blooms appear. Place these in a well-defined spot. Otherwise you may accidentally dig into them while they are incognito.

Summer Bulb Placement

Most summer- and fall-blooming bulbous plants such as irises, dahlias, and crocosmias look good in an herbaceous perennial border, since their foliage stays green and lush throughout the gardening season. Specialty beds of the summer bloomers such as cannas, caladiums, dahlias, lilies, or a combination of bulbous plants are also attractive, although lilies have foliage that isn't as likely to be pretty after the bulbs finish blooming. In a mixed border the leaves of other perennials will hide their stalks, but in a bed where only lilies grow you may want to grow ferns or other plants to screen the fading foliage in late summer.

Gladioli are difficult to use effectively in perennial flower borders, although they can be attractive if you plant the tall ones in color groupings at the middle or back of a border. They are excellent for floral arrangements, however, and like many gardeners we grow them either in the cutting garden or in a row in our vegetable garden.

Good Companions

Certain ferns make good companion plants for bulbs, particularly spring bulbs or summer lilies. In our climate most spring bulbs bloom before the ferns begin to grow, but if you are combining summer bulbs with ferns, you must plant those that are the proper height to be compatible. Choose ferns carefully because some demand more shade and moisture than a normal sunny border provides, and others become too invasive to control easily. Many also require somewhat acidic soil to thrive. Here are some attractive species that grow well in a variety of soils:

Christmas fern (*Polystichum acrostichoides*). 1 to 2 feet. Sun or shade. Leathery fronds with each individual leaflet shaped like a Christmas stocking. Evergreen.

Lady fern (*Athyrium filix-femina*). 2 to 3 feet. Sun or light shade. Likes moist soil; easy to grow.

Maidenhair fern (*Adiantum pedatum*). 8 to 20 inches. Light to medium shade. Especially beautiful, lacy foliage is nearly orbicular.

Spring Bulbs

PLANT	MARCH	APRIL	MAY	JUNE
Crocus vernus and hybrids	▓▓			
Eranthis	▓▓			
Galanthus (snowdrop)	▓▓			
Iris reticulata	▓▓			
Bulbocodium vernum	▓▓			
Chionodoxa (glory-of-the-snow)	▓▓▓	▓		
Narcissus (early varieties)	▓▓▓	▓		
Puschkinia scilloides (striped squill)	▓▓	▓		
Anemone blanda		▓▓		
Tulipa (early and species tulips)		▓▓▓	▓	
Muscari (grape hyacinth)		▓▓		
Scilla siberica (squill)		▓▓		
Narcissus (later varieties)		▓▓	▓	
Hyacinthus (hyacinth)		▓	▓	
Fritillaria imperialis		▓	▓	
Scilla tubergeniana (scilla)		▓	▓	
Frittillaria meleagris (guinea-hen flower)			▓▓	
Tulipa (Darwin Hybrids, Early Double, Early Single, Lily-Flowered, Mendel, Triumph Tulips)		▓	▓	
Convallaria (lily-of-the-valley)			▓▓	
Erythronium (trout lily)			▓▓	
Iris (Dutch iris)			▓▓	
Leucojum vernum (spring snowflake)			▓▓	
Ornithogalum (star-of-Bethlehem)			▓▓	
Camassia			▓	
Eremurus (foxtail lily)			▓	
Tulipa (cottage, Darwin, parrot tulips)			▓	
Endymion hispanicus (scilla)			▓	▓

Summer and Fall Bulbs

PLANT	EARLY SUMMER	MIDSUMMER	LATE SUMMER	FALL
Caladium	▨	▨	▨	▨
Colocasia	▨	▨	▨	▨
Oxalis	▨	▨	▨	▨
Tuberous begonia	▨	▨	▨	▨
Anemone	▨	▨	▨	
Ranunculus asiaticus	▨	▨	▨	
Lilium	▨	▨	▨	
Gloriosa (Rothchild gloriosa-lily)		▨	▨	
Hymenocallis (spider-lily)		▨	▨	
Ornithogalum thyrsoides (star-of-Bethlehem)		▨	▨	
Gladiolus		▨	▨	
Canna		▨	▨	▨
Crocosmia (montbretia)		▨	▨	▨
Tigridia pavonia (tiger flower)		▨	▨	▨
Zantedeschia (calla lily)		▨	▨	▨
Dahlia		▨	▨	▨
Polianthes tuberosa (tuberose)		▨	▨	▨
Lycoris		▨	▨	
Colchicum (meadow saffron)				▨
Crocus (autumn crocus)				▨
Cyclamen (most species)				▨

Use this chart to help you plan your garden. By selecting carefully, you'll be able to have bulbous plants in bloom from early spring to late fall. The flowering times listed are approximate for plants in zones 5 and 6. In zone 4 add two weeks; in zone 3, add about four. In warmer zones subtract two to four weeks. The table is only a guide. Where spring comes late and is very short — as in zones 2, 3, and 4 and near the ocean — the early, midseason, and late spring flowering bulbs all tend to bloom close to the same time.

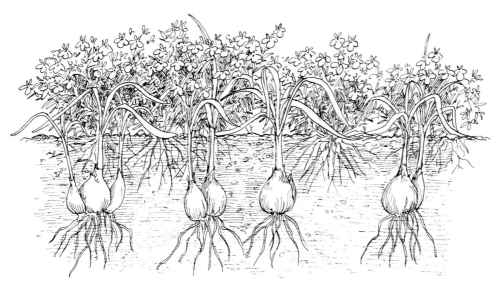

Plant shallow-rooted annual bedding plants like alyssum or lobelia on top of bulbs as soon as their foliage begins to die.

Royal fern (*Osmunda regalis*). 2 to 6 feet. Sun or light shade. Excellent for wet places similar to that needed for *Iris versicolor*.

Underplantings

Occasionally we hear about gardeners who wanted an underplanting where their bulbs were growing, so they planted myrtle, pachysandra, ajuga, bishop's weed, or another ground cover among their lilies, irises, or other summer-blooming bulbous plants. Because the competition was too much, the bulbs didn't bloom well and eventually petered out. If you want an underplanting for nonaggressive bulbs, choose an annual such as alyssum, a biennial such as forget-me-nots, or some other nonthreatening plant. Even the low-growing, silvery lamb's ears (*Stachys*) and certain dead nettles (*Lamium*) are aggressive and hard to control in some locations. Forget-me-nots (*Myosotis sylvatica*), English daisies (*Bellis*), and violas or pansies make fine ground covers for tall-growing spring bulbs such as daffodils or tulips because many bloom at the same time and you can select compatible color combinations. They are annuals or biennials and seed readily, so they can come back again and again. If you plant forget-me-nots, make sure you like them, because their seeds scatter freely and are difficult to eliminate, especially if they get into your compost pile.

Bulbs in Containers

When we think of the places bulbs grow, our thoughts usually turn to borders filled with masses of bloom, naturalized hillsides, or even pots forced for indoor winter blooms. But once you've seen bulbs in an outdoor container, you may stop feeling sorry for people who have to garden that way. In fact you will probably wonder why you haven't been doing more growing on your porch, terrace, deck, or breezeway. Spring bulbs such as the miniature daffodils and summer bloomers such as tuberous begonias thrive in containers and are often planted in

BULBS CLASSIFIED ACCORDING TO HEIGHT

HEIGHT	SEASON	COLORS
Tall: 30 inches or more		
Allium	late spring to early	lilac, purple, rose, white
Fritillaria	summer	dark purple, red, yellow
Medium tall: 20 to 30 inches		
Tulips: Cottage, Darwin,	late spring	various colors
Lily-flowered, Parrot, Triumph	late spring	various colors
Medium: 12 to 20 inches		
Tulips: fosteriana	spring	various colors
Narcissus	spring	various colors
Medium short: 8 to 12 inches		
Hyacinths	spring	various colors
Tulips: Double Early, greigii hybrids	spring	various colors
Tulips: kaufmanniana hybrids	early spring	blue, pink, red, white
Low: 4 to 8 inches		
Anemone blanda	spring	blue, white, pink
Chionodoxa	spring	blue, pink, white
Crocus	early spring	blue, purple, white, yellow, mixed
Crocus, autumn	fall	lilac, lavender
Colchicum	fall	pink, lilac, white, mixed
Cyclamen	fall	pink, white, red
Galanthus	early spring	white
Muscari	spring	blue, white, purple
Tulips: species	early spring	various colors

window boxes, for example. With imagination you can create a courtyard entirely of bulbs, or use them combined with foliage plants, annuals, or other perennials.

In some ways container growing allows you more freedom than you have when the bulbs are growing in a garden bed, because you can move containers around to provide more or less sunlight and quickly replace bulbs that are either past their prime or not doing well. Gardening in raised containers is especially appealing to anyone who finds it difficult to bend over to weed and tend plants at ground level. By using sterile potting soil, there is little likelihood of weeds, and the danger of soil-borne diseases is minimized.

In other ways, container growing is demanding, however. The plants need more attention because the soil in pots dries out quickly, and the roots can't reach out into surrounding soil for moisture, fertilizer, and lime. In fact, plants may need daily watering unless you set up a mechanical watering system. Frequent watering leaches out soil nutrients rapidly, so if you use chemical fertilizers you must feed them more frequently than you would if they were in the ground. Organic fertilizers such as compost, alfalfa meal, manure, or slow-release chemical

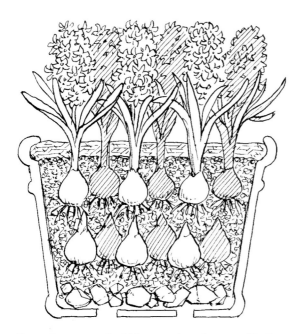

For a long period of bloom, plant layers of bulbs in containers. Here, hyacinths bloom before the later-flowering tulips below.

fertilizers such as Osmocote or Mag-Amp are excellent for containers because one application at planting time usually lasts the entire gardening season.

Large pots, tubs, urns, and whisky barrels cut in half all make fine containers. Whatever you choose must have good drainage, though, because bulbs that are wet for an extended period will rot. Be sure the holes in the base are large enough to carry off rains and excess waterings without becoming clogged. Place a layer of small rocks or pieces of broken clay pots in the bottom before you fill a container with soil.

Spring Bulbs in Containers

Plant spring bulbs in potting soil in the container in the fall. You won't have to plant them as deep as in the ground, and also you can plant them closer together. It won't do any harm if they touch each other, but do not set them too close to the edge of the container because, lack-

SPRING BULBS FOR CONTAINERS

Anemone blanda	giant windflower
Galanthus	snowdrop
Iris danfordiae and *I. reticulata* hybrids	miniature iris
Leucojum	snowflake
Muscari armeniacum and *M. botryoides album*	grape hyacinth
Narcissus (especially the shorter-stemmed & miniature-flowering kinds)	
Puschkinia scilloides	striped squill
Scilla siberica	early flowering Siberian squill
Scilla campanulata also called *Endymion hispanicus*	later-flowering Spanish bluebells

ing the insulation of the soil, they may suffer frost damage. After planting, water them thoroughly and place an inch of organic mulch on top of the soil.

The bulbs you choose should be right for your climatic zone and always plant them early enough so they will grow a good clump of roots before they freeze. Set the containers in a sheltered place out of the wind, or in sub-zero climates store them in an unheated but protected area such as a closed shed or garage. In warm climates keep them in a cool place out of the sun, and avoid using dark-colored containers that collect heat. You don't want the bulbs to start to grow during a late winter warm spell and then be injured when the temperature falls again. In areas that are frost-free or mostly frost-free, chill the bulbs in near-freezing temperatures (40°F) in a refrigerator for a few weeks before planting.

Bulb experts from the Netherlands suggest several creative container plantings guaranteed to make spring a delight.

A Barrel of Bloom. Plant several different layers of bulbs in a barrel or large tub for a long series of blooms. Plant those you want to bloom latest as the bottom layer where it is coolest, 6 to 8 inches from the soil surface, with subsequent layers above. Spread a layer of soil between each layer, and don't plant one large bulb directly on top of another.

The bottom layer (which, of course, you should plant first) might be Lily-flowered tulips in white, bright yellow, and pink such as 'White Triumphator', 'West Point', and 'Mariette'. The top layer, and first to bloom, might be pink and yellow hyacinths, perhaps 'Anna Marie', and 'City of Haarlem' plus the daisy-flowering white Anemone, 'White Splendour'.

A Pot of Fragrance. This planting will provide two months of fragrance in three planting layers: crocuses, hyacinths, and tulips. For the bottom layer you might use the fragrant orange tulip cultivar 'Orange Sun', planted first; for the middle layer, the fragrant orange tulip 'General de Wet'; and for the top layer, crocuses, such as 'Snow Bunting' and the cobalt blue grape hyacinth, Muscari armeniacum.

Patriotism in a Pot. Plant two containers, with one layer of light blue and white Chionodoxa (glory-of-the-snow) and the red species tulip 'Red Riding Hood' for the early blooms. In the second pot, plant one single layer of Lily-flowered tulips 'Red Shine' and 'White Triumphator' mixed with blue wood hyacinth (Endymion hispanicus). If you are lucky you may get the proper colored blooms for Memorial Day.

Blue Magic. For a stunning mass of blue loaded with spring fragrance, plant a wide, shallow pan with lots of blue hyacinths such as 'Blue Giant' or 'King of Blues.'

Colorful Ground Cover. If your climate lets you grow small trees in big planters, set a grouping of flowering bulbs at their bases to enhance them and give you one more spot for spring color. Mix the early blooming blue Chionodoxa bulbs with miniature narcissus such as 'Tête à Tête.' After the flowers fade, plant annuals to hide the dead foliage and provide summer color.

Summer Bulbs in Containers

Container planting is not limited to spring bulbs, of course. After their blooms fade, you can either plant annuals on top of spring bulbs or dig out the bulbs, discard or store them, and plant summer-blooming bulbs such as some of the shorter Asiatic lilies, dwarf gladioli, dwarf dahlias, tuberous begonias, or the shorter-growing varieties of cannas.

Whether you decide to plant your containers entirely with bulbs of one kind to give a mass of color or with a mixture of bulbs is a personal decision. Both can be very attractive, and we feel that if a planting has given pleasure to the grower, it has been an unqualified success.

Bulb Viewing

Impressive displays of flowering bulbs are not limited to the Netherlands (see box on page 26). At the end of every cold winter in North America, many thousands of spring-hungry people flock to indoor spring garden shows, such as the Philadelphia Flower Show (sponsored by the Pennsylvania Horticultural Society), the New England Flower Show in Boston (sponsored by the Massachusetts Horticultural Society), and the Garden Clubs of Toronto show. Later, when spring actually arrives, colorful bulb extravaganzas appear at botanical gardens and arboretums all over the North to inspire gardeners with new and unusual cultivars.

Many American towns have spring festivals featuring a certain bulb, particularly in areas where the Dutch settled in North America. For over sixty years the citizens of Holland, Michigan, have sponsored "Tulip Time Festival" in mid-May, an event filled with bulbs and Dutch culture. Likewise, Orange City, Iowa, celebrates its ancestry with tulips and other Dutch attractions. Pella, Iowa, too, has had a tulip festival for nearly sixty years.

In New England, the island of Nantucket is known for its extensive welcome-to-spring daffodil plantings each year in April. Among other places that enjoy daffodil shows or festivals are Meriden and Greenwich, Connecticut; Dublin, New Hampshire; and Brewster, Massachusetts.

"Bulb Days" in some communities consist simply of floral displays in parks, open private gardens, or indoor exhibits of cut flowers. In other towns, community organizations may sponsor a parade, dinners, and sporting events, as well. Garden clubs and civic groups find bulb plantings worthwhile because as they multiply and become more impressive each year, they are a source of pride for local citizens as well as a tourist attraction.

The best place for bulbs, of course, is nestled in your own gardens, yard, or woodland. No botanical display anywhere gives more satisfaction than one you've planted and tended yourself.

For addresses and further information about bulb displays, see Appendix (page 203).

THE GREATEST BULB SHOW ON EARTH

Keukenhof Gardens, near the town of Lisse, a 30-minute drive from Amsterdam, has the best-known bulb display in The Netherlands. For two months each spring, from late March until the third week in May, 6 million bulbs (more or less) bloom in 70 acres of landscaped gardens. Many tulip varieties bloom throughout the spring, with peak bloom at the end of April. If you go, plan on a full day to wander through the colorful displays, open from 8 a.m. until 7:30 p.m. Most bulbs for sale at Keukenhof have been cleared by the USDA for shipping to the U.S. Another reliable bulb source is at the Frans Roozen Show Gardens in Vogelenzang, near Lisse.

Most commercial bulbs are grown in a narrow strip of land on the west coast of The Netherlands near the North Sea, from Leiden northward to Haarlem; and north of Alkmaar along the coast, as well. A trip through these fields by bicycle, car, bus, or train during the height of the tulip season is a feast of color. Growers concentrate on bulb production rather than scenery, and barges are filled with the flower heads they chop off in full bloom.

Bulb viewers can find blooms in many places other than these. Some search out botanical gardens, including the venerable *Hortus Botanicus* of Leiden University, not far from Keukenhof in Leiden, dating from the sixteenth century. Near Amsterdam, visitors are welcome at Aalsmeer's Flower Auction, the largest in the world, where several million flowers change hands each day. Flowers are sold retail from barges on Amsterdam canals at the floating market. At various times local parades throughout Holland exhibit different flowers: a large spring bulb parade from Haarlem to Noordwijk features narcissus-, tulip-, and hyacinth-covered floats that are illuminated at night.

For travel information, see Appendix.

Choosing Bulbs

WHEN YOU LOOK through the colorful photos in a specialty bulb catalog and see the huge number of beautiful cultivars available, you may feel a bit like a kid in a candy store, not knowing which to choose. We're sometimes tempted to make bulb decisions by throwing darts at a board covered with pictures of tulips, lilies, or irises, or simply to pick up a bagged assortment in a garden shop. But there are better ways.

Gardeners today can make choices not only from the widest selection of cultivars ever available, but also from the finest bulbs ever grown. You'll find lists of recommended species and cultivars in each section of individual bulbs in the following chapters, but don't be constrained by them. There are many wonderful cultivars of each species, and exciting new ones appear each year.

To get the best kinds for your garden, buy them early, as soon as they appear in stores and garden centers, or make out an order as soon as the catalogs arrive. If you wait until the end of the planting season they'll be picked over in the stores and possibly unavailable from suppliers. Spring-blooming bulbs won't have time to root and become well-established in your garden before winter if you plant them late in the fall.

When you're choosing bulbs from a bin at a garden center, pick out the largest and firmest ones. They'll provide the best flowers, and some will produce two stalks instead of one. Check each bulb to be sure it is firm and has no spots or blemishes that might indicate disease. Sometimes you'll find a double bulb or a large one with a small bulblet attached; don't separate them but leave them together when you plant them. If they've begun to sprout plant them anyway. If you set them at the proper depth, the sprouts will be covered. Mulch them with a thick layer of leaves or similar material to keep the soil cool and dark so they won't be encouraged to grow further.

A mail-order nursery that carries a large assortment of bulbs is the place to buy from if you want more unusual plants than those you can find locally. Specialty nurseries often have exceptionally wide assortments (see Appendix). Even though catalog photos aren't always accurate and sometimes the colors are enhanced, they'll give you a general idea of what the blooms look like. If you are requesting a catalog for summer-blooming bulbs, do it early in the year so you can plant before growth starts. Ask for spring bulb catalogs in early summer so you can order the bulbs in time for fall planting; when the catalogs appear, don't hesitate to order right away. Often by ordering early you can enjoy a discount in price. The supplier will deliver the bulbs at the proper time to plant in your area, usually in peak condition. If your catalog offers a variety of bulb sizes, get the ones described as "top-sized," unless you want a large number for a mass planting and are not concerned about getting the best blooms the first year.

Most spring-flowering bulbs are grown in northern Europe, especially the Netherlands, Belgium, and Great Britain, although some are grown in North America in New York (Long Island), Michigan, Oregon, Virginia, and other states. Lilies and other summer bloomers are grown on the West Coast in large numbers and in smaller amounts in nurseries throughout the country.

Imported bulbs are distributed by many firms in the United States and Canada, so there is no need to order them directly from Europe. Inspections are thorough and it is rare to get diseased bulbs, unlike half a century ago when gardeners often received bulbs that were infected with viruses.

Most summer- and fall-blooming bulbs can be shipped long distances safely, with the exception of lilies. They do not become as completely dormant as spring bulbs and can't be stored for long periods. For best quality, buy lily bulbs grown in North America.

Getting a Bargain

Many first-class, reputable businesses offer top-quality bulbs at a discount from time to time to lure new customers or to dispose of surplus plants. These kinds of bargains are an excellent investment. A few firms, however, lure customers with low prices and catalog pictures of flowers far too brilliant to be believable, and they ship bulbs that are not of top quality. You'll occasionally see fantastic offers in Sunday newspapers or pulp magazines, or get them by direct mail. They might offer 100 gladiolus corms or tulip bulbs for only a few dollars. We once took the tantalizing bait in one of these ads and got exactly what we paid for. "Bargain" bulbs are usually small culls that do not measure up to industry standards either in size or quality and are unlikely to bloom until the second year, if they grow at all.

If you are unsure about the trustworthiness of the firm offering a bulb bargain, choose a supplier from the list in the Appendix, or buy bulbs from a garden center where you can see what you are getting. Caveat emptor. It will save you time and disappointment.

Bulb Hardiness

If you are unfamiliar with the plant hardiness zone where you live, check it out on the map on page 30. The bulbs at a local garden center should be appropriate for your climate, and catalogs usually indicate the outdoor planting zones to which a bulb is hardy, but sometimes they aren't completely accurate. Tender bulbs that originated in tropical areas can't, of course, survive northern winters outdoors; hardy bulbs that need a chilling period aren't meant to grow in the deep South. Nevertheless, you can grow many tender bulbs in the North by lifting and storing them for the winter. Spring bulbs will bloom in the frost-free South if you give them a chilling period before setting them in the ground. If your heart is set on growing a bulb that is listed as not quite hardy in your zone, we'd suggest giving it a try. For years we've been growing montbretia (*Crocosmia*) successfully in zone 3 without protection, even though it is widely described as being hardy only to zone 7.

Buying Bulb Plants in Bloom

Each year florists, garden centers, supermarkets, and department stores sell thousands of potted hardy spring bulbs — crocuses, hyacinths, tulips, and narcissus — in bud or bloom during the late winter and early spring. By purchasing flowering plants you can see exactly what you are getting, and by keeping the plants watered and fertilized after they bloom, you should be able to plant them outdoors safely as soon as hard frosts are over. They won't bloom again that spring, but with proper care, they should produce flowers the following spring. (See chapter 7 for detailed information on how to handle forced bulbs.)

Tender bulbs must be handled differently. Potted plants such as tuberous begonias can be set in the ground as soon as frosts are over, dug in the fall, stored, and replanted the following spring. Easter lilies are not good choices for outdoor gardens in cool planting zones because they are tender bulbs, and the new hybrids have been developed especially for indoor blooms. We have planted them outdoors in the spring and taken them indoors before fall frosts, but they produced only one or two disappointing blooms per plant the following Easter.

Endangered Bulbs

Named cultivars are, as the name implies, cultivated plants, so when you buy them there's no need to be concerned that you might be buying bulbs that are endangered. Wild species

— referred to as *species bulbs* — are a different story, however. Some have already become nearly extinct, and many others are classified as endangered. For many years local collectors have gathered wild "minor" bulbs in the rural areas of Turkey, western Europe, Asia, and Africa and sold them to European and American importers. Species bulbs are in demand because, although they are less showy than the cultivars and may bloom for shorter periods, they need less care and flower year after year without replacement. Some of these wild species, therefore, make excellent choices for rock gardens, semi-wild plantings, and for naturalizing. They are often much cheaper than cultivated bulbs, too, although careless digging and handling may result in a high mortality rate.

Collectors today are still digging and exporting these wild bulbs, because it is an excellent source of income for people in remote areas. Wholesale digging, however, has led to their rapid depletion. Furthermore, new settlements in formerly remote areas have resulted in increased cultivation and grazing of the land and caused the widespread destruction of many wild habitats.

Most nurseries that sell species bulbs handle only those that are commercially cultivated and proudly advertise this fact. Dutch suppliers, as of 1990, have marked wild species bulbs "grown from wild sources," and since 1992 they have marked cultivated bulbs "grown from cultivated stock." Their labeling program will cover all bulbs beginning in 1995. However, all wild bulbs do not come from Dutch suppliers, and other countries do not always indicate the origin of their bulbs. Unfortunately, some American nurseries still import and sell wild endangered species. For more information, write to the Natural Resources Defense Council (see Appendix for address).

At present the only way to end this practice is for gardeners to stop buying endangered bulbs

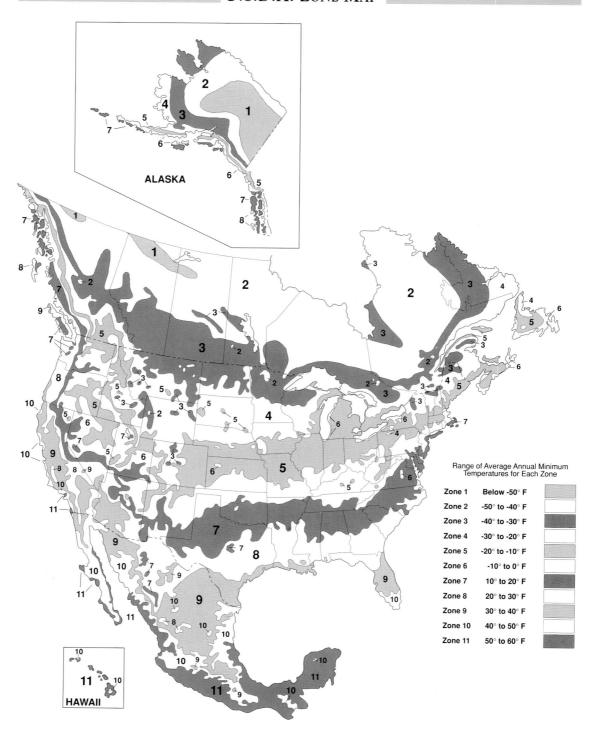

ALASKA

HAWAII

Range of Average Annual Minimum
Temperatures for Each Zone

Zone 1	Below -50° F	
Zone 2	-50° to -40° F	
Zone 3	-40° to -30° F	
Zone 4	-30° to -20° F	
Zone 5	-20° to -10° F	
Zone 6	-10° to 0° F	
Zone 7	10° to 20° F	
Zone 8	20° to 30° F	
Zone 9	30° to 40° F	
Zone 10	40° to 50° F	
Zone 11	50° to 60° F	

collected from wild sources from nurseries that still import and sell them. Look for the notation, "Commercially Propagated," and if you don't find it, ask about the origin. Not only will your conscience be clear, but nursery-grown bulbs are more likely to arrive in better condition and be more certain to live and bloom. In addition to buying species bulbs from reputable nurseries (see Appendix), you may be able to get them from other gardeners. Many wild bulbs clump up so fast that most people are happy to split off a few bunches and share them.

SOME WILD SPECIES CONSIDERED ENDANGERED

Anemone blanda. Windflower is a tuberous-rooted Greek native.

Arisaema triphyllum. Jack-in-the-pulpit has been widely dug throughout North America and is now in short supply.

Cardiocrinum giganteum. A tall-growing (up to 12 feet) native of the Himalayas, it can produce as many as two dozen fragrant, funnel-shaped flowers on each stalk in July.

Cyclamen. A group of native bulbs from southern Europe and Sicily, cyclamen grow from corms and are related to the florist's lily, *C. persicum*, which is often raised as a pot plant and isn't endangered.

Cypripedium. Lady's slipper and other wild species of the orchid family grow wild in North America.

Dracunculus. These tuberous-rooted plants are natives of the Canary and Madeira islands and Asia Minor.

Eranthis cilicica. Winter aconite is a tuberous-rooted native of Greece and Asia Minor. *E. hyemalis*, which grows wild in parts of North America, is also endangered.

Galanthus. Snowdrops are natives of Europe and Asia and, except for *G. nivalis*, are considered endangered.

Iris. Several species are considered threatened, including *I. acutiloba*, *I. paradoxa*, *I. persica*, and *I. tuberosa*.

Leucojum aestivum. The summer snowflake, as well as *L. vernum*, the spring snowflake, has been in cultivation for many years, but both are still sometimes collected from wild areas of central and eastern Europe.

Narcissus asturiensis. This tiny trumpet daffodil is a native of Spain and Portugal. *N. bulbocodium conspicuus* and *N. b. tenuifolius*, from southern France and Morocco, are also considered endangered. Others are *Narcissus cyclamineus*, *N. juncifolius*, *N. rupicola*, *N. scaberulus*, *N. triandrus albus*, and *N. t. concolor*.

Pancratium maritimum. Tender bulbs from Europe are grown as house plants, much like amaryllis.

Sternbergia. All species of this "fall daffodil" are considered endangered.

Trillium. Certain species.

Urginea maritima. The sea onion is an old-time house plant, too tender for outdoor growing except in zone 9. It is native to South Africa.

Uvularia. The merrybells are North American natives with a bulblike root.

The Nitty Gritty of Successful Bulbs: Planting and Culture

A DORMANT BULB with its unattractive drab wrapping is somewhat like a chrysalis, the hard-shelled pupa of a butterfly. In time, and with the proper conditions, a beautiful flower will emerge, just as the butterfly comes from the chrysalis. Fortunately, bulbs are tough objects in their dormant stage, but even so, if they are to fulfill their potential, we must handle them properly.

Spring Bulbs

Most dormant spring-booming bulbs we buy in late summer or fall originated from little bulblets that grew around "parent" bulbs in a nursery. Propagators have painstakingly cared for them with what amounts to force feeding, then dug, graded, and shipped the bulbs so they reach us at the proper time for fall planting.

When you plant bulbs in early autumn, small feeder roots grow from their bases in soil that is still warm from summer's heat. If newly planted bulbs are to bloom their best in the spring, feeder roots must grow before freezing weather arrives, which can vary from mid-September in the North to early November in southern regions. If you live where cool fall weather arrives late, don't plant your new spring bulbs too early in the fall, hoping to get better rooting. They may decide that their summer resting period is over, and, feeling warm earth around them, begin to grow. (Bulbs that stay in the ground all summer know better than to do this.) If in doubt, a good rule is to plant them about six weeks before the ground is likely to begin to freeze at night where you live. If you guessed wrong and notice some sprouts coming from your newly planted bulbs, pile a thin layer of compost over them, or after a cool night cover the bed with leaves or evergreen boughs to darken the soil and keep them cool. Hopefully, with that treatment they will reconsider their early awakening.

STORING BULBS

Before planting your bulbs, keep them in a dry, dark, cool place in a paper bag or open container rather than in an airtight can or plastic bag. They need air circulation so they don't collect moisture and rot.

If you plant spring bulbs so late in the fall that they have no chance to grow the roots they need to absorb moisture and nutrients, they will probably bloom anyway, using the stored energy of the bulb. The flowers are not likely to be as nice as they would have been if they had faced spring with a better root system, however, although they should recover and bloom well in future years.

When you must plant spring bulbs late, you may be able to give them extra rooting time by spreading a thick mulch over them to keep the ground from chilling for a few extra weeks. Don't forget to take most of it off in very early spring, so the plants won't need to struggle through it.

After the bulbs have been planted, they need a period of chilling, which nature provides during the winter months in temperate climates. Spring bulbs can tolerate freezing temperatures, but they don't need them as long as the temperature stays as cool as 32° to 40° F for six or eight weeks. Like lilacs and other cool-weather plants, spring bulbs need this chilling period to survive and will not bloom well in areas that are frost-free unless they are chilled artificially.

As winter draws to a close and temperatures become warmer, leaves and buds begin to grow from the bulbs. Eager snowdrops are first to break their dormancy and push through the snow, followed by crocuses, narcissus, hyacinths, and tulips. We are always surprised when the sprouts pop through the ground as soon as it thaws and the weather warms, but are alarmed when cold days return and snow covers the budding plants. Fortunately, the plants go on growing as if they didn't mind this weather change a bit. They are certainly our kind of flower.

Summer-Blooming Bulbs

The list of hardy and tender bulbous plants that can brighten our summer months is a long one. Some such as lilies and irises will survive when left in the ground all year, as long as they are hardy in your planting zone. It is safe to plant the winter-hardy kinds in either spring or fall, or to buy them as potted plants and set them out anytime, even when in bloom.

The tender kinds such as dahlias and gladioli, which originated in tropical climates, can't tolerate freezing temperatures, so you must either treat them as annuals and replace them each spring or dig up the roots in the fall and store them over the winter. (See chapter 11 for how to do this.)

Fall-Blooming Bulbs

Plant the fall-blooming bulbs, such as autumn crocus and lycoris, early in the spring before they start to grow or anytime throughout the summer, when they are dormant. Follow the instructions you receive with the bulbs or see chapter 12 for planting directions.

You can move bulbs within your garden safely even when they are in bloom if you take a large clump of soil with them. If you want to break the bulbs apart to extend your plantings, however, wait until they are dormant.

When bulbs arrive too late to plant outdoors, you can often salvage them by potting and forcing them for late winter blooms indoors. Occasionally, however, this advice won't work. Friends once called us in early winter to say, "We just realized that we haven't planted the 200 daffodil bulbs that came in September. Got any ideas?" Obviously they had too many to pot, so we suggested they plant the bulbs close together — top side up — in deep flats of potting soil, put them in a cold root cellar or cold frame for the winter, and set them out in the spring as early as they could dig in the ground.

They reported that the bulbs did bloom after they planted them out in the spring, al-though not as well as they would have other-wise. The next year they bloomed beautifully, however, so all was not lost. Narcissus, cro-cuses, and the smaller bulbs are more likely to survive this treatment than tulips and hya-cinths.

Another of our gardening friends was ill in the fall and left her tulip bulbs in a bag in an unheated garage. In early spring, as soon as the ground thawed, she soaked them in water overnight and then planted them at the recommended depth. Every one survived and produced foliage, and many of them bloomed. It just goes to show that bulbs are often more resilient than we think.

Getting Started with Bulbs

If you choose the bulbous plants that are suit-able for your planting zone, select a good location, prepare the soil well, and plant them at the right time and proper depth, the chances for success are excellent. Because different spe-cies and cultivars vary in their requirements, however, see the instructions for individual bulbs in chapters 8 through 12 for specific planting directions.

The Planting Site

Most bulbs and bulblike plants need sun-shine. The ones that do best in shade will be discussed later. Spring bulbs can stand summer shade during their dormant period, and some even need it, but they require the bright spring sunshine during the time they bloom.

Nearly all garden plants, and especially bulbs, need good drainage. When we first started to garden, we were confused when direc-tions specified soil with good drainage, but well supplied with moisture. How could one have both? We learned that it meant soil that was loamy enough to hold moisture between show-ers and waterings, but not so heavy it would create soggy conditions for long periods. Heavy soil inhibits good root growth on bulbs and en-courages rot. Such soils can be improved by adding sand or humus such as compost, well-rotted manure, or peat moss, and by putting an organic mulch over the soil.

Soil Preparation

Many bulbs need to be planted fairly deep to bloom well, and some, like lilies and alliums, are so large they need a deep, loose soil. You'll save future work and frustration by preparing the bed well initially for all bulbs except those that are going into naturalized plantings such as in a lawn (see chapter 6). When you dig the bed only to the planting depth of the bulb, it doesn't give the feeder roots at the base any loose soil to grow in, so till or spade the soil to a minimum depth of at least 1 foot and pulverize it thoroughly, removing all weed and grass roots. When you've finished the preparation, the soil should be loose enough so that when you plant your bulbs it will pack tightly around them and leave no air pockets that would dry them out. Till in compost or manure to supply humus and nutrients, including the trace elements that plants need.

Although our favorite soil additive is compost, which is safe to use on everything, we also spread some dry commercial plant food over our soil and till it in deeply so it is incorporated into

SIMPLE COMPOST, THE EASY WAY

The benefits of recycling organic household and garden wastes into compost are so compelling that gardeners without a compost pile are at a disadvantage, as is the environment. Although chemical fertilizers provide the necessary nutrients for plants, they do not supply the moisture-retentive humus and trace minerals that make plants thrive. Nor do chemicals encourage soil-improving earthworms as moist, humus-rich organic soils do.

Compost-making can be as simple or as complicated as you want. Entire books are written about the subject, and some people are fascinated with the elaborate ceremony some of these recommend. Composting is a simple process, however, that nature uses all the time in the woods and on farms as vegetative and woody wastes decay.

To make it in small amounts as fast as possible, use a shredder to grind up your garbage, garden wastes, and leaves before you start, since small pieces of organic material rot much more quickly than larger ones. Use one or more large garbage cans in which you have made some large holes for ventilation. As you accumulate the organic wastes alternate them in layers approximately 6 inches thick with layers of soil 1 inch thick. Moisten everything slightly, but never let it become swampy wet. Set the can in a place that stays well above freezing and the materials will turn to a rich, dark soil builder within a few months.

If garbage cans don't provide enough compost for your needs, an outdoor garden compost pile is the solution. Some people enclose piles with concrete blocks; others build a three-sided wooden enclosure or buy one of the many compost bins on the market. Alternate 6- to 10-inch layers of organic matter such as garden wastes, garbage, leaves, and similar materials with 2-inch layers of soil. We avoid putting meat, bones, and eggshells in ours because they attract wild animals. The pile would rot faster if we shredded the organic matter first, but even corn cobs eventually rot without shredding.

Each of us who makes compost has a different method for handling the piles. Most of us find it easiest to have three piles — one to which we add fresh materials, another rotting, and the third ready for use. Gardeners with small plots often build only one narrow pile, however. They continually add material to the top, and dig out the finished compost from the bottom.

You can hasten decomposition by keeping the pile moist and by turning it with a spading fork once a month. Some gardeners add bacterial activators available at organic suppliers to their pile. Although earthworms usually appear on their own, to speed up the rotting process you can buy those that are commercially grown that are advertised in garden magazines. The neighborhood boys have always found our pile a good source of bait for their fishing trips.

the area around the base of the bulbs that will be planted there. We use something less tempting to animal pests than bonemeal. Alfalfa meal, dried seaweed, or small amounts of a complete chemical fertilizer all work well. The Netherlands bulb experts recommend a 9-9-6 (9 percent nitrogen, 9 percent phosphorus oxide, and 6 percent potassium oxide) bulb fertilizer, which many garden centers carry. The gardeners we know all have their favorite plant foods with other formulas. It is wise to keep in mind that twice as much is never twice as good. Cultivate any dry chemical fertilizer into the soil rather than leaving it on top. The nitrogen it contains is volatile, and can easily be lost into the air.

Some gardeners maintain that manure should be forbidden near all bulbs because it makes them rot. We are strong believers in organic plant foods and have never had trouble from using aged poultry, horse, cow, or sheep manure, or any dry manure, on any plants. If we buy some of the fresh product from a nearby farm, we use it as a fall mulch or mix it in with the green material in our compost to age for a season before use.

Most garden bulbs do best in soil with a pH that ranges between 5.5 and 7. Many soils are more acidic than 5.5 if no lime has been spread there in recent years, so if you aren't sure about the pH, check it with an inexpensive soil test kit. Ten pounds of garden lime spread over 100 square feet of soil (a bed 5 x 20 feet) will raise the pH about one point. Mix it into the soil at planting time, if possible, so it will be near the roots. If you missed that opportunity, and your bulbs are already planted, either sprinkle it over the surface and water it heavily to wash it in, or apply it just before a heavy rain and let nature do the job.

Planting Tools

There are many ways to dig holes for bulbs. We like a round-pointed spade, whether we dig a hole for each individual bulb or make long trenches for several. The long-handled spades may be best for digging deep holes or leaning on, but we prefer those with shorter handles.

For planting a few small bulbs that are not set deep, a trowel is also handy. Dibbles — stainless steel tools that look somewhat like sharpened pencils — are also fine for small bulbs, but we haven't found them useful for narcissus, tulips, and lilies that need deep planting. A dibble makes such a small hole that only small bulbs

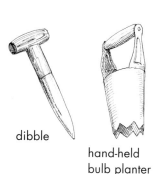

dibble

hand-held
bulb planter

trowel

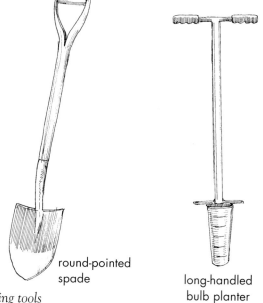

round-pointed
spade

long-handled
bulb planter

Bulb-planting tools

can drop to the bottom, and even then a pocket of air can easily be left underneath to dry out the roots. Nursery catalogs and garden centers offer bulb planters with either short or long handles. These tools are made so that when you press them into the soil and withdraw them, they leave a hole into which you can place a good-sized bulb. The theory is wonderful, but we've found it takes a lot of force to thrust a hand-held planter deep enough into even loose soil to plant a tulip or lily bulb, and it can be difficult to shake moist soil out of the planter when you are ready to bury the bulb. The long-handled types operated by foot power are easier to get into the soil, and some of those offered by bulb companies and garden centers are especially rugged. Although expensive, it may be a tool worth considering if you have lots of bulbs to plant.

The Planting

After your soil is prepared, you are ready for the fun of planting. If you didn't fertilize the bed at tilling time, dig each hole about 2 inches deeper than you will set the bulb, and put an inch of loose soil back in the hole. Cover the soil with a tablespoon of a complete fertilizer. Then spread an inch of soil on top of the fertilizer, and place the bulb on the soil with its base at the recommended depth from the soil's surface. Then pack loose soil around it. If you have rodents,

put a mothball beside the bulb before covering with soil.

If you prefer, instead of digging a hole for each bulb you can dig a trench for planting. People who plant large numbers of bulbs in parks and display gardens first remove all the soil from the planting area, excavating to slightly below the depth they want to set the bulbs. They till the area to loosen the soil that is left, spread a layer of complete fertilizer, and cover the fertilizer with a thin layer of soil so the bulbs will not be in direct contact with it which could "burn" them. Then they set the bulbs on top of the soil and replace the excavated soil. This type of planting ensures that each bulb is spaced at exactly the same depth and at the proper distance apart.

In the many garden books we have read, the recommended depth for planting bulbs often varies by several inches for the same kind of bulb, indicating that the depth you plant doesn't need to be absolutely exact. If the soil is not too heavy, some bulbs, by the action of their contractile roots, are able to move far enough upward or downward over a period of time to satisfy their preferences. Still, we suggest that you follow the recommendations in the chapters on the various bulbs, because these seem to have gotten the best results from a variety of expert growers. When a bulb that should be set 6 inches deep is planted at only 2 inches, it is likely to split quickly into small bulblets and

loose soil

fertilizer

loose soil

To plant bulbs in a trench, loosen the soil at the bottom, spread a layer of fertilizer, then cover with more loose soil and set bulbs on top of soil. Replace the rest of the excavated soil.

not bloom well. Those that have been set too deep, on the other hand, have trouble forcing their sprouts to the surface, especially in heavy soil. Consequently they bloom later, if at all, and increase in numbers much more slowly.

The conventional wisdom is to set each bulb so that its top sits two to three times as far from the soil's surface as the height of the bulb. This rule works well for most bulbs but not for tulips, which should be planted with their bases from 6 to 8 inches below the surface. Madonna lily bulbs are another exception to the rule. They are large, but they grow well only if they are set with their tops 1 inch deep.

Get your bulbs started in the right direction by planting them top side up. One of our customers confessed to putting in a foundation planting of daffodils when she was beginning to garden, and when the bulbs didn't come up in the spring after a reasonable length of time she dug up a few and discovered that she had planted them all with their tops downward! Bulbs planted upside down become contortionists and eventually emerge by twisting their stems upward, but they have a tough struggle, and it takes them a long time to reach the surface of the soil. Most true bulbs, such as tulips and narcissus, have pointed tips that obviously

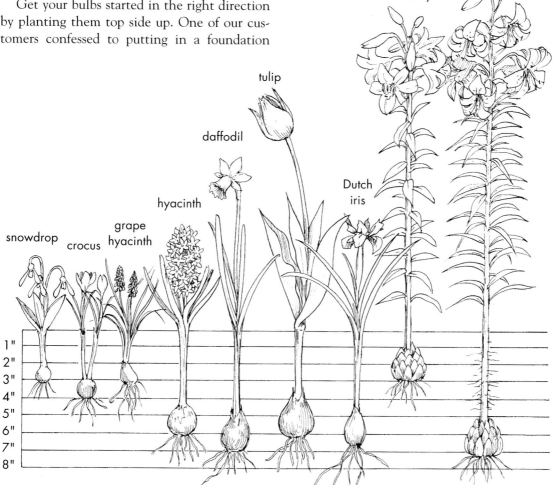

Proper planting depth at bulb base

After planting bulbs, firm soil with your foot and water thoroughly. Spread a 1- to 2-inch layer of mulch over the planting.

should face upward and a basal plate from which the roots emerge. Corms, tubers, and rhizomes usually show sprouts on their upper sides, so keep these on top when you plant them. When you plant the bulb, pack the soil around it firmly with your foot. Even a small amount of air left in the pocket will dry out the bulb, and if its base doesn't touch the soil, the roots will have a tough time.

Always water the area thoroughly after planting unless rains are heavy. We are surprised when gardeners who faithfully water their newly set shrubs and trees in the spring forget that moisture is just as necessary in the fall to help plants get started.

Most bulbs sprout in their proper season and send a shoot straight upward, although the underground stems of certain lilies tend to twist around before breaking through the surface. We planted a bed of regal lilies for a customer many years ago, spacing them carefully in several straight rows as she wanted. When the plants came up she was distressed because they were not evenly spaced. They grew in a tangled fashion that bore no resemblance to the rows we'd set them in, and it was difficult to explain that lilies seem to have minds of their own.

Mulching

We like to spread a layer of organic mulch an inch or two thick over our bulb plantings. The bulbs easily push through it, and it helps them in many ways. Nature doesn't like bare soil and tends to carpet it with weeds unless we cover it first. Also, bulbs need lots of moisture during their short, speedy growing season, and a mulch keeps the soil from drying out between showers or waterings. It also protects fall-planted bulbs from an early frost and gives them extra rooting time in regions like ours where winters come early. In very cold climates, a mulch provides extra insulation during winter when the alternate freezing and thawing of the earth can heave bulbs out of the ground. It also keeps the soil from freezing deeply, which protects tender bulbs. And, as an extra bonus, an organic mulch adds fertility and humus to the soil as it decomposes.

We mulch our flower beds with leaves each fall, but you can use any similar material that will gradually decompose — bark, wood chips, cocoa or peanut hulls, seaweed, and citrus pulp are all good. We don't recommend using sawdust, however, because it packs too tightly and steals nitrogen from the soil.

Good Mulch Materials

Material	Source
Bark (best if shredded)	Buy from garden centers, mills
Grass clippings	Lawns
Hay, spoiled ensilage	Farms, old meadows
Leaves	Woods, roadsides, community maintenance workers
Pine needles	Woods, roadsides
Hulls, peanut shells	Buy from garden centers
Salt hay, seaweed	Buy, collect from beaches
Shavings	Buy, collect from mills
Straw	Buy, get from farms

Bulb Care As Time Goes On

Because nursery-grown bulbs, including narcissus, tulips, and hyacinths, are treated so well in their early stages, their blooms are almost certain to be good the first season after you plant them, whether you fertilize them or not. When the blossoms are not as spectacular in the years that follow, the fault is usually lack of nutrients. Keep the bulbs well supplied with food and water during their growing period, but be careful not to overfeed them. Although they benefit from a light annual feeding, overfertilizing results in lots of leaf growth at the expense of blooms, and excessive amounts of chemical plant foods can kill the bulbs. Lack of fertilizer is one of the chief reasons that all bulbs deteriorate over the years. Many of those recommended for naturalizing last for many years if they are fertilized occasionally.

Spring is a good time to apply fertilizer, spreading it over the bed just before you add new mulch. The fertilizer will then be covered and ready to feed the plants over a longer period. Choose a fertilizer that contains both nitrogen and potash as bulbs need these more than they do phosphorus. Neither super-phosphate nor phosphate rock contain these elements, and the much-recommended bonemeal is rich in phosphorus, but not in nitrogen and potash. Wood ashes are a good source of potash, and they also increase the soil pH, which is of benefit to most bulbs. A light sprinkling of ashes once a year is about right.

There are many other reasons besides lack of fertilizer that bulbs bloom less satisfactorily as time goes on. When bulbs that initially bloomed beautifully stop blooming well, check to see if they are becoming overcrowded. If so, dig, divide, and replant them at the recommended depth as soon as they die down after blooming. Diseases and insects may also be reasons for poor bulb health (see chapter 5). Or, it may be that growing trees or large shrubs either shade the plants or have spreading root systems that compete for moisture and nutrients. Heavy growth of weeds, grass, competitive perennials, or ground covers can also crowd bulbs. Avoid planting them together with invasive ground covers, and keep other types of competition controlled by frequent weeding, mowing, mulching, or by applying one of the safer herbicides such as Roundup.

Most bulbous plants need water during their growing season to do well and may suffer during dry years if extra water is not provided. Some, such as iris and certain alliums, need frequent division and will deteriorate if the clump becomes too large.

Always keep seed pods from forming on the larger bulbs such as narcissus, tulips, lilies, and hyacinths, because the plant uses lots of energy to mature them. On the other hand, let the seeds grow on the small bulbs such as *Chionodoxa* that you are raising for naturalizing because these plants spread rapidly by seeds.

After-Bloom Care

After the colorful blossoms of the spring bulbs fade and die, the leaves of small bulbs such as snowdrops, crocuses, and grape hyacinths die quickly, but the process takes longer for the larger "major" bulbs —narcissus, hyacinths, and tulips. The after-bloom period is critical for the future of each bulb. During that time the sugars, proteins, and starches in the foliage that were used by the bulb during its growing and blooming periods must be replenished so that the embryonic plant and flower of the coming year can form. Because the dying foliage is ugly, it is tempting to mow or clip it off, but unless you plan to buy and plant new bulbs each year, never interrupt this pre-dormancy process. Allow the leaves to die completely on their own. Don't let anyone convince you to braid up the browning leaves on your daffodils to make them less obvious in the garden, as friends persuaded us to do years ago. The leaves need sun and air circulation around them to complete this stage of their life cycle.

After the foliage has died and the bulb or corm is again filled with nutrients, the plant will be somewhat dormant for the summer season, although it doesn't rest completely since it forms small bulblets or cormels. The corm of some bulbous plants, such as crocus, dies each year and is replaced by a completely new one.

Most spring bulbs thrive when they spend the summer in the soil, but tulips are an exception. They do best if you dig them after their foliage dies, let them dry, store them over the summer, and replant them in the fall. See chapter 8 for the best methods of handling them.

Each bulb, no matter when it blooms, has a built-in dormancy period following the blossoming. For the proper treatment of summer and fall bloomers and tender bulbs during this time, see sections on individual bulbs in chapters 10 to 13.

Remove spent flowers and seed pods from tulips and other large bulbs (but be sure to leave the foliage).

WHY DON'T MY BULBS BLOOM?

If your newly planted bulbs fail to bloom well the first spring after planting, it may be because the bulbs were of poor quality or diseased when you bought them, or any of the following:

❖ STORAGE. If the bulbs have been stored in temperatures that were too dry or too warm (over 80°F) they won't bloom. The flower buds of tulips will be killed.

❖ DEPTH. Bulbs may be planted at the wrong depth. Check and replant if necessary.

❖ TIMING. Bulbs may have been planted too late in the fall. Fertilize, and they should do better the second year.

❖ LIGHT. The bulbs may not be getting all the spring sunshine they need.

❖ SOIL. The soil may be too heavy or sandy.

❖ ANIMALS. Rodents sometimes eat crocus, hyacinths, tulips, muscari, and other bulbs. Deer and rabbits may eat tops in the spring.

Labels and Records

Throughout the gardening season you can keep an eye on most of your annuals and perennials whether they are blooming or not. But you can't see the foliage of spring bulbs during the summer and autumn, and fall-bloomers such as autumn crocus and lycoris produce leaves in the spring but then disappear until they bloom later in the season. Unless your memory is better than ours, it's wise to use labels and keep records, so you don't plant a clump of phlox on top of dormant hyacinths, or cannas over the autumn crocuses. Labels and records help you keep track of the names of new cultivars and when you planted them. You never know when you may want to order more of a particularly nice cultivar, or replace bulbs that the mice devoured.

Many kinds of garden labels are good, including homemade ones. After years of experimenting, we've settled on the aluminum sort sold by garden stores because they are more permanent than either wood or plastic. We emboss them with a ballpoint pen and fasten them to small metal or bamboo stakes which we buy, or onto pieces of used ½-inch black plastic water pipe that we've cut into 6-inch lengths. We

place them inconspicuously near the plants, where they last for years.

For most gardeners, keeping records is a bore. It's much more fun to spend time planting and pruning. Many gardeners never write down a thing and remember the names and location of everything in the garden, but we are not among them. We need to label everything we plant and record it promptly, a habit we formed when we operated a plant nursery for many years. It helped us to better buy, plan, and organize our bulbs and other plantings.

To make a garden journal more fun, include your own comments and those of visitors: "a nasty bindweed is assaulting the Madonna lilies." Record changes of the weather and uninvited animal guests. Jot down details about plants' blooming times, heights, and vigor, and which insects and diseases are around, as well as remedies that worked or failed.

We note which plants should be moved to another spot and try, somewhat unsuccessfully, to keep track of the sequence of bloom and color arrangement in the landscape. We always write down the dates we apply fertilizers and those of the spring and fall frosts. We've never been sorry that we took the time to keep records and couldn't garden without them.

A garden calendar, like a birthday calendar, can help you get through the year without missing important events. Most of us need to be reminded to purchase potting soil, plant food, labels, and pest control materials long before we need them. We need reminders of when to order spring flowering bulbs; when to pot up crocuses, daffodils, and tulips for forcing; and when to take them from cold storage for a succession of late winter blooms.

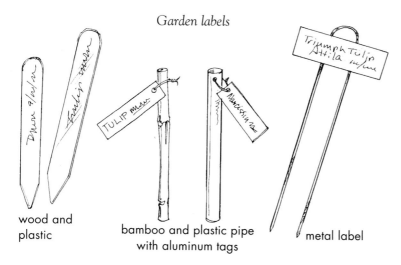

Garden labels

wood and plastic

bamboo and plastic pipe with aluminum tags

metal label

Protect early-season bulbs against frost with a floating row cover.

Lengthening the Season

A couple of weeks before the daffodils and tulips bloom in our backyard, one of our neighbors always has a beautiful display of them in front of her home. Our bulbs are in a windy, cool spot where the snow stays late, but hers are sheltered by the house in a warm, south-facing bed.

If you garden in a short season, you may be able to convince some of your bulbs to bloom early by planting them in a protected sunny spot. Another way to "force" them is to build a miniature greenhouse by simply placing a sheet of clear plastic over the bed, but lift it off on warm, sunny days so the tender sprouts won't be burned by bright spring sunlight. Bulbs that sprout early are more vulnerable to spring frosts, so as soon as the bulbs sprout, replace the clear plastic with a floating row cover such as Reemay. This material is so light that it moves up with the plants as they grow, and it provides better protection from frost than plastic. Remove it as the season warms.

Row covers are also an excellent protection for tender, summer-blooming bulbs such as dahlias, gladioli, and tuberous begonias. By starting the plants indoors and setting them outdoors early with row cover protection, you can often get a jump of two or three weeks on the blooming season. The lightweight covers won't crush the growing plants and they also keep out flying insects that lay eggs on the leaves. Anchor the edges of the coverings with stones, bricks, or boards so they don't blow away. The fabric is fragile, but if you handle it carefully you can use it for more than one year.

Bulb Problems

COMPARED WITH THE PESTS that attack our fruit trees and cabbage plants, those that menace bulbs seem insignificant, both in numbers and in the devastation they cause. Bulbs are amazingly free from troublesome pests, but — like all plants — they attract certain diseases, insects, and four-footed creatures. Most of their plagues are the same as those that trouble our herbaceous perennials — diseases such as blights, mildew, and rots, and sucking insects (aphids), chewing ones (beetles), and nematodes and worms that assault roots. Animals that find bulbs tasty range in size from mice to moose. Check the entries for individual bulbs for their susceptibility to these problems.

Although insects or disease might strike your bulbs at any time, bulbs — like humans — better resist and overcome such troubles if they are healthy. Try to avoid difficulties by starting with good bulbs, giving them a favorable location, and supplying them with adequate moisture and nutrients.

Even with the best of care, however, things can go wrong. Most gardeners are realistic enough to know that 100-percent success with every plant is rare. Still, there is usually a reason when a bulb doesn't thrive, and it can't always be blamed on disease, insects, or animals. Check first for physiological conditions that might be affecting your bulbs. Is the spot where they are planted too wet, too dry, too sunny, or too shady? Abnormal growth and poor flowering can occur when bulbs are planted too deep, not deep enough, or wrong side up.

Diseases

To prevent fungal diseases, especially rots, treat any bulbs, rhizomes, corms, or tubers you store for any length of time with a fungicide such as sulfur. Place them in a paper bag, pour in a small amount of dry fungicide, and shake the bag so all are dusted. Although many commercial bulbs have already been treated with fungicide, it can also be good insurance against troubles for the bulbs you buy to do this just before planting. If for any reason you didn't treat glads and dahlias before storing them, do it

BUD BLAST

A common complaint of bulb growers is a condition called *bud blast*. The buds of affected bulbs develop normally, but before they open they become deformed and often discolored. The malady is not limited to bulbs, since many perennials such as daylilies and peonies and even certain houseplants are sometimes affected.

Bud blasting may be caused by a variety of things, including disease, insects, and physiological conditions. Botrytis and other blights, for example, are often culprits, as are insects that feed on the buds. These pests are difficult to identify, and a small magnifying glass is often necessary to spot them. The soil may lack moisture or contain too much or too little of a nutrient or trace element.

To help prevent this condition, plant only healthy bulbs, put them in good soil, and give them the light conditions they prefer. Provide nutrients and the moisture they need, and don't allow them to become too crowded.

---

just before planting. Whenever you separate bulbs, treat any cut surfaces with fungicide, too, because they are a prime target for disease.

A few decades ago many imported bulbs were infected with viruses that caused growers problems, but nurseries are far more careful now, and shipments are carefully inspected. Fungal or bacterial diseases such as rots can occur in storage, however, even if the bulbs were healthy when they were dug and shipped, so always inspect them before planting. Discard any that are obviously sick, since bulb diseases can spread rapidly once they get into the soil. Bulbs can also pick up diseases such as botrytis, leaf spot, powdery mildew, rots, viruses, and wilts from other garden plants.

Botrytis, or **gray mold,** is one of the most common diseases that affects bulbs and other perennials. This fungus blight first shows up as a browning of plant tissue that later turns black and finally changes to gray-brown masses of downy spores on the leaves and stems. Since botrytis is most prevalent in warm, humid weather, unless the bulbs are shade lovers, plant them in a sunny spot where a gentle breeze will blow now and then. Don't allow the plants to become overcrowded, either. Water early in the morning whenever possible so that the leaves will not stay wet for long periods and the top of the soil or mulch will dry out quickly and not contribute to the humidity.

Unless the problem is very serious, you can often check botrytis by cutting off the affected parts. Remove and destroy all dead foliage on the summer-blooming plants in late fall, too, so the fungus can't overwinter there and infect new plants in the spring. In extreme cases, spray with a fungicide beginning early in the season, and continue the treatment as long as necessary.

Leafspot is a black or brown fungus on leaves and sometimes on flowers. In extreme cases, leaf drop may occur. Good air circulation helps prevent it. Spray with a fungicide if necessary.

Powdery mildew, a common problem, first appears as reddish spots, then as a white or gray powdery fungus on leaves, stems, and flowers. Later you may notice a gray or white woolly growth that causes flower buds to "blast" without opening and leaves to wither. Mildew grows and spreads in much the same way as botrytis, and the recommended methods of prevention are much the same: water carefully, encourage air circulation, and clean away dead foliage in the fall. If the disease is problematic year after year, spray or dust several times during the season with a fungicide, beginning early in the summer before obvious signs appear. It is usually too late for treatment if you wait until your gardening neighbors are starting to notice it.

Rots of various kinds attack bulbs and may be either fungal or bacterial in origin. They get their start either in the soil or in storage, so in some cases the bulbs may be diseased when you buy them. If they are soft and mushy or show other signs of rot, or if they are dry, small, and hard, discard them immediately (but not on your compost pile where you can later spread the trouble over your garden).

Infected bulbs may not grow at all, or if they do, the foliage is likely to be weak, yellowish, and prone to wilt. To help prevent rots, grow bulbs only in very well drained soil, dust them with a fungicide before planting, and store them only in a dry, cool place.

Viruses on bulbs, as on all plants, are the hardest diseases to control. Suspect a virus when plants are stunted with deformed flowers and leaves that sometimes show various shades of green. Viruses invariably weaken a bulb and sometimes kill it. Since there is no cure, try to keep viruses out of your plantings by buying only healthy plants and quickly removing any infected ones before they contaminate others. Since most viral diseases, including mosaic, are carried by aphids or other sucking insects, control them by regular spot spraying with an insecticide such as pyrethrum. Cover the sprayed plants with a floating row cover for two days after spraying if you wish, to keep beneficial insects from reaching the spray. Never replant bulbs in the spot where infected bulbs have been grown unless you first grow a cover crop there for two or three years or sterilize the soil.

Wilts are caused by fungi that live in the soil. They cause plant yellowing, wilting, stunting of growth, and eventually death. As with viruses, there is no cure. Remove any infected plants immediately, and do not plant new bulbs where you have recently grown wilt-susceptible vegetables such as tomatoes. Also, do not plant new bulbs in a spot where infected bulbs have grown unless you sterilize the soil first.

DISEASES AND INSECT PESTS OF COMMON BULB-TYPE PLANTS

PLANT	DISEASES	INSECT PESTS
CROCUS	rot, rust, scab, virus	aphids, bulb mites
DAHLIA	crown gall, wilt (fusarian and verticillium), root rot, powdery mildew	aphids, borers, caterpillars, leafhoppers, wireworms
GLADIOLUS	blight, crown rot, leaf spot, scab, virus, wilt	aphids, beetles, maggots, mealybugs, nematodes, scale, tarnished plant bugs, thrips, wireworms
IRIS	blight, leaf spot, rot, rust, mosaic virus, scorch	aphids, borers, flies, nematodes, slugs, thrips, weevils
LILY	botrytis blight, canker, chlorosis, crown rot, leaf spot, mold, rust, virus	aphids, borers, bulb flies, bulb mites, nematodes, thrips
NARCISSUS	basal bulb-rot, blight, leaf scorch, leaf spot, rot, virus	aphids, bulb flies, mealybugs, millipedes, nematodes, thrips
TULIP	anthracnose, blight, crown rot, virus	aphids, bulb flies, millipedes, nematodes, wireworms

Insect Pests

Aphids, tiny little plant lice that cluster on leaves and stems, show up on nearly every kind of plant including those grown from bulbs. When there are large numbers of them, they weaken a plant by sucking out its juices. Even worse, they transmit viral diseases. Because they are so tiny, you often don't notice them until you see that the plant is failing. Sometimes other insects, such as ladybugs, are able to keep

BULB PEST ALERT: THE RED LILY LEAF BEETLE

Lilliocerus lilii, the red lily leaf beetle, a common pest in Europe, first appeared in the Boston area in 1992, although infestations have occurred in Montreal, Canada, since 1943. In adult and larval stages they devour lily foliage until only bare stalks are left, and they've been known to eat leaves of other bulbous and herbacious perennials as well.

LIFE CYCLE. The red adult beetles, about the size of thin ladybugs, lay clusters of eggs on the undersides of leaves. Within ten days they hatch into ugly brownish grubs, soon covered with black excrement. They eat for twenty days, then pupate for twenty days. Unfortunately, each can produce several generations each year. Thus far, no biological methods of control have been found.

CONTROL. (1) Hand-pick as many grubs as possible and kill them by squashing, burning, or soaking in alcohol; (2) spray all lily foliage with an insecticide as soon as the creatures appear; (3) drench the soil with insecticide in the fall to kill overwintering beetles.

aphids in check, but if not, control them with applications of an insecticide such as pyrethrum, rotenone, or an insecticidal soap. (To protect ladybugs and other beneficial predators, cover plants with floating row cover for a couple of days after spraying.) Some gardeners have had good luck with the new, highly refined oil sprays (see Appendix for sources).

winged aphid

wingless aphid

Beetles such as the Japanese beetle, cucumber beetle, and rose chafer feed on bulb leaves, stems, and blooms. They chew holes in the leaves and their larvae may feed on the roots. Pick off the large ones and drop them in alcohol, or a jar of water with a squirt of detergent. If necessary, spray the plant with an insecticide.

Japanese beetle

striped cucumber beetle

Borers feed on leaves, stalks, and roots. If they are present, the bulb leaves will be spotted and look water-soaked. Rot often follows borer activity. To control borers, remove and destroy infected parts. If necessary, spray an insecticide as often as required, beginning in early spring.

rose chafer

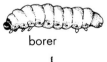

borer

Maggots of the narcissus bulb fly (*Lampetia equestris*) are small, whitish, legless worms about ¾ inch long that feed on bulbs, and a soft rot may result. The leaves

maggot

become infected, and the plant stops growing. Control it by discarding all infected bulbs.

Mites are very tiny, but the wrinkled leaves they cause indicate their presence. Cyclamen mites hit other plants as well as cyclamen. Control them with an insecticide, and keep them from infecting other susceptible garden plants such as strawberries and delphiniums.

Nematodes, microscopic worms that feed on roots, are most common in cultivated soils in warm climates but may be present anywhere. They multiply rapidly, causing plants to become stunted and discolored, and small galls often show up on the roots. If they are a problem, it may be necessary to sterilize the soil before planting and rotate the plantings occasionally.

How to Avoid Diseases and Insects

- ❖ Buy healthy bulbs, inspect them before planting for signs of disease, and discard any in dubious condition.
- ❖ Store all bulbs in a cool, dry, well-ventilated place (*never* in an airtight container).
- ❖ Plant bulbs in soil and light conditions they prefer, and in a spot with good air circulation and excellent drainage.
- ❖ When watering bulbs, always do it in the morning, and/or use a drip hose to avoid wetting leaves.
- ❖ Use sanitation practices: remove dead leaves and clean away foliage of summer- and fall-blooming bulbs in the autumn.
- ❖ Inspect your plantings frequently for problems, and keep in mind a couple of clichés: "The footsteps of the gardener are the best medicine" and "A stitch in time saves nine."

Some gardeners report that they've controlled mild infestations by growing smelly varieties of marigolds among the bulbs. Chemical nematocides are also available.

Slugs and **snails** are slimy creatures that like dark, damp areas. A nuisance to most gardeners, they multiply rapidly and eat holes in leaves at night. Snails have shells but slugs do not. Remove their hiding places, such as old leaves and other debris, and use slug baits if the damage becomes widespread. If the infestation is serious, dust the area with diatomaceous earth.

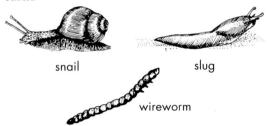

snail   slug

wireworm

Wireworms are long, jointed, brown to yellowish beetle larvae with hard, shiny skin, ⅓ to ½ inch long. They attack bulbs, corms, rhizomes, and even stems, sometimes killing the plant. You will find a few in most soils but they are not usually a problem. You can help control them by rotating bulb plantings with a cover crop of rye or millet once every few years. Some gardeners trap them in pieces of potato they spread in the garden.

Beneficial Insects

Most people prefer to do as little spraying as possible, even with the so-called "safe" sprays. One of the best ways to control plant-eating insects in the garden is to encourage plenty of "good guy" insects that prey on them. You can buy them from suppliers listed in garden magazines or in the Appendix. Unless you have sprayed heavily in the past, your garden no doubt is already home to many beneficial

BENEFICIALS AND THEIR TARGETS

INSECT	CONTROLS
ant lions	ants, small insects
chalcid wasps	aphids, scale, cabbage worms
green lacewings	aphids, scale
ground beetles	aphids, flea beetles, leafhoppers
hover fly larvae	aphids, leafhoppers, mealy bugs, scale
ichneumon wasps	caterpillars, borers
ladybugs	aphids, spider mites
praying mantis	aphids, beetles, caterpillars, leafhoppers, wasps
tachinid flies	beetles, cutworms, grasshoppers

ant lion   green lacewing   ground beetle

hover fly   ichneumon wasp   ladybug

praying mantis   tachinid fly

insects. If you do have to resort to spraying, protect the local population of beneficial insects by covering the sprayed plants with floating row cover for a few days. See the box for some of the best, listed with what they help to control.

Natural Repellents

Organic gardeners often use other plants to ward off harmful insects, and although they are seldom 100-percent effective, they can be helpful. Unfortunately, many plants that help the most — catnip, horseradish, mints, tansy, and thyme — become so weedy that they, too, can be problems. If you use these plants, put them in a tub that you've sunk partly into the ground, so they can't escape. Garlic, other members of the onion family, and marigolds are insect repellents that are easier to control.

The sprays made from some plants can also be effective deterrents to insects. Stewed rhubarb or tansy leaves, garlic juice, and similar plant sprays are less toxic than most chemicals, but because they are not long-lasting, repeated applications may be necessary. Growers have also had success by collecting harmful insects, crushing them in an old blender (use it *only* for this purpose, not for food), and mixing them with water to make a spray that repels the same kind of insect on the plants. Bird houses and berry-producing shrubs encourage the birds that also control many insects.

When using pesticides of all kinds, be careful to read the label on the package or bottle. Make sure it is for the problem you have, and follow the directions carefully.

Bulbs Least Attractive to Mice and Other Rodents

Spring

Allium	Galanthus
Camassia	Hyacinth
Convallaria	Narcissus
Fritillaria	Scilla

Summer- and Fall-Blooming

Acidanthera	Cyclamen
Agapanthus	Dahlia
Anemone	Gladiolus
Begonia, tuberous	Lycoris
Caladium	Ornithogalum
Calla	Oxalis
Canna	Polianthes
Colocasia	Ranunculus
Crocosmia	Tigridia

Animal Pests

Woodchucks, rabbits, deer, mice, and other creatures sometimes devastate bulb plants in suburban and city gardens, as well as in the back country. We frequently get calls from gardeners asking what could possibly have dug up their newly planted bulbs. Invariably they followed planting directions and used a generous amount of bonemeal in the soil, which proved irresistible to dogs and doglike wild animals — coyotes, wolves, and foxes.

Moles get bad press for eating bulbs each winter, but they usually eat only insects, especially grubs. They do, however, burrow networks of tunnels in lawns and gardens, which make great subterranean routes for gophers, mice, and voles that have lusty appetites for bulbs, especially tulips. You can sometimes discourage them with traps, baits, mothballs, or electronic controls sold by some nurseries. Or plant only those bulbs that rodents don't eat.

The bulbs and foliage of narcissus and most scillas are poisonous to animals, and when in a mixed planting with other bulbs, the toxic bulbs sometimes protect the others.

Electric fences are effective barriers to some of the larger bulb-eating animals, but woodchucks easily burrow beneath them. We have heard that planting a patch of clover nearby will lure both woodchucks and rabbits away from the bulb plants, but any wild creatures we have known prefer to eat the most valuable crops. Some gardeners control woodchucks by using the gas bombs sold by farm stores.

American Nurseryman magazine lists the whitetail deer as one of the ten worst garden pests in the country, putting them in the same category as aphids and Japanese beetles. They certainly have been one of our biggest headaches. Since we live in a rural area, this is to be expected, but gardeners in the suburbs, where hunting is forbidden and the deer have no natural enemies except automobiles, have even worse problems. There seems to be no limit to what deer will eat or destroy. One fall night, a fat doe pulled up an entire row of our lilies just as they were going dormant, and left them on top of the ground to freeze.

Noisemakers have been largely ineffective for us, but some gardeners have been smart enough to train their dogs to chase away deer and other wild creatures and then return home. Unfortunately, many dogs become deer killers and get into serious trouble with the local constabulary. Bloodmeal discourages the cloven-hoofed vandals during spring and summer, but in late fall the bloodmeal freezes and is no longer effective, nor are many other smelly repellents. Unfortunately this is also the time when much of the usual deer fodder freezes, and the period when they begin eating voraciously to store up fat for the winter. We finally constructed an 8-foot-high tight fence around our nursery and gardens that is effective.

Naturalizing Bulbs

SPRING BEAUTIES WERE one of the things we anticipated with excitement in the springtime as children growing up in the country. We called *Claytonia virginica* "mayflowers," and their tiny white flowers tinged with pink covered the floor of the maple woods, stretching magically around trees as far as the eye could see. As we went "mayflowering" and picked until our little hands were full of fragrant bouquets for May baskets, we didn't know they grew from corms. Nor did we know that the yellow trout lilies with mottled leaves (*Erythronium americanum*), which filled our fields a bit later, also grew from corms. Only much later did we realize that the patches of red "nosebleeds" and their elegant painted-trillium cousins also grew from bulbous roots. What we *did* know, though subconsciously, was that these natural woodland areas with their profusion of blooms were some of the most happy places we'd ever been.

And these days, we try to imitate nature's lavishness by planting "naturalized" bulbs.

No one has defined naturalizing better than Louise Beebe Wilder in her classic 1936 book, *Adventures with Hardy Bulbs:*

> In its narrow sense, to naturalize bulbs means merely to plant them in an informal and unstudied manner in contradistinction to their use in formal beds; but in the broader and more accepted sense, it means to broadcast them on a generous scale in woods, in meadows, by pond and streamside, along winding paths, on rough banks or about the outskirts of the garden, to suggest, as best we may, nature's handicraft, not man's.

She goes on to say that it isn't easy for a gardener to bring about a perfectly natural and spontaneous effect. Nevertheless, it can be

Once established, a naturalized planting of narcissus provides a breathtaking display each spring.

done, and once the bulbs are installed in a location they enjoy, a naturalized planting is the easiest kind of gardening. Year after year the plants bloom on their own, taking care of themselves and expanding until you're likely to forget that you had anything to do with them. They may even outlive you and delight future generations.

Choosing Bulbs

The bulbs you choose for your naturalizing project should grow well in the climate, light, and soil conditions of your location. They should also be vigorous types that can flourish for years with only minimal fertilizing and pest control.

Many hardy spring-flowering bulbs fit this description. The inexpensive, older types, including wild species known as *botanicals,* are better for naturalizing than the higher-priced fancy cultivars you'd choose for a formal border. They need less care than the more refined plants and can grow happily for years without division. (See comments on endangered bulbs, page 31.)

Bulbs in the *Narcissus* genus, especially the

Star-of-Bethlehem (Ornithogalum umbellatum)

Summer snowflake (Leucojum aestivum)

Lily-of-the-valley (Convallaria majalis)

Grassnut, triplet lily
(Triteleia laxa)

Striped squill (Puschkinia scilloides)

old rugged types, are particularly adept at growing in a natural planting, and fortunately rodents and deer don't like them. When we think of daffodils, a home near the highway in Stowe, Vermont, comes to mind. The gray weathered shingle house is attractive, but the sloping field next to it covered with gold and white narcissus is the spot that catches the eye. When summer arrives, the field becomes a neatly mowed lawn without a hint of the enchanting flowers that bloomed there throughout the month of May. It is a naturalized planting at its best, appearing unplanned and somewhat wild, as if nature had arranged it without the help of human hands. The charming lady of the house told us she'd started the planting with bulbs she'd dug up in the country

(Left to right) Tulipa greigii *'Mary Ann'* and *'Peach Blossom'*, *with* T. fosteriana *'Purissima'*

beside an old cellar hole, after getting permission from the owner.

Other large-flowering major spring bulbs that naturalize well are crocuses, and some of the botanical tulips including the early-flowering *Tulipa kaufmanniana* and *T. fosteriana* varieties and hybrids, and *T. greigii* with their mottled or striped foliage. (For other species, see the individual listings at the end of this chapter.) The bulbs are smaller than those of the cultivars, the largest reaching only about 1 inch in diameter. Unlike crocuses and narcissus most tulips do not compete well with grass and weeds and should be kept weed-free for best results.

Many of the smaller spring bulbs also naturalize well. We recall, on springtime walks in the English countryside, masses of bluebells (*Endymion non-scriptus*, also known as *Scilla non-scripta*) surrounding woodland paths, and aromatic white garlic (a variety of *Allium*) thick under the trees. Those and many other attractive bulbs can be easily naturalized. The tiny

A wild drift of white trillium is one of the delightful surprises of the spring woodlands.

Snowdrops (Galanthus nivalis)

white snowdrops (*Galanthus*) and yellow winter aconite (*Eranthis*) come early, followed by glory-of-the snow (*Chionodoxa*) and deep purple grape hyacinths (*Muscari*). Then come blue, white, and pink squill (*Endymion hispanicus*, also known as *Scilla hispanica*), the deep purple *Iris reticulata* with its yellow crests, and the fragrant bells of lily-of-the-valley (*Convallaria*).

In the summer and fall, not as many hardy bulbous plants adapt well to a natural setting, but wild lilies, certain *Alliums*, and autumn crocuses (*Colchicum*) are sometimes used.

For a planting to be effective, it must be large enough to give the illusion of mass, even in a

Siberian iris quickly multiply to make a spectacular early summer display.

RICHARD BROWN

RICHARD BROWN

Autumn crocus (Colchicum speciosum)

small space. If your budget can handle it, start with one of the collections of up to 100 bulbs for naturalizing offered by mail-order nurseries. Many list purple crocus or yellow narcissus in a mixture of cultivars that bloom at different times and can provide drifts of the same color for a month of more. Some sell naturalizing mixtures of colorful, short (8 to 10 inch) species tulips.

When you are choosing bulbs for a natural planting, avoid masses of multicolored bulbs because no matter how lovely each bloom is individually, the overall effect will appear disordered. Even tiny plots can appear large, however, when they consist entirely of one kind and color of plant, such as all yellow crocuses, or vivid blue squill. A grouping of daffodils near another of squill can be beautiful, but intermingled, they would be less effective. Bulbs that are mixed do not resemble those in a natural wild setting.

Since rules are made to be broken, you can probably think of effective color combinations and intermingled groupings that work. An assortment of crocuses in their spring garbs of yellow, purple, and white seems to shout, "Spring is here!" and who would say they should all be color-coordinated?

For a long season of bloom, gardeners not only use plants of the same genus that bloom for a long time, such as early, midseason, and late narcissus, but they also interplant bulbs of a different genus that bloom at different seasons. Snowdrops and tulips are good companion bulbs, since the snowdrops are gone when the tulips bloom. Dwarf iris can be used to follow the tulips.

Choosing the Location

Choosing the proper location for your naturalizing project is crucial to its success. Each genus has its own requirements, and it's a good idea to do some research before you invest in huge numbers of an unfamiliar bulb. If you are doubtful about whether a plant will naturalize in the place you want to put it, do a small test planting before you scatter hundreds of bulbs there. Within a couple of years, you'll have the answer.

Most of us have some spot that would be ideal for a natural planting — in a lawn or meadow, lining a path or walkway, nestled under an apple tree or lilac bush, near the edge of a woodland, alongside a stream, surrounding a pond, or in deciduous woods. A sloping hillside is a wonderful showcase for naturalized bulbs, and we like to plant them in out-of-the-way spots to surprise people when they come upon them unexpectedly.

Nearly all bulbs need spring sunlight. Spots under deciduous trees and shrubs are ideal for many early-blooming spring bulbs because, as we mentioned before, the flowers will have faded and the plants begun to go dormant by the time the leaves appear and start to shade them. Before you plant, keep in mind that the foliage of some bulbs looks sick after the blooms have faded, but you must leave it intact until the bulb has completed its regeneration process. Daffodils, for example, need from four to six weeks after blooming before you should cut them; in cool, damp climates, the process may take longer. Choose a spot for such bulbs where their unkempt appearance during early summer will be something you can endure.

Crocuses and many early-blooming minor spring bulbs have foliage that disappears quickly after blooming, and these are the types of bulb to use on a lawn that you want to look neat. *Chionodoxa*, *Scilla*, *Puschkinia*, *Ornithogalum*, and *Galanthus* all have blooms that are only 3 to 6 inches tall, and their foliage dies back before mowing is necessary. (A good time to plant them is when you are reseeding the lawn.)

Few bulbs do well in damp areas because they tend to rot, but there are exceptions. *Fritillaria meleagris*, which has a charming, unique, tiny purple-checked flower, is one that does well in moist sunny places. *Iris cristata* enjoys moist spots in light shade, and wild ginger (*Asarum canadense*) also grows in moist, lightly shaded spots. Most other bulbous plants need soil that is well drained.

Controlling Competitive Plants

Even the best bulbs for naturalizing cannot withstand aggressive competition. Choose a place where the turf is not thick, and fertilize only lightly so you don't encourage excessive weed and grass growth. Plowing or cultivating is unnecessary when you plant tough, hardy bulbs, but you should be able to dig through the soil easily. Crabgrass, quackgrass, and aggressive ground covers can give bulbs a hard time, as do shallow-rooted trees such as willows and poplars or trees with spreading roots such as maples. Deeply rooted trees such as elms and oaks offer less competition for moisture and nutrients.

We keep our naturalized area from becoming overgrown with hay, brush, or weeds by mowing it at least once a month after the bulb foliage has died completely. We use a 2-wheel power string mower. One of our friends, who enjoys using her head to save her back, lets her horses pasture in her naturalized area from time to time throughout the summer. Other gardeners put a light mulch of old hay or leaves over their plantings in the fall to suppress excessive competitive growth, and some spray herbicides when the bulbs are dormant to thin out weeds and grass whenever too many appear.

Designing and Planting

Straight lines and formality rarely exist in nature, so avoid straight edges unless you set the bulbs along a hedge, path, or road. One way to achieve asymmetrical edges is to take a garden hose, swing it around an area to make graceful curves along the border, and then set the bulbs within that area.

Since well-organized clumps don't belong in a natural planting, arrange the bulbs haphazardly, varying the space between them. One of the charms of bulbs that naturalize well is their tendency to multiply quickly, so there is no need to crowd them when planting. Most at least double each year, and many produce offsets that also grow into new plants. If you are uncertain about spacing, use the old rule of planting: set large bulbs 8 to 12 inches apart, medium-sized ones 4 to 6 inches apart, and small ones 3 to 5 inches apart. Even though they will look sparse the first year or two, they will fill in, and with the wider spacing you won't have to dig and separate them as soon. A patch of only a hundred daffodil bulbs can explode to over three thousand in just five years under ideal conditions.

One oft-recommended way to plant is to take a handful of bulbs and toss them over the section you want to plant. Then plant them

Use garden hose to outline a graceful, natural-looking planting area for bulbs

where they land. Many people swear by this method, but we've found, perhaps because we're not very good at guessing distances, that some bulbs land far too close together and others too far apart. Consequently, we trudge around with a bucket of bulbs and plant them as randomly as possible.

Whether you use a spade or planting tool is up to you. For larger bulbs, dibbles aren't very easy and may leave an unwanted air pocket, but for small bulbs that are set at a shallow depth, a dibble may be the best choice. An acquaintance of ours made one by sharpening the end of an old broom handle like a pencil. We simply open the soil with a spade, insert the bulb at the proper depth, and close it again, packing the soil around it carefully. If the lawn or field looks bumpy when you're done, don't worry. By spring it will have settled into place.

You can help bulbs expand quickly if you fertilize them in the fall or very early in the spring each year. Sprinkle a complete fertilizer over the area, just as you would feed a lawn. Professional bulb growers use chemical fertilizers with higher levels of nitrogen and phosphorus (such as 9–9–6, 7–7–7, 5–10–10) at the rate of about ½ pound per 100 square feet or as recommended on the package, or they spread compost or dried manure over their plantings.

Selecting Naturalized Bulbs

The chart on the following pages lists bulbous plants that naturalize well, as long as they have the conditions they like. Unless otherwise noted they are suitable for planting in zones 3 through 8. The number of bulbs listed per square yard is only a suggestion if you want fast results. If you are in no hurry for complete coverage, plant far fewer.

When ordering bulbs, buy only from reputable dealers so you will be sure they are nursery grown, rather than collected from the wild. For a list of endangered species, see chapter 3.

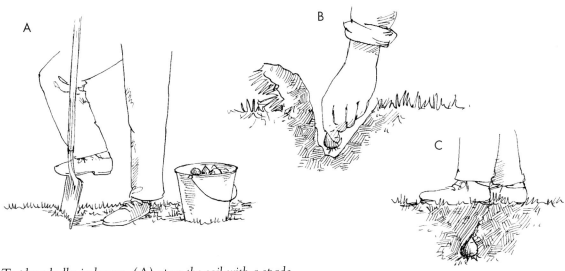

To plant bulbs in lawns, (A) open the soil with a spade,
(B) insert bulb at proper depth, and
(C) close the opening, packing the soil carefully with your foot.

BOTANICAL AND COMMON NAMES	COMMENTS
Allium, Flowering onion	Plant small bulbs in sun, 4 to 6 inches apart; larger ones, 12–18 inches apart.
A. aflatunense, Ornamental garlic	Height, 2½ to 5 feet. Lavender. 'Purple Sensation', 3 feet tall, is a nice cultivar.
A. karataviense, Turkestan onion	Height, 10 inches. Pale pink.
A. moly, Golden garlic, lily leek	Height, 18 inches. Will grow in sun or shade. Yellow.
A. neapolitanum, Daffodil garlic, Naples onion	Height, 15 inches. White with pink stamens. Blooms early spring.
A. oreophilum, Ornamental garlic	Height, 6 inches. Fragrant, rose-colored blooms.
A. sphaerocephalum, Ballhead onion, drumsticks	Height, 30 inches. Reddish purple.
Anemone blanda, Windflower, Greek anemone	Height, 2 to 8 inches. Sun or part shade. Plant 144 per square yard. Cultivars include 'Blue Shades', 'Pink Star', and 'White Splendour'.
Asarum canadense, Wild ginger	Height, 6 inches. Interesting plant for moist, lightly shaded spots. Unusual brown, three-petaled, trumpet-shaped flowers. Large, heart-shaped leaves. Blooms in early summer.
Camassia cusickii, Cusick camas	Height, 18 to 24 inches. Pale blue flowers. Sun or light shade. 64 per square yard.
Chionodoxa, Glory-of-the-snow	Height, 5 to 8 inches. Sun or light shade. 100 per square yard.
C. luciliae	Bright blue.
C. l. 'Gigantea'	Gentian blue.
C. sardensis	Deep blue.
Colchicum autumnale, Autumn crocus, meadow saffron	Height, 8 inches. Sun or light shade. Blooms in late fall. Plant 24 per square yard. 'Autumn Queen' is a light purple cultivar with dark purple checks.
C. speciosum	Rose to purple flowers with cultivars ranging from white to red. To 12 inches tall.
Convallaria, Lily-of-the-valley	Height, 8 inches. Light to medium shade. Tiny, white, very fragrant blooms. Plant 36 per square yard. Blooms in early summer.

BOTANICAL AND COMMON NAMES	COMMENTS
Crocus, Crocus	Height, 3 to 5 inches. Sun. Spring blooming. Plant 144 per square yard. Great for naturalizing. Species live longer than showy Dutch crocus, *C. vernus*. Species include *C. angustifolius*, *C. chrysanthus*, *C. sieberi*, *C. speciosus* (fall bloomer), *and C. tomasinianus*. See p. 78 for list of bunch-flowering crocus good for naturalizing.
Eranthis hyemalis, Winter aconite	Height, 2 to 6 inches. Sun or shade. 144 per square yard. Yellow-gold flowers. Blooms as early as snowdrops.
Galanthus, Snowdrop	Height, 4 to 8 inches. Sun or light shade. Plant 144 per square yard.
G. *nivalis*, Common snowdrop	White.
G. *elwesii*, Giant snowdrop	White, larger flowers and leaves.
Iris cristata, Dwarf crested iris	Height, 4 inches tall. Blue flowers and stiff leaves can make a carpet of green in moist, lightly shaded spots. Blooms in May. White form, 'Alba', adds a bright bit of contrast to darker-colored flowers and leaves in shaded locations. Plant 80 per square yard.
I. reticulata, Dwarf iris	Height, 4 to 6 inches. Sun to light shade. Plant 80 per square yard. The species has violet flowers with a bright orange-yellow blotch on the falls. Good cultivars are 'Clairette' (blue standards with deeper blue falls), 'Harmony' (sky blue standards with royal blue falls marked with gold), and 'Pauline' (violet purple with a white blotch on each fall).
Leucojum vernum, Snowflake	Height, 9 to 12 inches. Plant 3 to 4 inches deep and the same distance apart in light shade. Plant 144 per square yard.
Lilium, Lily	Height, 2 feet or more. Sun or light shade. Plant 16 per square yard. Best for naturalizing: *L. canadense*, meadow lily (Canada lily), *L. lancifolium* (tiger lily), *L. martagon* (Turk's-cap lily), *L. philadelphicum* (wood lily).
Muscari armeniacum, Grape-hyacinth	Height, 5 to 8 inches. Sun or light shade. Plant 125 per square yard. Cultivars include 'Blue Spike' (double and flax-blue) and 'Early Giant' (blue with white edges).
M. botryoides, Grape-hyacinth	'Album' is a white cultivar. Height to 12 inches.

BOTANICAL AND COMMON NAMES	COMMENTS
Narcissus, Daffodils	Height, 6 to 20 inches. Sun, light shade. Plant up to 25 per square yard. The cultivars of most narcissus can be used for naturalizing, but the vigorous ones are best. These include 'Arctic Gold' (goldenrod yellow), 'Barrett Browning' (white with orange cup), 'Cheerfulness' (double white with creamy yellow center), 'Duke of Windsor' (white with orange-yellow cup), 'General Patton' (ivory and yellow), 'Ice Follies' (white with lemon yellow cup that turns white), 'King Alfred' (yellow), 'Mount Hood' (white), 'Mrs. R. O. Backhouse' (light pink), 'Peeping Tom' (yellow), 'Salome' (coral pink cup, white petals), 'Silver Chimes' (white with primrose yellow cup), 'Spellbinder' (yellow petals and green-yellow trumpet), and 'Sweetness' (yellow; late bloomer).
N. cyclamineus	Perianths have reflexed petals. Height, 8 inches. Bloom early. Cultivars are yellow unless otherwise marked. They include 'Jenny', 'Salome', 'Tête-à-tête', 'February Silver' (white with yellow crown), and 'February Gold'.
N. poeticus, Poet's narcissus	Usually white, fragrant, with a small yellow cup edged in red. 'Actaea' is the principal one available; it tolerates damp soil.
N. jonquilla, Jonquil	Various shades of yellow. Fragrant.
Ornithogalum umbellatum, Star-of-Bethlehem	Height 6 to 12 inches. Sun, light shade. Plant 100 per square yard. White or green and white. Can become invasive.
Puschkinia scilloides, Striped squill	Height, 3 to 6 inches. Sun or partial shade. Plant 144 per square yard. White with pale blue stripes.
Scilla	Height, 5 to 10 inches. Sun or light shade. Plant up to 125 per square yard.
S. bifolia, Twin-leaf squill	Gentian blue.
S. litardierei, Meadow squill	Bright blue.
S. siberica, Siberian squill	Blue. Foliage dies early so this is a good lawn plant. 'Alba' has white flowers.
Triteleia laxa (*Brodiaea laxa*), Grassnut, triplet lily	Height, 1 to 2 feet. Sun. Plant 100 per square yard. 'Queen Fabiola' is deep blue.

BOTANICAL AND COMMON NAMES	COMMENTS
Tulipa, Tulip	Various heights. Full sun or partial shade. Plant tulip species for naturalizing in cultivated areas. Keep weed-free, either by mulching or using herbicides (after dormancy). Plant up to 144 per square yard.
T. clusiana, Lady tulip	White inner petals and white outer petals with wide red band from top to bottom. Naturalizes well in mountains and plains. Hardy to zone 4 and most of zone 3. 8 inches tall.
T. Fosteriana, Foster tulip	Grows about a foot tall. Red. Blooms early. Hardy to zone 4 and most of zone 3.
T. greigii, Greig tulip	Orange-red flowers with black center, mottled leaves. Height, 8 to 12 inches. Hardy to zone 4 and most of zone 3.
T. kaufmanniana, Water-lily tulip	Height, 6 to 10 inches. Petals open like water lilies in full sun. Also thrives in light shade.
T. tarda (*T. dasystemon*)	Height, 6 inches. Up to 5 blooms on a stem. Greenish white exterior and white with yellow interior.

Forcing Bulbs

IN FEBRUARY THIS YEAR we heard from two friends, one in Switzerland and another in Portland, Oregon, both announcing that crocuses were blooming on their lawns. We should have been envious as we peered out at four-foot snowbanks and a thermometer that showed -20°F, but we weren't. A pot full of beautiful yellow narcissus was blooming in our living room, and the green tips of tulip foliage poked through the soil in a container in a sunny, southern-facing window.

Anyone can enjoy the beauty and fun of an early spring without the hassle of a trip south and have a garden of crocuses, hyacinths, narcissus, and tulips blooming indoors during the winter months. Almost any other spring bulb can be forced to bloom early, too, including snowdrops (*Galanthus nivalis*), winter aconite (*Eranthis hyemalis*), glory-of-the-snow (*Chionodoxa luciliae*), grape hyacinth (*Muscari*), and even certain late-bloomers such as *Alliums, Iris reticulata*, and lily-of-the-valley (*Convallaria*). Almost everyone has grown at least one of the

tender bulbs such as amaryllis, *Freesia*, or *Narcissus tazetta*, the paper-whites.

Within each genus of plants, some are better suited for forcing than others. (See chart on page 74.) Specialty bulb catalogs often offer collections of different kinds of bulbs that force easily.

The normal life cycle of a hardy, spring-blooming bulb passes through several stages, including: (1) dormancy, which happens naturally after blooming; (2) development of the small feeder roots that the bulb needs to absorb moisture and nutrients so it can bloom well the following spring; (3) a chilling period, to initiate the biochemical activity that starts the development of the embryonic flowers, and finally (4) exposure to light and warmth that results in the growth of leaves, buds, and flowers.

When you plant bulbs outdoors in the fall, their seasonal cycle occurs naturally. After planting, the dormant bulbs develop the roots they need for spring growth on warm fall days, and as the days grow cooler, they get the necessary chilling. Winter keeps them cold until the warm spring days stimulate them to sprout and grow.

When you "force" bulbs, you simply provide the fall and winter conditions that simulate those they would have if they were planted in the ground, but you encourage them to bloom earlier by providing them with heat and light sooner than nature would. The usual method is to pot them in mid- to late October and keep them fairly moist at a cool temperature (40 to 45°F) until January. After that you can bring them into the warmth and light anytime and they will start to grow.

Containers

Bulb pans, available in garden centers, are usually 4 or 5 inches deep and are made specifically for forcing bulbs. They are shallow because it isn't necessary to plant indoor bulbs as deep as those in the ground. A shallow container is better than a standard pot because it doesn't require as much potting soil, it doesn't tip over as easily, and a clump of bulbs looks best when blooming in a shorter pot. If you don't have a bulb pan handy, however, a regular pot works just fine.

The container you choose should be large enough in diameter for the bulbs you want to grow but no larger, since bulbs look best when massed together. It *must* have good drainage holes, because even though bulbs need moisture at all times, good drainage is vital to their health and they'll rot if waterlogged. Place at least a half inch of pebbles, pottery fragments, or other drainage material at the bottom of the pan before adding the soil, so the holes won't become clogged.

Whether you use plastic or clay pots is an individual decision, and both have their advocates. Since moisture evaporates more quickly through clay pots, before planting the bulbs soak the pots in water for several hours.

If you're using a recycled pot for forcing, always clean it thoroughly to avoid possible disease contamination. Once you've cleaned out the old pieces of soil, you can sterilize old pots by running them through the dishwasher. Or sterilize them by rinsing in a solution of 1 part chlorine bleach to 5 parts water.

Forcing Bulbs in Soil

It will take from sixteen to eighteen weeks from the time you plant most bulbs until they flower. If you can't pot them when you receive them, store them for a few weeks in a dry spot in a ventilated container, where the temperature stays between 45 and 55°F. Keep in mind, though, that they are alive, and treat them accordingly.

Any standard mixture will do for potting soil, but a good medium is a combination of one-third each of peat moss, perlite or vermiculite, and potting soil that is sterilized to make it

A shallow bulb pan is designed specifically for forcing bulbs indoors.

free of plant diseases and weed seeds. If you intend to transplant the bulbs to the garden after they bloom, add a tablespoon of slow-acting fertilizer, such as dried manure or Osmocote, to the mixture before planting. Put some of the mix into the pots and set in the bulbs. Netherlands bulb experts recommend that you put in as many bulbs as will fit in the container, placing them close together — about ½ inch apart — but not touching each other or the sides of the pot (see illustration below). Plant tulip bulbs with their flat side facing the outside of the container, since the first leaves will come from this side and, when facing outward, will make the pot more attractive.

Set the bulbs on top of the soil so that their pointed tips or the tops of the corms are nearly even with the top of the pot. Then add the soil until its surface is ¼ to ½ inch from the top of the pot so that you can easily water it. Don't press down hard on the soil. It should be loose enough so it will drain well and the roots can form easily.

Water the pot thoroughly. A good way to do it is to set the container in a bowl of water and leave it there until the top of the soil is moist.

APPROXIMATE NUMBER OF BULBS IN A 6-INCH POT

Some bulb growers recommend buying the jumbo or top-sized bulbs for forcing in order to get the largest blooms. We like using medium-grade ones, because the plants are shorter and the blooms less heavy, so they are less likely to need staking. It is possible, too, to get more blooms in a pot. The number given here is approximate, depending on the size of the bulb. After potting, all of these need a period of chilling and holding that lasts approximately three months.

BULB	NUMBER	LIGHT REQUIRED
Chionodoxa	5	bright, no direct sun
Crocus	8–15	sun
Galanthus	6	bright, no direct sun
Narcissus	6	sun
Hyacinthus	3	sun
Iris reticulata	6–10	sun
Iris danfordiae	5	sun
Tulipa	4–5	sun

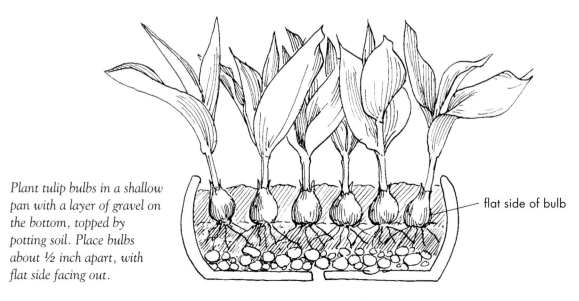

Plant tulip bulbs in a shallow pan with a layer of gravel on the bottom, topped by potting soil. Place bulbs about ½ inch apart, with flat side facing out.

flat side of bulb

Then — and this is very important — let the pot drain for at least a day before chilling, so the soil will not be soggy wet. Finally, label the pot with the name of the plant and date of planting.

The Big Chill

For the next twelve weeks or more keep the pots in a dark place such as a root cellar where the temperature is between 35° and 48°F. If the bulbs aren't chilled long enough the plants will be small, take longer to force, or may not bloom at all.

Ideally, root development is best if you can keep the temperature at about 45°F for five or six weeks, then lower it to 35°F for the next six to eight weeks to slow the growth. Precise temperature control is easiest if you are lucky enough to own a spare refrigerator; but don't combine bulbs with fruits in the same refrigerator or root cellar, since some fruits emit ethylene, a gas that can kill the flower buds of the bulbs. Many gardeners have good luck storing their pots in an unheated spare room, a portion of their basement, or a cool garage. Cover the pots with burlap, old sheets, or other cloth to hold in moisture and keep out light.

The soil should be moist but never wet throughout the chilling period to ensure the development of good roots. Check the pot every week or so for dryness, but you'll probably find they don't need watering more often than every three or four weeks. Check on them, also, to be sure that mold is not forming; if it is, remove the covering to improve ventilation.

An outdoor cold frame is a good place to replicate nature's chilling and rooting period, if you live where heavy snows don't prevent getting the pots when you want them in midwinter. After potting, put them in the frame, but leave them uncovered until the ground begins to freeze. Then mulch them with leaves or salt hay. They won't need water because the surrounding earth will keep the humidity high.

If you don't have a cold frame, it is possible to dig a trench in the ground and treat them the same way. The disadvantage of this method is that some years the pots freeze into the ground and can't be dug out during the winter.

Preparing for Blooming

After the bulbs have had their chilling period, you can make springtime appear whenever you wish by taking them out of cold storage. If you have enough pots, it is fun to bring out a new one or more every week and have continuous spring throughout the winter months.

Three to four weeks before you want the blooms, take the pot from the storage area to a moderately warm spot (approximately 60°F) in your home or greenhouse. The bulbs should have a few sprouts by this time. Handle them carefully so you don't damage the flower buds developing inside the sprouts.

Since the pale shoots are tender, don't expose them to bright sunlight immediately. Keep them in indirect light for a few days, or cover them with a sheet of newspaper. When the shoots turn green, move them to a spot that gets direct sun but relatively cool temperatures (less than 65°F in the day and between 50° and 55°F at night). Water the bulbs regularly as they grow, as you would a houseplant. To get the tallest blooms on hyacinths, see the box below.

After the flower buds have begun to show color, move the pot to a spot out of direct sunlight, with cool temperatures. Keep the pot away from hot air registers and radiators, and move it to a cool room overnight. These conditions imitate those they would experience outdoors on a cool spring night, and extend the blooming period by several days.

As the days get longer it takes less time for the blooms to develop, so if you are on a schedule you should allow less time for the growing

GETTING TALLER HYACINTH BLOSSOMS

Most spring bulbs receive the same treatment, but hyacinths are an exception. If you want tall blooms that look the way they do in the garden, after their chilling period keep their stems absolutely in the dark. Some growers use dark construction paper to make little collars that are open at the top for each stem; others surround the pots with tall boxes that have their tops and bottoms removed. When the bulbs have grown several inches, in about two weeks, remove the collars or boxes and let them come into bloom in full sun.

period as spring approaches. Crocuses that would take three weeks of light in January may bloom within only two weeks in early March.

Low-growing plants obviously need no staking, but some taller types of daffodils and tulips grow rather leggy, with crooked stems. You can use the green-colored bulb supports available from garden supply stores to unobtrusively shore up drooping stems and foliage. Bamboo plant stakes and green yarn are another possibility

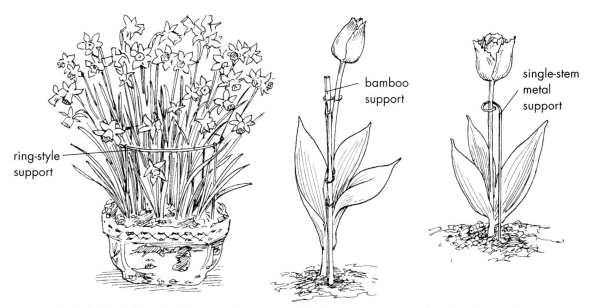

ring-style support

bamboo support

single-stem metal support

Stake bulbs before they bloom with commercial bulb supports or green bamboo plant stakes and green yarn or string.

FORCING LILY-OF-THE-VALLEY

For lily-of-the-valley blooms out of season, dig six or ten bulbs (pips) from your own patch or buy them in the fall when they are dormant. Pot them in a bulb pan, and leave them in a dark, cool place until a few weeks before you want them. Then put the pot in a saucer of water to ensure humidity, and set them in a sunny window at a temperature between 65 and 70°F. In a short time the flowers will fill the room with a sweet perfume.

---

for staking, and a friend of ours who likes Chinese food uses wooden chopsticks as stakes. Try to hide the supports under the leaves where they will not distract from the blooms. Since it's difficult to repair the damage if the blooms and foliage have already fallen over, stake tall-growing plants well before they bloom. Some gardeners sink the entire pot of leggy, top-heavy plants into a deeper, slightly larger pot and pack in the empty space with damp florist's moss for support.

A late-winter garden show is a good place to see forced bulbs. Whenever we attend a large flower show, we are overwhelmed by the beautiful displays of spring bulbs in natural-looking settings and are impressed by the skillful growers who got them into full bloom at just the right week. Although we can't hope to match those displays, we enjoy the few bulbs we force at home. Potted bulbs make good gifts for nursing-home patients, who enjoy watching them develop from bud to bloom. They can also be a learning experience for children, both at home or in youth groups in school, clubs, or church. Some organizations regularly use forced bulbs as money-raising projects.

Saving the Bulbs

Although you shouldn't try to force the same bulbs indoors two years in a row, you can transplant most of them outdoors after blooming if you grow them in a soil mix as described above. (Bulbs forced in water, as described on pages 72-74, cannot be reused.) It usually takes a year for them to recover from their interrupted life cycle, so don't expect the best blooms until they have lived in the ground for two years. To help the bulbs replace the nutrients they expended and prepare them for a summer in the earth, give them a helping of liquid fertilizer just as they begin to bloom (follow the directions on the package). After the flowers fade, cut them off, but leave the foliage and flower stalk intact. Continue to water the pots, but less often as the leaves begin to die.

When the weather warms in the spring, pop the bulbs from their pots, separate them from each other, and replant them in the garden at the depth recommended in chapters 8 and 9. Even if the leaves have not died down completely, you can leave on the tops and transplant them successfully. Disturb the attached roots as little as possible and water them immediately after planting. Mix in a small amount of liquid fertilizer with the water to help the bulbs become established in their new home.

Forced tulips need special treatment after blooming if they are to recover, just as they do if they're growing in the ground. Allow their foliage to die completely, and let the soil dry. Then cut off the stalk and gently shake both soil and bulbs from the pot, separate the bulbs, and dry them a few days more. Store them for the summer in an open container or open paper bag in a cool, dark, dry place such as a closet. In the fall, replant them at the proper depth in the ground as described in chapter 8.

Remove lily-of-the-valley clumps from the pot, along with their soil, and set them into the garden without separating the bulbs. They should recover nicely, spread, and bloom the following year.

As frugal Yankees we can't bear to toss out bulbs that might grow again; we started our present bed of miniature narcissus from potted plants given us in midwinter. After they had finished blooming, we fertilized them with liquid fertilizer and kept them watered. When spring arrived, their foliage had died back and we removed the bulbs from their pot and planted them outdoors. Although they didn't bloom very well the following year, by the third spring they had multiplied, and they flowered beautifully. They've been expanding ever since.

We have saved potted Easter lilies and planted them in the garden in the spring. Because they are tender bulbs, and our climate doesn't resemble that of Bermuda, they haven't wintered over even with a mulch. One year we tried repotting them in the fall, but we got only a few small blooms on each plant. Obviously we weren't able to duplicate the conditions that are possible in warmer regions or in a modern greenhouse. Like trying to save poinsettias from year to year, we feel it isn't worth the trouble.

Forcing Tender Bulbs

The directions for forcing tender bulbs such as *Freesia* and *Ornithogalum arabicum* (star-of-Bethlehem) are not as involved as those for hardy bulbs, since they don't need a chilling period. Pot them in the fall, water them thoroughly, and place them in a cool indoor room (50°F). Keep the soil moist and soon roots will develop. Then move them into sunlight and warmer temperatures (60°F). When buds develop, move them again into indirect light for a longer blooming period.

After blooming, gradually reduce the amount of water you give them until finally they are dry. Hold them over the summer in dry

soil, and repot them in the fall.

For growing the tropical bulbs such as amaryllis that are ordinarily grown as house plants, see chapter 13.

Forcing Bulbs in Water

Everyone is familiar with the fragrant paper-white narcissus that grow and bloom in a shallow container filled only with tiny stones and water, and hyacinths that bloom beautifully without soil in a water-filled container. Crocus, too, can be forced in water, as can a special tulip called 'Jingle Bell'. As the name implies, these red tulips are usually forced for the Christmas season, and suppliers prechill them before shipping in early December. Bulbs forced in water cannot be reused because they have expended their stored energy in blooming, and have had no nutrients to renew it.

Forcing Paper-Whites

Paper-white narcissus (*Narcissus tazetta*) are popular for winter blooms because they are so reliable and will grow and bloom during the darkest months. Furthermore, they are not at all fussy about humidity and temperature. They bloom within six weeks after planting and, if kept cool and out of the sun, will stay in bloom for many days. No soil is needed because they'll grow in water. Their powerful fragrance can permeate a large room, and although some people love it, others find it much too pungent.

Paper-whites have been preconditioned for forcing, so a cooling period is unnecessary. Don't store them for more than one month, and during that time, keep them in a dry room at room temperature. Unless they are already preplanted in a pot, use approximately six bulbs in a 6-inch pan or twelve bulbs for a 10-inch pan.

You can control the timing of the blooms by keeping them warmer or cooler. Keep them cool

1. Choose a shallow bowl or bulb pan with no drainage holes in the bottom.
2. Fill bowl ⅔ full of pebbles, gravel, marbles, or seashells.
3. Place as many bulbs as will fit on the stones, about ½ inch apart, with pointed sides upward.
4. Fill in the spaces around them with pebbles, leaving the top-half of each bulb exposed.
5. Add water just to the base of the bulbs and maintain it at this level.
6. Place container in a cool, dark spot, and roots will appear within two weeks.
7. When green shoots appear, move the container to a cool, sunny spot. If they don't get enough light, the stems will become leggy and fall over.
8. Three to four weeks after the shoots appear, they will bloom with heavily scented white flowers.
9. Discard bulbs after flowering. They won't bloom another year.

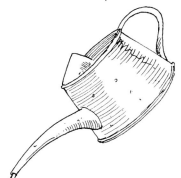

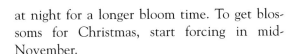

Keep water level just to base of bulb.

at night for a longer bloom time. To get blossoms for Christmas, start forcing in mid-November.

Forcing Hyacinths in Water

In nineteenth-century parlors, it was popular to force hyacinths in water in special colored bulb glasses, and now specialty garden shops and mail-order suppliers offer replicas in cobalt blue, deep rose, and similar colors. We bought a simple modern one of clear glass last week at our local florist's shop. A hyacinth glass is shaped like a large, open-topped hour-glass with a narrow collar. The bulb rests in the upper "cup," and roots grow in the water below.

Prechilled hyacinths are available for winter forcing but if you need to condition your own, keep them in the refrigerator or in a cold, dry, ventilated place for about three months. When you are ready to force the bulb, place it in a bulb glass or any container with a narrow top that will hold it out of the water. Fill the glass with water so that the base of the bulb just touches it, and add a piece of natural, aquarium-type charcoal to the water to prevent algae growth.

Keep the bulb in a cool, dark place, perhaps in a closet or cellar, until the roots become well developed. When the shoots are 3 to 4 inches tall and you can see

Hyacinth glass

the flower buds, bring them into the light and a temperature of 65 to 70°F. Add more water as needed to keep it just touching the base of the bulb. As the plant grows, rotate it so it doesn't lean toward the light. Within three to four weeks you should be sniffing a whiff of spring. Hyacinths are particularly effective when grown this way because, unlike most bulbs, a single bloom is very striking, both for its beauty and its fragrance. Don't try to save the bulbs for planting outdoors later. By the time they have finished blooming they have used all their energy and it's best to discard them.

BEST CULTIVARS FOR FORCING

Although most bulbs can be forced, some consistently do better under forcing conditions than others. Bulb growers recommend the following, but by no means is the selection limited to them.

CROCUS
Use only large bulbs for the best results.
'Flower Record' — purple
'Jeanne d'Arc' — white
'Peter Pan' — white
'Pickwick' — striped
'Remembrance' — lavender

TULIPS
Use medium- to large-sized bulbs. Besides the ones listed, the early-blooming species such as Tulipa kaufmanniana *are excellent for forcing.*

APRICOT
'Apricot Beauty'

BICOLORED (red and yellow)
'Abra'
'Kees Nelis'

LAVENDER
'Atilla'

ORANGE
'General de Wet'

PINK
'Cantor'
'Christmas Marvel'
'Gander'
'Peach Blossom'

RED
'Carpi'
'Electra'
'Jingle Bells'
'Ruby Red'
'Trance'

WHITE
'White Hawk'

YELLOW
'Bellona'
'Golden Melody'
'Schoonoord'

HYACINTHS
Use medium- to large-sized bulbs.
All kinds force well.

NARCISSUS
Use double-nosed bulbs for more blooms. Medium-sized bulbs are best unless you want fewer and larger blooms per pot.
'Barrett Browning' — small cup, white with orange cup
'Bridal Gown' — double, creamy yellow
'Carlton' — large cup, yellow
'Cragford' — large cup, white with orange cup
'Dutch Master' — large trumpet, yellow
'February Gold' — miniature yellow
'Flower Record' — large cup, white with orange cup
'Golden Harvest' — large trumpet, yellow
'Ice Follies' — large cup, white with yellow cup that turns white
'Jack Snipe' — miniature, white perianth, yellow trumpet
'Mount Hood' — large trumpet, white
'Peeping Tom' — miniature yellow
'Tête-à-Tête' — dwarf, with small golden yellow blooms
'Unsurpassable' — large trumpet, yellow

The Big Four Spring Bulbs

The flowers that bloom in the spring,
Tra la!
Bring promise of merry sunshine.
— *The Mikado*
W.S. Gilbert

GILBERT'S WORDS FROM *The Mikado* evoke little argument, for no matter how much we enjoy our lilies, gladioli, and dahlias during the summer, whenever we hear "flowering bulbs" it is crocuses, daffodils, hyacinths, and tulips that usually come to mind. These and many other cheery bulbous plants announce the end of the dark winter months at a time when we are hungry for color, greenery, and flowers. We're thrilled when the precocious snowdrops *(Galanthus),* winter aconite *(Eranthis),* and crocuses begin to appear as if by magic, poking through the snow.

Spring-blooming bulbs adapted to cool climates millenniums ago, and all of them have in common the need for a chilling period in order to bloom. The fall and winter temperatures in temperate climates provide a natural refrigerator, and in the spring, after their hibernation, they are able to grow and bloom more quickly than herbaceous plants because they have a built-in storehouse of nutrients to spur them on.

Among the many nice things about spring bulbs is that you don't need to wait for years for them to look their best, as you would for a flowering tree or lilac hedge. Top-sized bulbs will bloom beautifully the first season after you plant them, and those you plant en masse for naturalizing become more impressive each year as they blanket large areas. All are easy to grow, not especially susceptible to diseases and insects, and even the tallest seldom need staking. They are inexpensive, and most last for many years.

A Child's Bulb Garden

The quick growth of spring bulbs makes them especially delightful to children, and a few bulbs in a patch of their own make an ideal first garden. They are easy to plant in the fall, and once the warm spring days arrive, the waiting time is short from the time the first sprig of green sprouts until the leaves, buds, and flowers appear. Daffodils and tulips are close to children's heads, and their imaginations can easily find elves, fairies, and gnomes among them.

The familiar crocus, hyacinth, narcissus (daffodil), and tulip are considered "major" spring bulbs. We're particularly fond of the indomitable crocuses and narcissus because both multiply rapidly and naturalize easily. We're just as devoted to the magnificent tulips and fragrant hyacinths, but because they are not as durable and need more care in our climate, we plant fewer of them at home and enjoy the mass plantings in parks and botanical gardens.

Croci or Crocuses?

For years people debated over whether the plural of crocus and narcissus should be, as in Latin, croci and narcissi, or crocuses and narcissuses. Finally horticulturists agreed that Latin would lose and the same word would be used for both singular and plural of narcissus, whether we had one bulb or a thousand narcissus. More than one crocus, however, would be crocuses. We still find it tempting to speak of croci or narcissi, with a glance back at Caesar and Latin II.

Crocus (KRO-cuss)

COMMON NAME: crocus
TYPE OF ROOT: corm
DEPTH TO PLANT (FROM BASE): 3 to 4 inches
PLANTING TIME: fall
BLOOMING SEASON: early spring
LIGHT PREFERENCE: sun

Each March someone always points out that the first spring day and the first day of spring seldom arrive at the same time. We feel that spring officially reaches our hilltop not on March 21, but whenever the first purple, yellow, and white crocuses begin to bloom on our lawn. Usually only a few hours intervene between the melting of snow and the flowers bursting out, and many times we see them poking through a late snowstorm to make their grand entrance. Although these tiny members of the Iris Family grow only 3 to 6 inches tall with grasslike foliage, their sturdy stems manage to hold the large blooms proudly upright throughout the fickle spring weather. (Other species of crocus bloom in late summer and autumn. See chapter 12.)

In cultivated gardens it is easy to disturb crocuses if you are digging near them when they are dormant and invisible; but they are ideal bulbs for lawns, in front of borders, mixed with foundation plantings, around trees, along paths, and in rock gardens. Though crocus foliage dies much more quickly than that of narcissus and tulips, if you grow them in your lawn, don't be too hasty to mow the grass. Their foliage, like that of all bulbs, should be allowed to die back naturally.

Culture

Plant the corms with the bases 3 to 4 inches deep and 3 to 4 inches apart early in the fall. The papery husks around the corm are actually old leaf bases because each year the old corm withers away and produces a new corm or two.

In another of nature's amazing adaptive mechanisms, the contractile movement of the roots shifts the new corm into the empty space left by the old one.

Crocuses look best when set in groups of a dozen or more together, rather than scattered sparsely throughout an area or set in a long single row. Grouping colors together also makes an effective mass, although some people prefer a multicolored effect. If your supply of corms is limited, don't be concerned. By spreading them around and letting them increase naturally, in a few years they will form a nice carpet of color. Mice, chipmunks, and other rodents are very fond of the corms, so scatter a few mothballs among them when you plant.

Crocuses are not fussy about soil, and if grass grows well in a spot, they will too. They can even grow under deciduous trees as long as they get the spring sunshine they need. The only care they need is a sprinkling of fertilizer either in very early spring or late fall. When they become so thick that they don't bloom well, it's time to dig them up and separate them. It's easiest to do this directly after the flowers fade because they are visible then; but if you can remember where they are, you can divide them successfully in the fall.

As your supply of corms increases you may want to dig out some of the extras in the fall for forcing (see chapter 7). They'll lift your spirits considerably when Groundhog Day rolls around.

Garden and Species Crocus

The large-flowering garden crocuses are known as Dutch crocuses, although the Dutch grow and sell many other crocus species as well. Dutch crocuses are hybrids of *Crocus vernus*, native to the mountains of central and southern Europe. Since they have the showiest flowers, they are the best to plant for a display. Of the other eighty or so crocus species, only a few are cultivated. The colors of these species do not vary greatly from the hybrids, but many of them naturalize better. Some bloom very early, so by planting a mixture of cultivars and species you can extend the blooming time over several weeks. Most of the species crocuses grow the same height (3 to 6 inches) as the Dutch cultivars, but their flowers are smaller. They are hardy from zones 4 to 8 unless otherwise stated, although in spots where snow comes early and stays all winter, most survive well in zone 3. A heavy mulch will help them survive the winter, but if you use it, take it off early in the spring so the sprouts won't need to push through it.

Some Spring-Blooming Crocuses

C. ancyrensis. This extra-early flowering species from Crimea has yellow blooms in abundance. 'Golden Bunch' is a deep orange-yellow variety.

C. angustifolius. Also called *C. susianus*, this is the cloth-of-gold crocus from Crimea. Orange blooms pop out early and in profusion.

C. biflorus. The Scotch crocus originated on the continent of Europe and in Asia Minor. An old-timer, it is white with purple stripes. Hardy in zones 6 to 9.

C. chrysanthus. This is known as the snow crocus because it blooms very early, just as the snow melts. It originated in the area from the Balkans to Asia Minor. Cultivars are as follows:

'Advance' — light yellow flowers striped purple
'Blue Pearl' — pale blue
'Cream Beauty' — light yellow
'Goldilocks' — golden yellow
'Lady Killer' — purple with white interior and edges
'Prinses Beatrix' — clear blue and yellow
'Snow Bunting' — white with a soft purple exterior

C. imperati. The Italian crocus from southern

Italy is an early bloomer with large, fragrant purple and white blooms. Zones 6 to 9.

C. korolkowii. From Turkey, this crocus has yellow blooms with touch of green or orange and is often used in rock gardens.

C. sieberi. This vigorous species from Greece and Crete has lilac blooms. 'Firefly' is a particularly deep purple variety. Grow best in zones 6 to 9.

C. tomasinianus. This Yugoslavian native is similar to the Dutch crocus. Cultivars come in various shades of lavender. One, 'Barr's Purple', has a soft lilac interior and a dark purple exterior. Zones 5 to 8.

C. vernus. A European native, this blooms early with lilac or white flowers, sometimes with purple stripes. Its hybrids are the well-known and widely planted large-flowering Dutch crocus. Among the many popular cultivars are these:

'Big Ben' — white with a blue stripe
'Haarlem Gem' — lilac blue
'Peter Pan' — white
'Pickwick' — blue white and violet
'Queen of the Blues' — soft blue
'Remembrance' — violet
'Striped Beauty' — lilac with white stripes
'Yellow Mammoth' — golden yellow

"Bunch-flowering" crocuses are cultivars that bloom early with clusters of smaller flowers and are good for rock gardens and naturalizing. Some popular kinds are the following:

'Blue Ribbon' — light blue
'Golden Bunch' — golden yellow
'Lady Killer' — purple with white interior and edge
'Purity' — pure white
'Taplow Ruby' — violet-red

Hyacinthus (hy-a-SIN-thus)

COMMON NAME: hyacinth
TYPE OF ROOT: bulb
DEPTH TO PLANT FROM BASE: 6 to 7 inches
PLANTING TIME: fall
BLOOMING SEASON: spring
LIGHT PREFERENCE: sun

This member of the lily family is unique because, unlike most spring flowering bulbs, its genus has only one species, *H. orientalis*. Louise Beebe Wilder, the doyenne of bulbs in the 1930s, called it the "fat Oriental hyacinth." Many other plants, such as *Muscari*, the grape hyacinth, resemble it, however, and are called by the same common name.

There are up to 100 varieties and a large number of hybrid cultivars in white and many shades of pink, purple, red, yellow, and blue. *H. orientalis* is a native of Greece, Syria, North Africa, and Asia Minor, and as with crocuses, narcissus, and tulips, most hyacinth bulbs sold in North America are grown in Europe. In France, the bulbs are cultivated for perfume.

Unlike crocuses and daffodils, the fragrant, showy hyacinth has a formal, somewhat stiff appearance, but after the first year of bloom the stiff florets "relax" a bit and flowers are usually smaller and more informal. The blooms can be effective even if they are not planted in masses in large beds as they were in the last century. A few bulbs scattered, in groups of three or five of one cultivar, throughout a border or in front of a hedge are all you may need for a lovely display.

Garden hyacinths grow from 8 to 12 inches tall, just the right height for edging a border, lining a path, or splashing a spot of color into a rock garden. Their bright springlike colors blend beautifully with the greenery of evergreen shrubs that are used as foundation plants. They are good choices for planting in window boxes or containers, too.

A limiting factor of hyacinths in cold climates is that they are not as hardy as most other spring bulbs. In zones 3, 4, and much of 5, you must mulch them heavily to be sure they will survive, unless a snow cover comes before the ground freezes hard and stays until spring.

Culture

You can buy named cultivars of hyacinths individually or in a collection of assorted colors. Try to get strong and healthy top-sized bulbs because those will produce the biggest and best flowers. Plant them early enough in the fall so they can grow a mass of roots before winter. Hyacinths will grow in sod if it isn't too heavy, but they don't bloom as well or spread as rapidly as they do in a bed that is free of grass and weeds. Set the bulbs about 6 inches apart (36 to the square yard). For further planting directions, see chapter 4.

Hyacinths bloom after crocuses and daffodils, along with the midseason tulips. After you have enjoyed their fragrant blossoms, cut off the flower stalk. Not only do the flowers emit an unpleasant odor at that stage, but removing the stalk is good for the bulb because it prevents seed production. Leave all the foliage, however, until it has completely withered. If you didn't do it in early spring, sprinkle manure, compost, or a tablespoon of a complete chemical fertilizer such as 9–9–6, 7–7–7 or 5–10–10 on each square foot of the bed. Although hyacinths will not produce as lush blooms the second year after planting as they do the first year, fertilizing will get them to continue to bloom each year, and they are likely to send up several smaller flower stalks as well.

Hyacinths aren't immune from pests. Mice enjoy the bulbs, and some gardeners plant a mothball along with each bulb to protect it. The mothball doesn't affect the bulb, but it steers the rodents away. Deer have been known to consume hyacinth stalks in early spring, but we feel it's a chance worth risking for the gorgeous flowers. For pest controls, see chapter 5.

Forcing

Hyacinths are popular for forcing because their bright colors and sweet fragrance are so welcome indoors during the winter. One of the nicest house gifts we ever received in midwinter was a "bouquet" of one single deep purple hyacinth that our friend had forced, in a special hyacinth vase. See chapter 7 for various methods of forcing.

Propagation

Although it is far easier to buy plants than to propagate them yourself, once many years ago we experimented with a method that the Dutch use to stimulate hyacinth bulbs to multiply faster than they usually do. We dug up a few bulbs after their leaves had completely died and, with a sterilized knife, cut two or three shallow notches across the base of each bulb. We replanted them and let them grow throughout the summer. In the fall when we dug them up, just

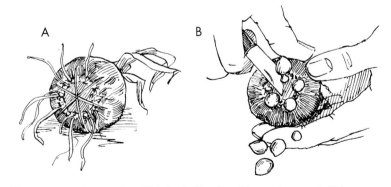

To propagate hyacinths, (A) dig bulb after foliage dies, and (B) cut two or three shallow notches at base of bulb and replant. Dig bulbs in the fall and pull off the bulblets that have formed on the notch.

as the book had promised, several tiny bulblets had formed along each notch. We pulled them off, separated them, and planted them in our cold frame where they spent the winter. In a few years they were large enough to plant in the flower border, where they bloomed beautifully for a few years.

We could have gotten fewer but larger bulblets by scooping out a small cavity in the base of the bulb. If you decide to attempt notching or scooping hyacinths, don't notch or scoop too deeply, because the bulb may not survive such a drastic operation.

You can also let a few hyacinths set seeds and plant them, but this method of propagation takes even longer. It is with seeds, however, that hybridizers originate new cultivars.

Varieties and Cultivars

H. orientalis, the parent of the many hybrid cultivars we now enjoy, has many varieties in a multitude of colors even in its native habitat. The variety *albulus*, the Roman hyacinth, is somewhat different from the species and not as hardy. Its small flowers in white or blue are not as stiff as those of *H. orientalis*, and it blooms earlier.

The following cultivars are among the special beauties available:

'Amsterdam' — red
'Anna Marie' — pink
'Blue Giant' — blue
'Blue Jacket' — bright navy blue
'City of Haarlem' — yellow
'Delft Blue' — soft lilac blue
'Gipsy Queen' — unusual combination of salmon and apricot
'Lady Derby' — pink
'L'Innocence' — white
'Pink Pearl' — pink
'Red Rocket' — red
'Topaz' — yellow
'Wedgewood' — light blue

Narcissus (nar-SIS-es)

COMMON NAME: narcissus, daffodil
TYPE OF ROOT: bulb
DEPTH TO PLANT FROM BASE: 6 to 7 inches
PLANTING TIME: fall
BLOOMING SEASON: spring
LIGHT PREFERENCE: sun

If there is a favorite spring flower it is probably the narcissus, or daffodil, as it is widely called. It is difficult, in our area, to find a home without at least a few of them in the yard in May. Their bright, cheerful yellow flowers have long been a favorite literary subject. Dickon, the redheaded Yorkshire lad in *The Secret Garden* by Frances Hodgson Burnett, called them "daffy down dillies," and sometimes, so do we.

When we were young, though, everyone called the narcissus with yellow blooms "daffodils," the white ones with red cups were "narcissus," and those that had several flowers on each stem were "jonquils." We didn't know that they were *all* narcissus (according to botanists). Horticulturally classified, a daffodil is a trumpet type of narcissus, and the term jonquil is reserved for a variety of the species *N. jonquilla* and similar plants. The narcissus belong to the Amaryllis Family, and although there are only about two dozen species in the genus, there are thousands of named cultivars.

Long ago the narcissus was named for the handsome son of the god Cephissus and the nymph Liriope of Greek mythology. Legend tells us that because he rejected the love of Echo he was punished by Aphrodite, who sentenced him to fall in love with his own reflection in a pool of water. He pined away for himself until he was transformed into a flower, leaving us with both the name of the narcissus and the term *narcissism*.

These days the mythological connections of the narcissus may be forgotten, but the poetry connected with them remains. No discussion of this bulb can be complete without a mention of the lines Wordsworth wrote nearly 200 years ago:

I wander'd lonely as a cloud
*   That floats on high o'er vales and hills,*
When all at once I saw a crowd,
*   A host, of golden daffodils;*
Beside the lake, beneath the trees,
Fluttering and dancing in the breeze.

The daffodils Wordsworth saw fluttering in the Lake District of England were probably *Narcissus pseudonarcissus*, a species that usually grows less than a foot tall with yellow petals that fold forward enough to partially cover the trumpet. Although they still grow wild, they are seldom offered for sale today because other kinds are so much more showy.

Gardeners have raised many different narcissus for centuries, but horticulturists didn't begin to work seriously with them until the 1800s. Thanks to many hybridizers, we now enjoy cultivars that bloom at various times from early to late in the spring. Their flowers come in an enormous variety of colors and forms, including those that are both single and double, ruffled and smooth, and from a miniature ½-inch in diameter to a huge 5 inches. Their stems range from 4 inches to more than 20 inches tall and the petals vary from lemons and golds to pure and creamy whites, with contrasting cups of pink, red, or orange. Some are very fragrant.

In 1919 the USDA put a quarantine on all plants entering the United States to prevent the importation of insects and disease. From then until its repeal in 1936, many Dutch bulb growers moved to the United States and British Columbia to protect the rich North American market. After the repeal of the quarantine, most western growers found they could not compete with the Dutch prices, and many companies folded. Nearly all the growing and breeding of new kinds takes place in the Netherlands today, but avid American hybridizers such as Brent and Becky Heath of the Daffodil Mart in Gloucester, Virginia, have also contributed hundreds of new hybrids. Before Jan de Graaff became involved with lilies, he also introduced many new daffodils in Oregon.

When we first began to study the photos of the new beauties in catalogs, we suspected they might be short-lived and difficult to grow, like the new cultivars of many other plants. We were also worried that the heavy blooms couldn't possibly stand up to a New England wind or a late spring snowstorm. Our fears were unnecessary. All of the many kinds that we grow have given us only the best results.

Culture

Most narcissus can stand fairly rough treatment, so about all you have to do, if the soil is reasonably good, is to dig a hole with a spade and drop in a bulb. Some of the newer cultivars deserve better treatment, however. Starting them in a well-tilled, compost-fertilized bed will eliminate competition from grass and weeds and help the bulbs get off to a better start and ensure the largest blooms.

Plant them with the bases 5 to 7 inches deep and 6 to 8 inches apart. They need sunshine, especially in the spring, but can get by with half a day of sun, such as they would get on the east side of a building, as long as they receive spring skylight all day. Most do best in a well-drained soil that has a pH of from 6 to 7, although *N. poeticus* 'Actaea' will grow in soil that is slightly moist. Narcissus contain poisonous crystals that are distasteful to rodents, and gardeners sometimes plant them near more appetizing bulbs such as tulips hoping they'll help repel the pests from all the bulbs.

Although some narcissus species and many older cultivars will grow for decades without attention, the bulbs of most modern narcissus

BICOLOR. Flowers whose corona is one color and whose corolla is another.

CALYX. The collective term for the sepals of a flower.

COROLLA. The collective term for the petals of a flower.

CORONA. The tubular part of the flower. Long coronas are called trumpets, short ones are cups.

CROWN. The base of a plant at ground level.

CUP. A term for a short corona.

DOUBLE-NOSED BULB. Two large bulbs joined together and planted as one.

PERIANTH. The collective term for the calyx, corolla, and corona of the flower.

PENDULOUS. Flowers that hang loosely.

PETAL. One of the series of flower parts arranged outside the stamens and pistil, and inside the sepals; collectively, the corolla.

REFLEXED. Petals that are curved backward toward the stem (recurved).

TRUMPET. A term for a long corona.

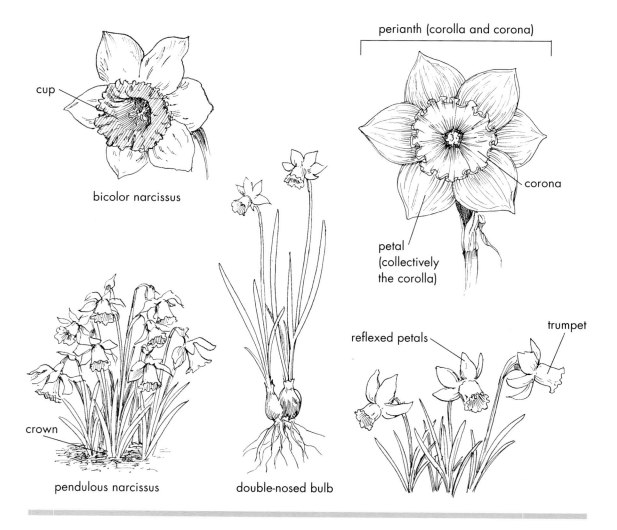

cup

bicolor narcissus

perianth (corolla and corona)

corona

petal (collectively the corolla)

crown

pendulous narcissus

double-nosed bulb

reflexed petals

trumpet

bloom better if you dig and separate them every 5 to 10 years — a good way to help a planting continue indefinitely.

The American Daffodil Society (see Appendix) maintains a detailed computer listing of cultivars and has published a book of recent and classic cultivar listings, *Daffodils to Show and Grow*. They also have compiled a list of the miniature daffodils.

Narcissus Classifications

The Royal Horticultural Society of Great Britain has classified the narcissus into twelve categories or divisions based on the length of the corona or other characteristics. Division 10 consists of wild species; the others have either been selected or hybridized and are called *garden narcissus*. The Society has also split some divisions into subcategories according to their color of bloom and size of the corona.

These classifications are indispensable to hybridizers and members of the American Daffodil Society (see Appendix), and any gardener with an interest in narcissus will find the divisions and terms helpful in distinguishing one bulb from another and describing them accurately. Once you have become familiar with the categories, you will probably look at each bloom in a new way and appreciate qualities you'd never noticed before.

The number of garden daffodil cultivars is tremendous, and the lists that follow contain only a few of those that you will find available in bulb catalogs and garden stores. Some firms carry only old-time familiar cultivars, so if you want to try some of the newer kinds, you may need to seek out specialty nurseries. (See Appendix.)

Division 1 — Trumpet Daffodils

Trumpet daffodils have one flower per stem, and the coronas are as long or longer than the perianth segments. They bloom from early to

NARCISSUS CLASSIFICATIONS

Division 1 — **Trumpet Daffodils**
Division 2 — **Large-Cupped Daffodils**
Division 3 — **Small-Cupped Daffodils**
Division 4 — **Double-Flowering Narcissus**
Division 5 — **Triandrus Narcissus**
Division 6 — **Cyclamineus Narcissus**
Division 7 — **Jonquilla Narcissus**
Division 8 — **Tazetta Narcissus**
Division 9 — **Poeticus Narcissus**
Division 10 — **Species and Wild Forms and Their Hybirds**
Division 11 — **Narcissus with split coronas (Butterfly)**
Division 12 — **Miscellaneous Narcissus**

midspring and grow from 14 to 18 inches tall. Miniatures in this group grow 5 to 6 inches tall.

'Beersheba'. Pure white. 14 inches tall.
'Dutch Master'. An improvement over the famous King Alfred with larger golden yellow flowers. 15 inches tall.
'Early Sensation'. Early yellow. 16 inches tall.
'General Patton'. Ivory perianth, yellow trumpet. 15 inches tall.
'Golden Harvest'. Large golden yellow. 14 inches.
'King Alfred'. A large yellow that is still popular, even though it is nearly a century old. 16 inches.
'Little Beauty'. Miniature creamy white with golden trumpet. 8 inches.
'Magnet'. Creamy white with yellow trumpet. 17 inches.
'Mount Hood'. Vigorous, outstanding ivory white. 16 inches.
'Peaches and Cream'. Creamy white, pink trumpet. 16 inches.
'Rosy Wonder'. Pink trumpet, white perianth. 18 inches.

'Spellbinder'. Yellow petals, green-yellow trumpet. 16 inches.

'Salome'. White perianth with a long pink trumpet. 16 inches.

'Unsurpassable'. Huge yellow blooms on 18-inch stems.

Division 2 — Large-Cupped Daffodils

Large-Cupped Daffodils have one flower to the stem. The corona is more than one-third the length of the perianth segments, but shorter than their total length. They bloom from early to midspring and grow from 14 to 18 inches tall.

'Ambergate'. Amber-orange perianth, red cup. 18 inches.

'Carbineer'. Yellow perianth, orange cup. 14 inches.

'Carlton'. Golden yellow. 14 inches.

'Ceylon'. Yellow, orange cup. Long-lasting. 14 inches.

'Fortissimo'. Large blooms, golden yellow perianth, red- orange cup. 16 inches.

'Ice Follies'. White with lemon yellow cup that turns white. 14 inches.

'Professor Einstein'. White perianth, orange-red cup. 15 inches.

Division 3 — Small-Cupped Daffodils

Small cups bear one flower per stem, and the coronas are less than one-third the length of the perianth segments. The 2- to 3-inch-wide flowers bloom early in the spring on stems that are 14 to 16 inches tall.

'Amor'. Creamy white with orange and red cup. 14 inches.

'Apricot Distinction'. Apricot perianth, red-orange cup. 15 inches.

'Barrett Browning'. Creamy white perianth, orange cup. 16 inches.

'Flower Record'. White perianth, yellow cup with orange rim. Good for naturalizing. 16 inches.

Division 4 — Double-Flowering Narcissus

These have double the number of the perianth segments or double cups, or both. The petals are all about the same size and replace the cup or trumpet. Most grow from 14 to 18 inches tall, but there are shorter-growing miniatures. Some cultivars may have more than one bloom to the stem.

'Bridal Crown'. Creamy yellow produced in clusters. 12 inches.

'Cheerfulness'. White with creamy yellow centers. Fragrant. 15 inches.

'Mary Copeland'. Fully double white flowers with small tufts of orange among the petals. 16 inches.

'Manley'. Huge yellow, high-class double. 18 inches.

'Sir Winston Churchill'. Large, double, creamy white outside petals and centers of saffron yellow. Several blooms usually appear on each stalk. 16 inches.

'Tahiti'. Large, fragrant, pale yellow blooms with gold and orange petals interspersed. 16 inches.

Division 5 — Triandrus Narcissus

These have several blooms per stem and were derived from the small species *N. triandrus*, a native of southwestern Europe. The flowers are small, nodding, with reflexed perianth segments. They bloom in late spring toward the end of the narcissus season and grow from 12 to 16 inches tall. The miniatures reach about 8 inches.

'April Tears'. Two to three yellow, trumpet-type blooms on 8-inch stems.

'Hawera'. Four to six small, pendulous lemon yellow flowers per stem. Good for rock gardens. 8 inches.

'Ice Wings'. Creamy flowers that turn white.
Reflexed petals frame a long cup. 12 inches.
'Liberty Bells'. Similar to Hawera, but taller
(to 15 inches).
'Thalia'. The popular orchid narcissus.
Three to five slightly fragrant, pendulous,
white flowers per stem. 14 inches.

Division 6 — Cyclamineus Narcissus

These hybrids are developed from the
multiflowered, early-blooming species, N.
cyclamineus. They grow one flower to a stem,
from 6 to 12 inches tall, with small flowers and
reflexed perianth segments. Miniatures in this
division grow only 6 to 8 inches tall, and
those such as 'Tête-à-Tête' are popular plants
for forcing.

'February Gold'. An early, golden yellow
bloomer with a long trumpet. 10 inches.
'February Silver'. A creamy white version of
February Gold. 10 inches.
'Foundling'. Reflexed, white petals surround
an apricot- pink cup. 12 inches.
'Jack Snipe'. Vigorous grower that spreads
fast and is good for naturalizing. White
blooms with lemon yellow cups. 10
inches.
'Peeping Tom'. A long trumpet and reflexed
petals both of golden yellow. 12 inches.
'Tête à Tête'. Golden yellow flowers, two to
a stem. 6 to 8 inches.

Division 7 — Jonquilla Narcissus

These hybrids are derived from the yellow,
fragrant, multiflowering N. jonquilla and similar
species. Their small, fragrant flowers have tiny
cups and narrow leaves. They grow from 12 to
16 inches tall and bloom from mid- to late
spring.

Baby Moon'. Lemon yellow, with several
blooms per stem. 7 inches.

'Pipit'. Bicolor of pale yellow with white
cup. 7 inches.
'Suzy'. Yellow petals and a flat orange cup.
16 inches.

Division 8 — Tazetta Narcissus

These fragrant flowers were derived from N.
tazetta, the polyanthus narcissus, a species native to southern France. Its small flowers grow
in clusters of four to eight or even more on a 18-
inch stem. Both paper-white narcissus and the
Chinese sacred lily are examples of this group.
They are hardy to zone 8, but are usually
grown indoors elsewhere in bowls of pebbles
and water. Their pungent fragrance can be
overpowering.

By crossing N. tazetta with N. jonquilla, hybridizers have developed cultivars that are
hardy in zones 5 to 10.

'Geranium'. White petals and an orange-red
cup. 14 inches.
'Grand Soleil d'Or'. Yellow petals frame an
orange cup. Fragrant. 12 inches.
'Minnow'. Pale yellow petals and a yellow
cup. 7 inches.
'Paper-White'. The best known of this
group, widely grown for its indoor pure
white winter blooms. Outdoors only to
zone 8.
'Silver Chimes'. Silver-white petals and a
primrose yellow cup. Blooms late. 12
inches.

Division 9 — Poeticus Narcissus

Members of this group have white perianth
segments and small cups that are either red, yellow with red edges, or greenish. Derived from
N. poeticus, a fragrant, late-blooming species,
they grow from 16 to 18 inches tall and usually
have one flower to a stem.

'Actaea'. White petals and yellow cup
with a green eye and red edge. Good for

naturalizing and tolerates damp soil. 18 inches.

Division 10 — Species and Wild Forms and Their Hybrids

All the native species and wild varieties are included in this division. Over two dozen species of narcissus exist, and you can find some of them in catalogs and at nurseries. Species are often more vigorous, less likely to need attention, and more pest resistant than cultivars so are sometimes better choices for naturalizing. They usually have smaller blooms, too, and tend to be shorter. All are designated hardy to zone 4 unless otherwise stated, but we have successfully grown some of those recommended for zone 6 in our zone 3 location. We plant them deep and are almost always certain of a good snow cover. Species narcissus are also well suited for wildflower plantings and rock gardens. All grow best in full sun or dappled shade. Among the commercially grown species available are:

N. asturiensis (N. minimus). This miniature daffodil, a native of Portugal, has tiny golden yellow blooms that come early in the season. 5 inches. Hardy to zone 6.

N. bulbocodium. The Petticoat narcissus is a native of Spain, Portugal, and southern France. It has a miniature yellow flower with an open trumpet that resembles the hoop of a petticoat. 15 inches. Hardy to zone 6. 'Conspicuus' is a variety.

N. cyclamineus. A bright yellow, early blooming miniature from Spain and Portugal. Hardy to zone 6.

N. jonquilla. The true jonquil, this bears two or three fragrant, deep yellow flowers per stem and blooms later than most others. From Algeria and Spain. 16 inches. Hardy to zone 6.

N. × odorus. The Campernelle jonquil is a very fragrant, bright yellow bloomer from France, Spain, and eastward. 12 inches. Hardy to zone 6.

N. pseudonarcissus. A trumpet daffodil, this is usually less than a foot tall. Flourishes in Britain and France.

N. tazetta. The polyanthus narcissus, from southern France, has small white flowers with pale yellow corollas and grows in clusters of 4 to 8 on an 18-inch stem. Hardy to zone 8.

N. triandrus. Sometimes called angel's tears, this narcissus has miniature bell-shaped yellow blooms with a white or creamy-colored cup. It is one of the oldest kinds of narcissus in cultivation. 12 inches tall.

Division 11 — Narcissus with Split Coronas (Butterfly)

This division is a fairly recent category known as the Butterfly or Split-Corona Narcissus. The segmented cup lies flat against the perianth. Members of this class vary considerably, and their inconsistent blooming habits make you wonder what the next bloom will be like.

'Cassata'. Wide-spreading split cup of lemon yellow that nearly covers the white petals. 14 inches.
'Dolly Mollinger'. White perianth with orange and white ruffled cup. 16 inches.
'Parisienne'. Orange cup and cream-colored petals. 20 inches.
'Pearlax'. White petals and a flat rose cup. 19 inches.
'Tricolet'. Orange cup and white perianth. 16 inches.

Narcissus for Naturalizing

Certain vigorous narcissus can go on producing blooms year after year with little care. Among those that have won such a reputation are these:

'Arctic Gold'
'Barrett Browning'
'Duke of Windsor'

'February Gold'
'Ice Follies'
'King Alfred'
'Mount Hood'
'Mrs. R. O. Backhouse'
'Salome'
'Spellbinder'
'Sweetness'

For a longer list of narcissus suitable for naturalizing, see chapter 6.

Division 12 — Miscellaneous Narcissus

This category includes all narcissus that don't fit into any other group.

The Miniatures

In almost every division of the *Narcissus* genus (with the exception of the *Poeticus* division) there are named cultivars of miniature daffodils. These diminuitive flowers are in a class by themselves, although the experts have difficulty defining precisely what is meant by the term "miniature" as it relates to daffodils. James Wells, a well-known authority on the subject, feels that a completely accurate definition is impossible, since there is such diversity of plants and growing conditions. In his book *Modern Miniature Daffodils*, Wells notes that the Royal Horticultural Society in England requires that a miniature flower "should measure no more than 2 inches (5 cm) in diameter," but he concludes that "dwarf" or "short stem" would be a more accurate description of the miniatures. (All are under 10 inches tall.) The American Daffodil Society has formulated rules for display and judging of these special bulbs and has compiled an officially "Approved List" of those that fit their description. If you are involved with hybridizing or showing them officially, contact the society for more information (see Appendix). Most of us simply want to use these delightful tiny plants in our rock gardens or special beds. They are particularly good for indoor growing, too. Wells has different miniature cultivars blossoming indoors in his greenhouse from late November into March and outdoors until late May, for a total of nearly seven months of bloom.

'Angel's Tears' (*Narcissus triandrus* var. *albus*). 4 inches. Clusters of creamy white blooms.
'Baby Moon'. 7 inches. Soft yellow. Fragrant. Late.
'February Gold'. 10 inches.
'Hawera'. 8 inches. Lemon yellow with recurved petals.
'Jack Snipe'. 10 inches. White perianth, small yellow trumpet. Early.
'Little Gem'. 6 inches. Yellow cup, yellow perianth.
'Minnow'. 8 inches. Pale yellow perianth with yellow cup.
'Tête-à-Tête'. 7 inches. Yellow. Very early. Good for forcing.

Tulipa (TEW-lip-a)

COMMON NAME: tulip
TYPE OF ROOT: bulb
DEPTH TO PLANT FROM BASE: 6 to 8 inches
PLANTING TIME: fall
BLOOMING SEASON: spring
LIGHT PREFERENCE: sun or partial shade

We aren't sure if children still draw tulips, color them, and paste them on school windows each spring, as we used to do in our art classes. In the second grade we didn't know if there were one or four blooms on a stem, but we thought four looked about right, and we made each bloom a different color.

Now that we know more about tulips, we still think of them in terms of spring and many colors. There is nothing like thumbing through a bulb catalog filled with colorful tulip photos to set our gardening juices flowing. We want to plant them all, from the short, early-flowering *greigii* and other botanical (species) tulips to the dramatic tall, late-blooming 'Black Parrots'. The new perennial types advertised to bloom beautifully for five years without replanting are especially tempting, too. Just when you'd think that breeders couldn't possibly come up with anything new in tulips, they do.

Tulips have changed a great deal since the seventeenth century, but the excitement they created then will probably never be surpassed by any other plant. The extraordinary tale of tulip mania, sometimes called tulipomania, began as early as the mid-1500s when the Holy Roman emperor, Ferdinand I, sent an ambassador from Flanders to the Turkish court. He became entranced with Turkish tulips and took some to Vienna. By the end of the century, they reached the Netherlands and botanists there had discovered some unusual streaked varieties caused by a botanical occurrence called a "break" — when a monochromatic plant produces a flower of unusual colors and markings.

Dutch plant breeders were unaware that their lovely blooms were the result of a virus spread through the soil, but they knew they had the makings of a fortune. In 1623 or 1624 a bulb producing a red and white flower with a blue-tinged base sold for the equivalent of $1,200 and the new owner sold two bulbs he had started from that one for $30,000.

By 1634, tulip bulbs, especially the "broken" tulips or "Rembrandts," as they were called later, were traded furiously, including seedlings that had not yet blossomed, and bulb "futures" were sold much like wheat and soybeans are today. In the furious pace of trading that followed, a market crash was inevitable, and only three years later in 1637, huge fortunes were lost as quickly as they were made. The Dutch government then took control of the bulb business and banned further speculation.

The Netherlands government still controls the tremendously successful tulip business. The combination of favorable growing conditions and centuries of experience are unbeatable, and today they are by far the world's leading grower and exporter of spring bulbs. In 1990 they exported 1.8 billion bulbs, worldwide.

The Nature of the Tulip

Tulips, unlike cheery little crocuses and breezy, natural-looking narcissus, are stately, formal flowers, and their solid stems and indelicate spreading leaves make many of them seem more suited for a formal garden than an informal border. They grow well almost everywhere as long as they have spring sunlight, including spots near deciduous trees where there will be no shade until after the blooms have faded.

Wherever they grow, they bring a cheerful spot of vivid color. Plant them where you will see them often during their blooming time — by the front door, bordering pathways or drives, or around the foundation of your garage; or set them in the border where their colors will stand out among the new green growth of the perennials. (Set them at the front if you intend to lift them after blooming, or in the back if you will leave them in the ground.) Some people plant a row or two in a cutting garden where they won't feel guilty about picking them for arrangements. We have seen them used effectively even around the stones in cemeteries where they bloom on Memorial Day.

Tulip Planting and Culture

In zones 3 through 5 plant tulip bulbs as soon as you get them in the fall. They need several weeks to grow roots before the soil becomes too cool, so that the plant will be able to absorb water and nutrients and bloom in the springtime. In warmer zones, wait until about six weeks before the first hard frost to plant. Otherwise the bulbs may start to grow. Those left in the ground over the summer seldom have this problem, however. For planting instructions and other cultural directions, see chapter 4.

For the best effect when planting tulips, place at least a dozen of the same cultivar together in each grouping, so they will be the same color and height and bloom at the same time. The shorter cultivars are ideal for growing outdoors in containers and for forcing indoors. For a listing of those most suitable for forcing, and directions, see chapter 7.

Tulips for More than a Year

We know of a community where groups and individuals spent hundreds of dollars planting displays of tulip bulbs one fall and had a grand festival the next spring. They widely advertised a repeat performance for the following May, but as the crowds arrived, the tulip festival committee was chagrined when instead of the great display of the previous year only a few lonely tulips appeared scattered through large beds.

What this community unfortunately didn't realize is that tulips bloom their best the first spring after they are planted. Propagators readying new bulbs for sale force-feed them to perfection, and the bulbs produce large blooms on sturdy stalks the first year. The care they get in the nursery is difficult to duplicate in a home garden, even if you fertilize the bulbs heavily hoping to get the same results the second year. They are likely to divide into smaller bulbs and the blooms become smaller each year, eventually petering out. The short life expectancy of tulips can be discouraging to new growers who are unaware of it. The poor blooming habits of most tulips during their second and subsequent years is why many people treat them as annuals.

Treating tulips as annuals and discarding them after blooming seems a waste of time and money, however, not to mention a loss of beautiful bulbs. It is possible to get an excellent second bloom and possibly even more from your bulbs by treating them as the Dutch do. During their growing and blooming season, fertilize them lightly. As the flowers begin to fade, pick them off so the bulb will not waste its energy making seeds. In Holland, bulb growers fill huge barges with discarded blooms throughout the season. Leave the stalk and leaves intact so that the nutrients in them will return to the bulb for next season's growth. Let the leaves wither in the bed, if the appearance isn't offensive to you, and dig the bulbs as soon as the foliage has browned and dried.

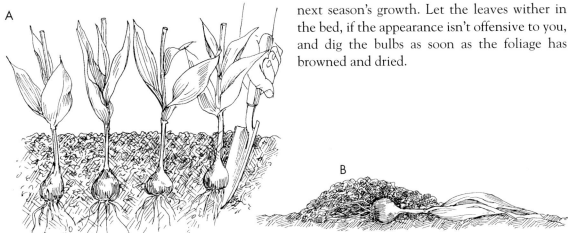

To get tulips to bloom in following years, (A) dig the bulb carefully leaving foliage undisturbed, (B) cover bulb with soil and compost until foliage withers, then store in a dry place.

Tulip Cultivars That Live Longer Than Most

(Includes both older and newer cultivars)

Type	Color	Blooming Time (zone 5)
Triumph Tulips		
'Don Quichotte'	rose	May
'Kees Nelis'	blood red, orange rim	April, May
Darwin Hybird Tulips		
'Apeldoorn'	cherry red	April, May
'Apeldoorn Elite'	red and yellow	April, May
'Beauty of Apeldoorn'	orange-yellow-red striped	April, May
'Golden Apeldoorn'	golden yellow	April, May
'Holland's Glory'	orange red	April, May
'Oxford'	scarlet flushed with purple	April, May
Lily-Flowered Tulips		
'Ballade'	reddish magenta, white edge	April, May
'Maytime'	reddish violet	April, May
'Red Shine'	deep red	April, May
'White Triumphator'	pure white	April, May
Fosteriana Series		
'Orange Emperor'	carrot orange	March, April
'Princeps'	red	March, April
'Purissima'	white	March, April
'Red Emperor'	red	March, April
'Yellow Purissima'	yellow with deeper yellow edge	March, April
Greigii series		
'Red Riding Hood'	red	April, May
'Toronto'	red with vermillion	April, May
Praestans series		
'Fusilier'	orange-red	March, April

Another way to treat them, to avoid having long-lasting unsightly foliage around, is to dig the bulbs directly after you have picked off the fading blooms but leave the foliage and stems attached. Bury the bulbs a couple of inches deep in a shallow trench in the corner of your vegetable garden or other out-of-sight bed. Keep them watered if the weather is dry, but let their foliage die naturally. Then dig and dry the bulbs.

An alternate, similar method recommended by a gardening friend who had seen it in the Netherlands, is one we've used with great success. After cutting the blooms, carefully dig the bulbs, leaving the foliage and stems attached. Then lay them flat on top of soil that is free of weeds and grass and has been loosened slightly in an out-of-the-way bed or garden. Cover the bulbs with a layer of a rich mixture of half soil and half compost about 3 inches thick, but leave the stems and leaves sticking out. With the roots buried, the tops die back slowly and as naturally as if they had never been disturbed. Since they are hidden away, their appearance doesn't offend anyone.

Whatever method you use to let your bulbs rejuvenate, after the foliage is dead and dry, dig them and tie them in bunches of the same color. Label them and hang them to dry in a warm airy place, or spread them out on raised screens. It is difficult to say exactly how long to dry them because conditions vary, but usually they'll be dry enough after only a few days if the weather is warm and dry. There is some latitude as to how dry they should get, but store them before they get so dry that they have lost vitality.

After drying, cut off the dead stems and put the bulbs in an open paper bag or other open container that allows air circulation, and store them in a dark, cool, dry place such as a closet. After years of experience, we recommend that you write yourself a reminder on a calendar to plant them in September or early October. One

year we found our bulbs still residing in the closet in midwinter, too late even to pot for forcing.

"Perennial" Tulips

There are exceptions to the rule that tulips are short lived. Hybrids of some of the early-blooming species often bloom well for more than one year. Among them are the *greigiis*, *fosterianas*, *kaufmannianas*, and *praestans* hybrids, as well as certain Darwins, Triumphs, and Lily-Flowered kinds. But it is the longevity of newly developed "perennial" tulips that is currently creating enthusiasm among tulip lovers. After years of testing, breeders have introduced a group of bulbs that will live and bloom beautifully for up to five years without the need for digging and replanting or replacing. They resemble the Darwins and grow between 24 and 30 inches tall. Some nurseries offer them according to color in pinks, reds, yellows, whites, and bicolors, and others offer named cultivars. If you grow the "perennials," add fertilizer to the bed each fall for continued good blooms.

No one expects that tulips will ever become as long-lived as peonies, even most of the perennial kinds begin to deteriorate after producing their third bloom. Nevertheless, their introduction is a worthwhile breakthrough, and it is likely that even longer-lived cultivars will follow.

Tulip Classifications

There are from 3,000 to 4,000 named cultivars of tulips which, along with the botanicals (species) and their hybrids, have been classified into fifteen groups according to their blooms and growth habits by the Royal General Bulb Growers' Association of the Netherlands. The following classification was made in 1987. (Some worthwhile cultivars are listed in each classification.)

TULIP CLASSIFICATION

Early Flowering
1. Single Early Tulips
2. Double Early Tulips

Mid-Season Flowering
3. Triumph Tulips
4. Darwin Hybrid Tulips

Late Flowering
5. Single Late Tulips
6. Lily-Flowered Tulips
7. Fringed Tulips
8. Viridiflora Tulips
9. Rembrandt Tulips
10. Parrot Tulips
11. Double Late Tulips (Peony-Flowered Tulips)
12. Kaufmanniana Tulips
13. Fosteriana Tulips
14. Greigii Tulips and its hybrids
15. Other Species and Their Varieties and Hybrids

Early Flowering

Single Early

These single tulips, some of which are fragrant, are 8 to 12 inches tall, one flower per stem.

'Apricot Beauty' — apricot and salmon pink
'Bellona' — fragrant yellow
'Christmas Dream' — pink
'General de Wat' — fragrant orange
'Keizerskroon' — old favorite, fragrant red with yellow edge
'Van der Neer' — lilac blue
'White Hawk' — white

Double Early

These have large, peonylike blooms on strong stems and are from 8 to 12 inches tall.

'Angelique' — semi-double pink
'Electra' — red
'Monte Carlo' — yellow
'Peach Blossom' — pink
'Schoonoord' — white

Mid-Season Flowering

Triumph

Crosses of single early tulips and late-flowering ones are responsible for most of this class. Blooms are single and cup-shaped, in numerous colors. 10 to 16 inches tall.

'Boccherini' — lilac purple and rose
'Dreaming Maid' — lavender edged with white
'Golden Melody' — light yellow
'Jo Ann' — pale pink
'New Design' — creamy yellow with pink and red
'Orange Wonder' — fragrant orange
'Page Polka' — white with pink border
'White Dream' — pure white

Darwin Hybrid

Most of these resulted from crossing *Tulipa fosteriana* with Darwin cultivars and from hybridization between botanicals and other tulips which have the same habit. The blooms are huge, on tall, strong stems. 12 to 20 inches. Excellent as cut flowers.

'Big Chief' — salmon pink
'Cream Jewel' — white
'Dover' — large, scarlet red
'Dutch Fair' — yellow with red markings
'Elizabeth Arden' — salmon pink with bluish overcast
'General Eisenhower' — large red
'Holland's Glory' — orange red
'Orange Sun' — orange
'Pink Impression' — large rose pink

Late Flowering

Single Late

In earlier classifications, these were Darwin, Breeder, and Cottage tulips but owing to hybridization, borderlines between the classes are no longer visible. They are among the tallest of all tulips, ranging from 14 to 30 inches tall, and bloom in many different colors.

'Anne Frank' — large white
'Aristocrat' — pink with lighter edge
'Balalaika' — red
'Cashmir' — red
'Cream Delight' — light yellow
'Daydream' — apricot
'Dreamland' — red with white
'Elizabeth Arden' — pink
'Kingsblood' — red
'Lafayette' — blue
'Mary Poppins' — rosy pink
'Maureen' — white
'Orange Sun' — fragrant orange
'Sweet Harmony' — yellow with white edge
'William Tell' — salmon pink

Lily-Flowered

Once called the Ottomans, their flowers are single and pointed, with reflexed segments, and the leaves are narrow. The tall stems tend to be weak and often need staking. 15 to 30 inches tall.

'Ballade' — purple edged with white
'China Pink' — pale pink
'Mariette' — rose pink
'Marilyn' — white with red markings
'Queen of Sheba' — deep red with yellow edge
'Red Shine' — red
'West Point' — yellow
'White Triumphator' — white

Fringed

Also known as crispa tulips, these have petals that are fringed. Many are mutants of other types of tulips.

'Blue Heron' — violet-blue with white base
'Fringed Elegance' — yellow with pink flecks
'Swan Wings' — pure white

Viridiflora

The distinguishing color of these flowers is green, as their name implies. They are shaped somewhat like the Lily-Flowered Tulips, and are exceptionally long-flowering.

'Greenland' — pale pink at the beginning, then green tones
'Spring Green' — creamy white with soft green feathering

Rembrandt

Oddly, Rembrandt was one of the few Dutch painters who didn't paint tulips. These are also sometimes called "broken tulips," and have stripes or blotches, often in brown, black, bronze, pink, purple, red on white, or red on yellow. These tulips originated with the Darwins and were the cause of the seventeenth-century tulip mania in Holland. Because it's thought that the effect was originally caused by a virus, there is controversy over whether planting them in your garden near healthy tulips or lilies will spread the virus. They are no longer being grown commercially in The Netherlands.

Parrot

These sports or mutations of other tulips have unusual feathery large flowers with twisted petals of various color combinations and streaks. Most have a green spot at the base of the petals. They grow up to 2 feet tall and should be planted in a protected area since they are easily devastated by wind.

'Amethyst' — blend of purple, rose red, and white
'Black Parrot' — velvety black
'Blue Parrot' — light blue

'Fantasy' — pink
'Firebird' — red
'Flaming Parrot' — yellow with red on a
    green base
'White Parrot' — white; with some green
    shading

Double Late

These are also called peony-flowered tulips because of their multiple petals. They grow up to 2 feet tall and need protection from the wind.

'Angelique' — fragrant rose pink
'Gold Medal' — clear yellow
'Mount Tacoma' — white with green
    markings

Species & Their Hybrids (botanical)

Kaufmanniana

Also known as water lily tulips, Kaufmannias are varieties and hybrids of *T. kaufmanniana*, a species from Turkestan. They have broad tapered leaves and large flowers, usually white, pale yellow, pink, or red with contrasting yellow or black centers. When open, their petals form a hexagonal star. These early flowering tulips are dwarf growing and good for rock gardens; their stems range from 4 to 8 inches and they sometimes have mottled foliage.

'Ancilla' — light pink with red center
'Cherry Orchard' — scarlet red
'Chopin' — lemon yellow
'Fritz Kreisler' — salmon pink
'Heart's Delight' — carmine and rose
'Pink Pixie' — pink with red center
'Shakespeare' — red with salmon pink
    center
'Showwinner' — scarlet
'Stresa' — yellow; red stripes on each petal

Fosteriana (botanical) (photo, page 55)

From central Asia, the Emperors are popular cultivars of this group. Blooms are yellow, or-ange, red, or white, and grow from 12 to 18 inches tall. Some cultivars have striped or mottled foliage. They bloom early.

'Orange Emperor' — salmon orange with
    deeper orange inside
'Purissima' — cream turning to white
'Pink Emperor' — pink, edged yellow, rose
    interior, black base
'Red Emperor' — bright red, very early
'Sweetheart' — lemon yellow with white edge
'White Emperor' — white, very early
'Yellow Empress' — golden yellow

Greigii (botanical) (photo, page 55)

T. greigii varieties and hybrids have wide, wavy-margined leaves that are distinctively mottled and striped reddish or purplish. Their bright-colored 3-inch flowers are borne on short 8- to 12-inch stems in shades of orange-red, yellow, and white, with a deep-colored center and pointed petals. They bloom later than *T. kaufmanniana*.

'Corsage' — rose with yellow edge
'Donna Bella' — red edged with cream,
    yellow inside
'Diantha' — salmon with orange overcast
'Golden Tango' — yellow
'Orange Elite' — orange-edged apricot with
    orange center
'Oratorio' — rose pink
'Plaisir' — red with creamy yellow edge
'Red Riding Hood' — scarlet

Other Species

There are additional species not in the above list, as well as their varieties and hybrids. See listing under "Botanical Tulips," page 95.

Multiflowered

Another grouping, though not an official class, are the multiflowered tulips. These various types all produce flowers in a similar way, although they vary in height and flower size. Their main stem branches into from three to seven secondary stems. They include the *T. praestans* varieties, a popular multiflowered type with 8 to 10 inch stems that naturalizes well. 'Zwanenburg', a large red, is a popular member of this group.

'Georgette' — yellow with red edge
'Red Bouquet' — all red

Botanical Tulips

Botanical is a term that describes both the species and their many varieties. Different species bloom throughout the season, from early to late spring, but most come early and are especially prized for their bright colors. The bulbs are tiny, the size of a nickel, and the plants are usually short. Most make good rock garden specimens and naturalize freely. Species bulbs last longer than those of the hybrids, so leave them in the ground to multiply naturally. All are hardy to zone 4 and most of zone 3 unless otherwise noted.

Till their bed before planting, just as you would for the cultivars, rather than just digging a hole in the ground as for the hardy narcissus. They do not withstand competition from other plants, though they can often cope with tough soils and severe weather conditions.

T. acuminata (*T. cornuta*), Turkish tulip. 12 to 18 inches. Yellow blooms with red markings. Blooms late spring. From Turkey.

T. aucherana. Dwarf, 8 inches. Starlike flowers are pink with brownish-yellow blotches. Inner petals are striped green. Blooms early. From Syria and Iran.

T. australis, southern tulip. 6 to 10 inches. Fragrant flowers, reddish outside, yellow inside, with pointed petals. From southern France and Algeria. Blooms late.

T. batalinii, Batalin tulip. Very dwarf, 6 inches. Flowers are yellow with blotches. Petals

are long and pointed, sometimes notched at top. From Bokhara (formerly U.S.S.R.).

T. clusiana, lady tulip, Clusius tulip, candy-stick tulip. 15 inches. Small, fragrant, medium-sized blooms are reddish purple at the base, white or yellowish at the top, with pink stripes. When open, petals form a star. Bulbs are small, and leaves narrow. Blooms late. From Afghanistan and Iran.

T. fosteriana, Foster tulip. 12 inches. Large, crimson flowers are darker at the base. Blooms early. From Turkestan.

T. hageri, Hager tulip. Only 6 inches tall.

Tulip Blooming Sequence

In some climatic zones, by planting the different kinds you can get flowers for up to two months; but in colder zones where the spring season is short, the blooming seasons greatly overlap.

Early Spring

Botanicals (species) — *T. aucherana, T. fosteriana, T. greigii, T. hageri, T. kaufmanniana, T. orphanidea, T. praestans, T. pulchella, T. saxatilis, T. tarda, T. turkestanica*
Dutch — Single Early, Double Early

Midspring

Botanicals (species) — *T. kolpakowskiana*
Dutch — Triumph, Darwin Hybrid

Late Spring

Botanicals — *T. acuminata, T. australis, T. clusiana, T. linifolia, T. montana, T. sylvestris*
Dutch — Single Late, Lily-Flowered, Parrot, Double Late, Rembrandt, Fringed, Viridiflora

Copper-yellow to reddish blooms appear in clusters on the stalk in early spring. From Greece and Asia Minor.

T. kolpakowskiana, Kolpak tulip. 6 to 8 inches. Petals are red outside, orange-yellow inside and form a star when open. Curved flower stems. Blooms midseason. From Turkestan.

T. linifolia, slimleaf tulip. 4 to 8 inches. Flowers are long, crimson, with a bluish base. Pointed petals. Foliage is grasslike. Blooms late. From Bokhara.

T. montana. 8 inches tall. Long bluish-green leaves. Flowers are crimson, with paler exterior. Outer petals are pointed. Blooms late. From Afghanistan and Iran.

T. orphanidea, Spartan tulip. 8 to 12 inches. Starlike orange-bronze to yellow blooms are greenish outside. May need protection in zones 3 and 4. Bloom early. From Turkey and Greece.

T. praestans, leather-bulb tulip. 12 inches. Flowers in clusters of up to four on a stalk. Petals are long, light red. Leaves are narrow. Many varieties. Blooms early. From Bokhara.

T. pulchella. Up to 6 inches. Large blooms are cup-shaped and form a flat star when fully opened. Cultivars are pinkish, violet, or white. Needs winter protection in zones 3 and 4. Blooms early. From Asia Minor.

T. saxatilis, cliff tulip. 12 inches. Fragrant, cup-shaped flowers are lilac colored with a yellow base and open to a star shape. Blooms early. From Crete.

T. sprengeri. Up to 12 inches. Orange-red flowers have a darker base and come late in spring. Leaves are long and narrow. Protect in the colder zones. From Armenia.

T. sylvestris, Florentine tulip, daffodil tulip. Up to 12 inches. Fragrant flowers are yellow and come in late spring. Native of Asia, Africa, and Europe.

T. tarda (*T. dasystemon*). 6 inches tall. Good for rock gardens. Golden yellow flowers usually come in clusters with white tips. Leaves grow in a flat rosette. Blooms early. From Turkestan.

T. turkestanica. 8 inches. White flowers have an orange yellow base and a black center. Each stem has up to nine flowers. Multiplies quickly and blooms early. From Turkestan.

The Minor Spring-Blooming Bulbs

MANY BEAUTIFUL UNCOMMON spring bulbs are unknown to backyard gardeners. Some of them we never see because they grow wild in unfamiliar corners of the world such as Siberia, northern Japan and high in the mountains of Europe and Asia. Others are native wildflowers, but even people who are familiar with plants such as jack-in-the-pulpit (*Arisaema*), spring beauties (*Claytonia*), and various *trilliums* often are surprised to learn that they grow from bulbous roots. Other bulbous plants, even though they are available and easy to grow, are familiar only to bulb specialists. Most of us have yet to experience the treats of bright yellow aconite (*Eranthis*) with our early snowdrops, lovely daisylike anemones in our borders, golden miniature lilies (*Erythronium revolutum* 'Pagoda') in the rock garden, or the common blue glory-of-the-snow (*Chionodoxa*) naturalized at the edge of the lawn. Several alliums also bloom in late spring (see pages 109 – 16).

Most "minor" bulbs worth considering as landscape plants are available either at garden stores, in specialty bulb catalogs, or at wildflower nurseries where they grow their own plants (see Appendix.) Most are inexpensive and have better root systems than the ones you could dig wild.

Never dig up plants growing in their native habitats for your garden. Because some native bulbs have been collected extensively they are now becoming extinct. (See page 31.)

See chapter 4 for detailed information about the planting and care of the following plants.

Anemone (a-NEM-o-nee)

(photo, page 107)

SPECIES AND COMMON NAME: *A. blanda*,
    Grecian windflower
TYPE OF ROOT: tuber-like rhizome
DEPTH TO PLANT FROM BASE: 1 to 2 inches
PLANTING TIME: fall
BLOOMING SEASON: late spring
LIGHT PREFERENCE: light shade

This 8-inch-tall daisylike bloomer grows nicely among trees with thin foliage or over grassy slopes. It is a member of the Buttercup Family. In warm zones the plants do best in partial shade. The flowers close up at night and during the day if the weather is cloudy.

Soak the rhizomes overnight or longer in slightly warm water before planting, because they are likely to be very dry. Lay them on their sides and bury them 1 to 2 inches deep and 4 to 5 inches apart in soil that is rich in humus. The plants spread from the roots, and also increase naturally by scattering seeds. If windflowers are well supplied with compost or peat moss, they don't usually need extra fertilizer.

The wild species, a native of Greece, has blue flowers and is on the endangered list. Buy the species plants only from a nursery that propagates them; or use cultivars such as 'Blue Star', 'Pink Star', and 'White Splendour.' Anemones are hardy to zone 5, but will grow in cooler zones if given winter protection.

Arisaema (ar-i-SEE-ma)

(photo, page 108)

SPECIES AND COMMON NAME: *A. triphyllum*,
    Jack-in-the-pulpit
TYPE OF ROOT: CORM
DEPTH TO PLANT FROM BASE: 2 TO 3 INCHES
PLANTING TIME: EARLY SPRING, FALL

BLOOMING SEASON: SPRING
LIGHT PREFERENCE: SHADE

It's always a delightful surprise to find this late spring, American wildflower in bloom in its native habitat in the light shade of deciduous woods, but there's no need to journey there. The plant is available in specialty bulb catalogs and will be happy in your own shady garden if you plant it in rich, moist, loamy soil. The compound leaves are divided in three, as the botanic name implies, and the flower consists of an erect spadix surrounded by a green and purple striped spathe that bends over the spadix, forming the "pulpit." A cluster of bright red berries follows the bloom later in the season.

The plant grows from a fat corm, which the Indians cooked for food, but when raw it has a very burning taste, which we discovered on a hike once when we were very young. Also, it is poisonous when raw, something we didn't know either, but which was no problem in that instance because we never swallowed it. These plants add interest to a wild or semi-wild planting because of the very different form and color of the blooms. It is native to North America and grows throughout the eastern and midwestern region, as far south as North Carolina. Plant the corms about 3 inches deep and in groups of three for an effective clump.

Camassia (ka-MASS-ee-a)

COMMON NAME: wild hyacinth, camass
TYPE OF ROOT: bulb
DEPTH TO PLANT FROM BASE: 4 to 5 inches
PLANTING TIME: fall
BLOOMING SEASON: late spring
LIGHT PREFERENCE: sun or light shade

These hardy plants with spiky flowers and grass-like leaves belong to the Lily Family and are natives of the Pacific Northwest. The bulbs were eaten by the Indians, who, it is said, shared them with members of the Lewis and Clark expedition. In the fall, plant the bulbs 4 to 5 inches deep and 6 to 8 inches apart in well-drained soil well supplied with humus, in either sun or light shade. Be ready to water them if spring weather is dry. They make attractive garden displays and are good choices for naturalizing. Don't disturb the bulbs until they become so overcrowded they no longer bloom well. Hardy to zone 3.

Camassia cusickii. The Cusick camass has light blue plumy flowers. 18 to 24 inches tall.

C. leichtlinii 'Alba'. White blooms. Up to 3 feet in height.

C. l. 'Coerula'. Dark blue and purple flowers. Up to 3 feet.

C. quamash. Light blue-violet flowers. From 1 to 2 feet.

C. scilloides, wild hyacinth. Spiky flowers in blue, white, or violet. Grows to 30 inches.

Chionodoxa (ky-on-o-DOK-sa)

COMMON NAME: glory-of-the-snow
TYPE OF ROOT: bulb
DEPTH TO PLANT FROM BASE: 3 inches
PLANTING TIME: fall
BLOOMING SEASON: early spring
LIGHT PREFERENCE: sun, light shade

These perennial favorites are some of the first plants to bloom in the spring. They grow from 3 to 6 inches tall, with grasslike foliage and small, star shaped flowers that come in clusters of eight to ten. Plant the bulbs about 3 inches deep in fertile soil. If they like the spot, they will spread rapidly both by seeds and offsets, though they are not invasive. Several varieties are available, all of which appear to be hardy to zone 3.

Because these bulbs are on the endangered list, buy only those that are commercially produced.

C. luciliae has large blue and white flowers. 'Gigantea' has large flowers of gentian blue. *C. l.* 'Alba' has white blooms and 'Pink Giant', a rare cultivar, is blush pink with white centers.

C. sardensis 'Deep Blue' has blue flowers with a small white center.

Claytonia (klay-TOH-nee-a)

COMMON NAME: spring beauty
TYPE OF ROOT: corm
DEPTH TO PLANT FROM BASE: 2 inches
PLANTING TIME: fall
BLOOMING SEASON: early spring
LIGHT PREFERENCE: light shade

Different species of these native plants bloom in early spring throughout North America. Plant the small corms 1 inch deep in light shade in moist, average to rich soil that is high in organic humus. Propagate them by dividing the corms, or by seeds. Different species grow from 6 to 12 inches tall and are good choices for wildflower plantings, on lawns, around shrubs, and in rock gardens. Hardy to zone 5.

C. caroliniana, the Carolina spring beauty, has small white flowers with pink veins in early spring. The foliage is quite wide and the blooms grow from 4 to 12 inches tall. It grows from a small bulb that was eaten by the early settlers who liked its starchy flavor.

C. megarhiza, a native of the western United States, does best where summers are cool. Its spiky blooms are white to dark pink.

C. virginica grows 6 to 12 inches tall, and the rose pink blooms have veins of deeper pink. It spreads by seeds and bulblets, and is good for naturalizing in light shade.

Convallaria (kon-val-AIR-e-a)

(photo, page 53)

COMMON NAME: lily-of-the-valley
TYPE OF ROOT: rhizome
DEPTH TO PLANT FROM BASE: 1 inch
PLANTING TIME: fall
BLOOMING SEASON: LATE SPRING
LIGHT PREFERENCE: LIGHT TO MODERATE
   SHADE

These old-time favorites have tiny white or pink bell-shaped, fragrant flowers in late spring on 8-inch stalks followed by small orange-red fruits. These are poisonous, although they were once used in small amounts as medicine.

Plant the small "pips," as the rhizomes are called, in the fall, 1 inch deep and 4 inches apart in moist, somewhat acidic soil in a shady location. They spread rapidly both from the roots and by seeds and are a good ground cover beneath deciduous trees or shrubs. They are not invasive, however. Native to eastern North America, Europe, and Asia. Hardy to zone 2.

Lily-of-the-valley is steeped in tradition and legend. For many years in the early twentieth century, it was such a favorite bouquet of June brides that few would have attempted a walk down the aisle without it. According to English folklore, the plant sprang from the drops of blood that fell from the wounds suffered by St. Leonard in a battle with a dragon in the woods of Sussex. In France the flowers are cultivated for their perfume. *Convallarias* need no special care, but if they are not growing well, give them a scattering of fertilizer in the fall. Insects rarely bother them. Sometimes the foliage becomes unattractive in late summer, and it helps to grow lycoris or other late-blooming plants among them to detract from their appearance.

C. majalis, the common species, has white blooms. A cultivar, 'Rosea,' is pink, and 'Prolificans' has double white flowers.

Cyclamen (SIK-la-men)

COMMON NAME: cyclamen
TYPE OF ROOT: tuber
DEPTH TO PLANT FROM BASE: 1 inch
PLANTING TIME: midsummer
BLOOMING SEASON: spring
LIGHT PREFERENCE: light shade

In addition to *C. persicum*, the familiar tender houseplant, there are several species, both spring and fall blooming, that are hardy to zone 6. Plant the spring bloomers in midsummer when they are dormant, in partial shade, about an inch deep in soil rich in leaf mold. Don't let the tubers dry out. They may not bloom until the second spring, although the leaves will sprout in the fall. They don't like an abundance of water, so be sure the soil is well drained. The tubers increase in size, and they also multiply by scattering seeds. They are ideal plants for the border, wildflower bed, and rock garden. *C. × atkinsii*, the Atkin's cyclamen (believed to be a hybrid of *C. coum* and *C. persicum*) is tiny, only 3 inches tall. The purplish magenta blooms come in very early spring and the plant is hardy to zone 6.

C. coum has pink or pink-white blossoms, and the leaves are spotted with silvery white markings. It is considered an endangered species throughout the world, so buy plants only from a nursery that grows them, such as the Montrose Nursery (see Appendix.) Hardy to zone 7.

Endymion (en-DIM-ee-on) (photo, page 107)

COMMON NAME: BLUEBELLS, WOOD HYACINTH
TYPE OF ROOT: BULB
DEPTH TO PLANT FROM BASE: 3 INCHES
PLANTING TIME: FALL
BLOOMING SEASON: SPRING
LIGHT PREFERENCE: MEDIUM TO HEAVY SHADE

This group of plants with bell-shaped flowers and grasslike foliage has apparently given taxonomists considerable trouble in classification, because different books list it variously as either *Hyacinthoides hispanicus*, *Scilla campanulata*, *S. hispanicus*, or *Endymion*. Set the bulbs 3 inches deep, 6 inches apart, in the fall in moist, humus-rich soil, in medium to heavy shade. Let them spread naturally by self-seeding and by offsets, and don't disturb them until they become too thick.

E. hispanicus (also *Hyacinthoides hispanica*, *Scilla hispanica*, or *S. campanulata*), wood hyacinth, Spanish bluebell. These plants grow to 20 inches, with clusters of blue, pink, or white flowers in late spring. 'Blue Queen' has large blue flowers, and 'Dainty Maid' has lavender-pink blooms. This species naturalizes well. Hardy to zone 5.

E. non-scriptus (also *Scilla non-scripta*), English bluebells. These were mentioned by Shakespeare, and Emily Bronte described them as "the sweetest flower." The bells are usually blue, but cultivars with pink and white blooms are also available. A native of Europe, it is hardy to zone 5.

Eranthis (e-RAN-this)

COMMON NAME: winter aconite
TYPE OF ROOT: tuber
DEPTH TO PLANT FROM BASE: 3 to 5 inches
PLANTING TIME: fall
BLOOMING SEASON: spring
LIGHT PREFERENCE: sun or light shade

This extra-early spring flower, a member of the Buttercup Family, often pokes through the snow to bloom about two weeks before the crocuses appear. It grows from a tuberous root, naturalizes easily, and is most effective when grown in masses. The flowers are buttercup yellow and grow only 3 to 6 inches high. It does not compete well with other plants, so is not the best flower for the lawn, but it grows well in a weed-free spot where the soil is rich.

Plant in late summer or early fall. Soak the tubers overnight before planting, and set them 3 inches deep and 3 inches apart in full sun or light shade. Mulch them so they will stay moist. The foliage dies down soon after the plants bloom in late spring, but you can plant shallow-rooted annuals over them for summer bloom. Be certain you're getting nursery-cultivated plants, since some *Eranthis* species are classified as endangered. They are hardy to zone 4.

E. hyemalis grows from 2 to 8 inches tall, with bright yellow flowers.

E. × Tubergenii, the Tubergen winter aconite, has large, deep yellow, fragrant flowers. Grows to 8 inches.

Erythronium (photo, page 108) (ee-ri-THRO-nee-um)

COMMON NAME: trout lily, dog-tooth violet
TYPE OF ROOT: corm
DEPTH TO PLANT FROM BASE: 3 inches
PLANTING TIME: fall
BLOOMING SEASON: spring
LIGHT PREFERENCE: sun, light shade

These familiar native American wildflowers are members of the Lily Family and resemble miniature lilies more than violets. Plant the corms 3 inches deep and 5 inches apart in late summer or fall in soil rich in humus. They grow best where they get plenty of sun in early spring and light shade thereafter and are easily naturalized. The flower stalks range from 6 to 24 inches, depending on the species, and most are very hardy.

E. americanum, a North American native, goes by the names of trout lily and adder's-tongue. Found on roadsides and in meadows in mid-spring, they are readily identified by their spotted leaves and yellow and brown lilylike blooms. They grow up to 12 inches tall and are good for wildflower plantings beneath deciduous trees, in rock gardens, or for naturalizing. They compete well with grass, so can be used in lawns. Plant them 2 to 3 inches deep and 4 inches apart. Hardy to zone 2.

E. dens-canis, dog-tooth violet. This species has leaves mottled with reddish brown and rose to purple flowers. It originates in Europe and Asia. Hardy, deep pink cultivars include 'Pink Perfection' and 'Rose Queen'. 'Album' has white blooms. 6 to 12 inches tall. Hardy to zone 2.

E. revolutum, mahogany fawn lily, is a West Coast native with pinkish blooms. Cultivars include 'White Beauty', with white flowers and brown basal spots on 12-inch stems and mottled brown and white leaves.

'Pagoda' is a vigorous cross between *E. revolutum* and *E. tuolumnense*. Golden yellow, on a 15 inch stem, with 4 or 5 blossoms to a stem.

Fritillaria (fri-ti-LAY-ree-a)

COMMON NAME: fritillary
TYPE OF ROOT: bulb
DEPTH TO PLANT FROM BASE: 5 inches
PLANTING TIME: fall
BLOOMING SEASON: midspring
LIGHT PREFERENCE: sun or light shade

Only a few of the seventy or more species of *Fritillaria* are used as garden plants. They have bell-shaped, pendant blooms and are easy to grow. Plant them in the fall in rich, well-drained soil in sun or light shade. Set the bulbs 5 inches deep and 7 inches apart as soon as they arrive in the fall, because they should not be allowed to dry out. Don't disturb the bulbs unless they become very overcrowded.

Buy top-sized bulbs because the small ones aren't likely to bloom for several years. They are good choices for borders and to tuck in among foundation plantings.

F. imperialis, crown imperial. This spectacular native of Persia grows about 30 inches tall and each stem sports eight to ten showy "bells" in midspring. They require good drainage to grow well. Be careful where you grow them, since the plants have an unpleasant odor that even the rodents don't like. 'Aurora' is orange-red; 'Lutea Maxima' is light yellow; 'Premier' has large orange blooms and is more tolerant of eastern wet winters than most of the others. 'Rubra Maxima' has large burnt orange-red flowers striped with purple. Hardy to zone 6 and the warmer areas of zone 5. The species is endangered, so buy only from reputable dealers.

F. meleagris, guinea-hen flower, checkered lily, grows about 12 inches tall with flowers of an interesting checkered purple and white. 'Alba' is a white cultivar. A native of Europe, it is well suited for California and often doesn't do well in wet eastern winters. It likes partial shade and is good for rock gardens. Hardy to zone 4.

F. persica, Persian fritillary, grows to 3 feet and produces bell-shaped, dark purple blooms along the stalk. A native of the Middle East, it is hardy to zone 8. The species is endangered.

F. pudica, yellow bell, grows up to 12 inches with yellow flowers and grasslike leaves. This California native is hardy to zone 5 as long as it gets full sun and good drainage.

Galanthus (ga-LAN-thus) (photo, page 56)

COMMON NAME: snowdrops
TYPE OF ROOT: bulb
DEPTH TO PLANT FROM BASE: 3 inches
PLANTING TIME: fall
BLOOMING SEASON: early spring
LIGHT PREFERENCE: sun or shade

These hardy, bell-shaped flowers are a familiar

sight in early spring, often pushing up through the snow. They grow 4 to 8 inches tall, depending on the species, and are members of the Amaryllis Family. The waxy blooms, named after the Greek words for milk and flower, are white with green markings. They like heavy soil that is somewhat moist and are good plants both for naturalizing under deciduous trees and for rock gardens.

The bulbs, with the exception of G. *nivalis*, have been widely collected in the wild and are considered endangered, so buy them only from sources where they are commercially propagated. (See page 31.)

Plant the bulbs about 3 inches deep and 3 inches apart in moist, rich, well-drained soil where they will get full sun or light shade in the spring. By leaving the bulbs undisturbed for years they will form large masses. Plant in combination with *Eranthis* for an attractive early spring show. Hardy to zone 2.

G. *elwesii*, the giant snowdrop, is a native of the mountains of Asia Minor. The flowers are emerald green at the base and apex.

G. *nivalis*, common snowdrop. The delicate flowers on 3-inch stems naturalize rapidly by seed. They thrive in partial shade, so the east or northeast side of a building is ideal. 'Flore Pleno' has double white blooms.

Hermodactylus (her-mo-DAK-ti-lus)

SPECIES AND COMMON NAME: *Hermodactylus tuberosus*, snake's-head iris
TYPE OF ROOT: tuber
DEPTH TO PLANT FROM BASE: 3 inches
PLANTING TIME: fall
BLOOMING SEASON: spring
LIGHT PREFERENCE: sun

Formerly *Iris tuberosa*, this fragrant plant is still sometimes sold under that name. A native of France, it has become naturalized in England and Ireland. It is closely related to the iris and grows from 10 to 18 inches tall. The unusual-looking flowers are similar to iris, with light green standards and purple falls that somewhat resemble the head of a snake. They make interesting cut flowers.

Plant the tubers 3 inches deep in early fall in rich, light soil, in a spot that gets full sun. Don't disturb the plants unless they become overcrowded. You can pot up the tubers in the fall, store them in a cool place, and force blooms in late winter (See chapter 7). Hardy to zone 5.

Ipheion (if-EE-on)

SPECIES AND COMMON NAME: *Ipheion uniflorum (Triteleia uniflora; Brodiaea uniflora)*, spring starflower
TYPE OF ROOT: bulb
DEPTH TO PLANT FROM BASE: 3 inches
PLANTING TIME: late summer and fall
BLOOMING SEASON: late spring
LIGHT PREFERENCE: sun or light shade

This little plant from South America is less than 8 inches tall with 1-inch, bluish white, star-shaped blooms in late spring. Its grasslike foliage smells like onions when crushed. It grows well only in zone 6 and warmer, where it flourishes almost neglected, needing no fertilizer or extra watering unless it is unusually dry. It naturalizes easily, sometimes spreading so rapidly it becomes invasive.

Plant the bulbs in late summer or fall, and the leaves will soon appear and last throughout the winter. After blooming the plants become dormant for the summer. A light mulch helps them survive the winter where they are borderline hardy.

Propagate by seed or by dividing the bulb clumps when they are dormant. Good cultivars include

'Album' — large white flowers

'Froyle Mill' — dark violet
'Rolf Fiedler' — clear blue

Iris (EYE-ris)

COMMON NAME: Dutch iris
TYPE OF ROOT: bulb
DEPTH TO PLANT FROM BASE: varies — see
    species.
PLANTING TIME: fall
BLOOMING SEASON: spring
LIGHT PREFERENCE: sun

There are several species of spring-blooming iris that grow from bulbs. (See chapter 10 for *I. xiphioides*, English iris, which blooms in midsummer.) The so-called Dutch hybrids were developed fairly recently by crossing Spanish iris, *I. xiphium*, with other species. They grow from 15 to 30 inches, in a wide range of colors, and make excellent cut flowers. They like a sunny location and soil that is warm and dry in summer so the bulbs in the ground can ripen before winter. Plant them 3 or 4 inches deep and 4 inches apart in the fall. Dutch iris are not as hardy as most other spring bulbs, but do well in zones 5 to 8. They bloom in midspring, and all are good for winter forcing. Good cultivars include

    'Apollo' — white with yellow falls
    'Ideal' — blue
    'Imperator' — dark lilac blue with a gold
      blotch
    'Lemon Queen' — yellow
    'White Superior' — white with a yellow
      stripe

Iris danfordiae, a dwarf iris, reaches a height of only 4 to 5 inches. It has a brown spotted stem, which shows up first in early spring, followed by 2- to 3-inch blooms that are yellow with brown spots. Finally the 2- to 3-inch leaves appear. Plant the bulbs in the fall, in a location with full sun or partial shade, 3 inches apart and a full 4 inches deep. At a more shallow depth they will propagate rapidly into numerous little bulblets that don't flower. The species is a native of Asia Minor. The bulbs are hardy to zone 4 but are short lived, so they need frequent replacement.

I. histrioides has a purple bloom with a white central blotch and a yellow ridge. 'Major' is a bright blue cultivar that blooms very early. It grows to 9 inches and is hardy to zone 4.

I. reticulata blooms very early and the charming flowers grow from 6 to 10 inches tall, although the leaves grow taller. Plant them 3 to 4 inches deep, 4 inches apart, in well-drained soil in a sunny spot or in partial shade. The species is violet-purple, bordered with white. The bulbs produce offsets rapidly, so are good for naturalizing. This native of the Caucasus is hardy to zone 3. Cultivars include

    'Cantab' — blue with a light yellow blotch
      on each petal
    'Clairette' — blue with white stripes and
      blotches
    'Harmony' — blue with gold markings
    'Pauline' — deep violet-purple with a white
      blotch on each fall.

Leucojum (lew-KO-jum)

COMMON NAME: snowflake
TYPE OF ROOT: bulb
DEPTH TO PLANT FROM BASE: 3 inches
PLANTING TIME: fall
BLOOMING SEASON: spring
LIGHT PREFERENCE: shade

These bulbs of the Amaryllis Family include the spring snowflake, *L. vernum*; summer snowflake, *L. aestivum (photo, page 53)*; and fall-blooming snowflake, *L. autumnale*. They are all natives of central Europe and hardy to zone 4. Since they are endangered in the wild, be certain to buy only those that are nursery grown.

L. aestivum blooms in late spring despite its common name, summer snowflake. Plants are taller than *L. vernum*, usually from 9 to 12 inches, and have bell-shaped white flowers. The variety 'Gravetye Giant' is a large, late-blooming, taller version, up to 20 inches.

L. vernum, spring snowflake, starts flowering about the time that snowdrops (*Galanthus*) finish. At 6 to 10 inches, they are taller than snowdrops and have bigger blossoms. The fragrant bell-like, white blooms are tipped with green. Plant them among shrubs, or in rock gardens or borders, about 3 inches deep and 4 inches apart. They like light sandy soil that is rich in humus. If they are growing happily, leave them undisturbed for years, and divide them only if you want more plants.

Muscari (mus-KAR-ee) (photo, page 107)

COMMON NAME: grape hyacinth, bluebell
TYPE OF ROOT: bulb
DEPTH TO PLANT FROM BASE: 3 inches
PLANTING TIME: fall
BLOOMING SEASON: spring
LIGHT PREFERENCE: sun or light shade

Widely used for naturalizing, these deep blue flowers that resemble little bunches of grapes are very effective in masses. Different species grow from 4 to 12 inches tall. Plant the bulbs about 3 inches deep, 3 inches apart, in deep, rich, well-drained soil in full sun or light shade. Choose a spot where they can multiply freely without spreading into perennial beds, because they can become a nuisance. They stay in bloom for three weeks or more, which is longer than most spring bulbs.

M. armeniacum grows to 12 inches. Different cultivars of this fragrant flower bloom in various shades of blue: 'Blue Spike', a double, deep cobalt-blue cultivar, has petals rimmed with white. Christopher Lloyd, the well-known English garden authority, prefers this beauty over other *Muscari* because of its compact foliage. 'Cantab' is light blue and blooms later; 'Early Giant', an especially vigorous cultivar, spreads rapidly. Hardy to zone 4. This species is good for forcing for winter blooms.

M. azureum blooms exceptionally early, with pale blue fragrant flowers. Grows to 8 inches and is hardy to zone 5.

M. botryoides is the common grape hyacinth, sometimes called bluebells. Grows to about 12 inches tall, with fragrant blue flowers. The cultivar 'Album' has white blooms. Hardy to zone 2.

M. comosum, tassel hyacinth, has unusual feathery light blue or violet blooms and wide leaves. Grows to 12 inches. Hardy to zone 4.

Ornithogalum (photo, page 53) (or-ni-THOG-a-lum)

COMMON NAME: star-of-Bethlehem
TYPE OF ROOT: bulb
DEPTH TO PLANT FROM BASE: 2 to 4 inches
PLANTING TIME: fall
BLOOMING SEASON: spring
LIGHT PREFERENCE: sun or light shade

Native American wildflowers, these members of the Lily Family are useful in the border or wildflower garden in zones 5 and warmer. Each star-shaped bloom has six separate parts and the fragrant flower clusters grow from 1 to 2 feet tall. The plants do well either in sun or partial shade. Plant them 2 to 4 inches deep, 6 inches apart, in well drained soil, in a spot where they can't do harm if they spread. *O. umbellatum*, especially, can become very invasive. The tender species are grown as houseplants or in a greenhouse.

O. arabicum, the fragrant Arabian star-of-Bethlehem, is hardy only to zone 7, but it is often used as a houseplant and for forcing.

O. nutans, nodding star-of-Bethlehem, has green and white flowers that are good for cutting.

O. umbellatum is the star-of-Bethlehem most of us know, with white flowers that are greenish outside. Although a native of Europe, Asia, and North Africa, it has become naturalized over much of northeastern United States and southern Canada. Hardy to zone 3.

Puschkinia (push-KIN-ee-a) (photo, page 54)

COMMON NAME: puschkinia
TYPE OF ROOT: bulb
DEPTH TO PLANT FROM BASE: 3 inches
PLANTING TIME: fall
BLOOMING SEASON: early spring
LIGHT PREFERENCE: sun or light shade

This genus is native to Asia Minor and the Caucasus. It is not widely planted, but is a good low-growing plant for naturalizing in large masses and for the rock garden. It spreads rapidly both by bulb offsets and by seeds, so plant it in a spot where it can be admired but not where it will be difficult to keep in its place.

Plant the bulbs in the fall, 3 inches deep and 3 inches apart in light, sandy soil, in full sun or light shade. Leave them undisturbed until they become overcrowded. Avoid using compost, manure, and fertilizer on them.

P. scilloides (also known as *P. libanotica*), striped squill, blooms in early spring and grows from 4 to 8 inches high. Clusters of bluish white flowers appear early and continue for three or four weeks. 'Alba' is a white-flowered cultivar. Hardy to zone 3.

Scilla (SIL-a) (photo, page 53)

COMMON NAME: squill
TYPE OF ROOT: bulb
DEPTH TO PLANT FROM BASE: 3 to 5 inches
PLANTING TIME: fall
BLOOMING SEASON: spring
LIGHT PREFERENCE: sun, light shade

We have always thought squill was not a very nice name for a plant, but through the many years it has been cultivated it hasn't collected any other widely used epithet. Scillas are members of the Lily Family and consist of over eighty species native to Eurasia. They spread readily both by seeds and offsets, and are especially popular in Europe. Most grow readily either in sun or partial shade, and the Siberian squill will thrive even in deep shade beneath evergreens. Plant the bulbs 3 inches deep, 3 inches apart in rich soil. A light mulch in the fall helps them grow better, and they benefit from an occasional dressing of fertilizer.

Scilla bifolia, twin-leaf squill, has gentian blue flowers; the cultivar 'Rosea' has pink flowers. About 6 inches high. Hardy to zone 3.

S. hispanica. See *Endymion hispanicus*.

S. litardierei (formerly *S. pratensis*) meadow squill, grows to 10 inches, with tiny, pale blue flowers in racemes of ten to thirty flowers. It is hardy to zone 5.

S. non-scripta. See *Endymion non-scriptus*.

S. siberica, siberian or blue squill, is the most planted squill in North America. The flowers are a deep blue on 6 inch stems; cultivars come in pale blue, pink, and white. It is excellent for naturalizing on a lawn and produces a blanket of bloom, spreading rapidly by both seeds and offsets in soil that is not too dry. 'Spring Beauty' quickly forms a blue carpet in midspring. 'Alba' has white flowers. The plants are very hardy and able to grow in zone 1.

Grape hyacinth (Muscari botryoides 'Album')

Bluebells, wood hyacinth (Endymion hispanicus)

S. mitschtschenkoana (S. tubergeniana) is similar to *S. siberica* but the effect is not as showy, since the blossoms are a paler blue. Also hardy to zone 1.

Trillium (TRIL-i-um) (photos, pages 56 and 57)

COMMON NAME: wake-robin
TYPE OF ROOT: bulbous
DEPTH TO PLANT FROM BASE: 2 to 4 inches
PLANTING TIME: fall
BLOOMING SEASON: spring
LIGHT PREFERENCE: spring sun, summer shade

Several native species of trillium are worth planting in a border or wildflower garden that gets spring sunshine and summer shade. The fleshy roots are not true bulbs, and the flowers consist of three petals and three sepals. The leaves are also in groups of three, and even the berry has three cells.

Trilliums are members of the Lily Family and natives of both North America and Asia. Plant

Trillium and wood anemone (Anemone nemorosa ovatum)

Jack-in-the-pulpit (Arisaema triphyllum)
(spathe)

Jack-in-the-pulpit (Arisaema triphyllum) *(fruit)*

them when they are dormant after they finish blooming, and set them in rich woodsy soil mixed with composted leaves. Buy only nursery-grown plants because some species have been classified as endangered.

T. cernuum, nodding wake-robin, grows from 6 to 18 inches tall and has fragrant white-to-pinkish flowers. It blooms in late spring or early summer.

T. erectum, purple trillium, has dark red flowers and is the one we always called "nosebleed" or "stinking Benjamin." Some varieties have white or yellow flowers without the foul scent. In early days, pioneers used the roots to treat a variety of illnesses, including tuberculosis.

T. undulatum, painted trillium. The white flowers with attractive red markings on each petal make this the most beautiful species. A native of the eastern United States and Canada, it is a cool-weather plant that grows well in acidic soil. It definitely deserves a place in the shady wildflower garden, but isn't an easy plant to cultivate. Hardy to zone 3.

Wood Hyacinth. See *Endymion*.

Erythronium (Erythronium tuolumnense)

Hardy Summer-Blooming Bulbs

ALTHOUGH THE TERM *bulb* always brings to mind the flowers of spring, gardeners know that summer has its share of beautiful blossoms grown from bulbs, corms, tubers, and rhizomes. Some, such as lilies, are hardy, but others, including dahlias and gladioli, are sensitive to frost and must be dug in late summer, stored for the winter, and planted out again in the spring in all but subtropical climates. Both the hardy and tender kinds furnish a wide range of colors, fragrances, sizes, and forms, and add much to summer's gardening pleasures. This chapter describes the hardy summer bloomers, and chapter 11 discusses the tender bulbs.

Allium (AL-lium) (photo, page 110)

TYPE OF ROOT: bulb
DEPTH TO PLANT: 2 to 3 times the diameter of the bulb
PLANTING TIME: early spring or fall
BLOOMING SEASON: late spring to fall
LIGHT PREFERENCE: sun

The Allium genus of over 400 species includes such tasty edibles as chives, garlic, leeks, shallots, and many kinds of garden onions, as well as attractive flowering perennials for the border in shades of lavender, purple, blue, pink, and even red and yellow. The globelike flowers come in

Allium *sp. and tulips*

umbels that may be either tight or loose and, when bruised or broken, have a distinctive onionlike scent, although some have blooms that are pleasantly fragrant. Most are hardy to zone 4 and often are able to live in zone 3 when they are set to their proper depth and are either mulched or insulated with a consistent snow cover during the coldest temperatures.

Wood sorrel
(Oxalis tetraphylla)

Some bloom in late spring and others in mid-summer.

Our maple woods are a carpet of wild leeks, also called ramps (*A. tricoccum*) in spring each year, and dairy farmers have to fence their cattle out of such areas until the plants die down. Otherwise, the milk tastes so much like garlic that the dairy processors won't buy it. When we were young it was fun to chew the tops whenever we wanted to be unpopular for a few hours, and we were surprised when we learned that our

Bearded iris (Iris × germanica)

RICHARD BROWN

Dwarf bearded iris (Iris pumila)

Bearded iris (Iris × germanica)

Montbretia (Crocosmia sp.)

French neighbors considered them a delicacy.

Many nurseries sell allium bulbs and seed companies such as The Onion Man (see Appendix) offer seed packets of the species that grow well from seed.

Plant the ornamental allium bulbs at a depth that is two to three times the diameter of the bulbs, and from 6 to 18 inches apart, depending upon the ultimate size of the plant. They need full sun and thrive in ordinary loamy garden soil. Snip off the flower heads after blooming if you don't want them to self-sow, and let the foliage die back naturally. Fertilize in early spring.

You can transplant the bulbs any time as long as you lift them with a clump of soil and keep them wet, so it is easy to move them around to change your garden decor. Or, if you prefer, leave them in a bed where they can grow undisturbed

Flame anemone (Anemone x fulgens)

Tender summer-blooming gladiolus combine with Asiatic lilies and anemones in this perennial bed.

Asiatic lilies bloom from mid-June to mid-July (in zone 5).

Oriental lilies bloom in August (in zone 5).

RICHARD BROWN

Container-grown Lilium sp.

Gardeners can choose from hundreds of beautiful, easy-to-raise Lilium cultivars.

Corn-lilies (Ixia *sp.*)

Allium senescens montanum

for years until they become overcrowded.

It is easy to start more plants: Either divide the bulb clumps, plant the seeds, plant the small bulblets that form around the parent bulb, or plant the bulbils that develop in the flower clusters at the top of some plants.

The alliums have no serious pests. Even those that bother vegetable onions are seldom problems for the ornamentals, and the rodents don't like them. Onion maggots, the small larvae of certain flies, sometimes attack young plants by burrowing into the bulbs. Control them by drenching the soil with an appropriate garden insecticide or by destroying the infected plants and starting a new planting a good distance away.

Downy mildew sometimes hits alliums in cool, damp weather, making the leaves turn yellow and die. Use a garden fungicide for control. See chapter 5 if other problems appear.

The following garden alliums are a selection of those readily available.

Allium aflatunense. Late spring. 2½ to 5 feet tall. A worthwhile garden plant with dense lilac purple flowers in clusters 4 inches across, and straplike foliage. 'Purple Sensation' is a tall-growing hybrid with darker-colored flowers. Hardy to zone 5.

A. atropurpureum. 20 inches. Midsummer.

DAVID CAVAGNARO

Dense umbels of wine red blooms over 2 inches in diameter. Attractive basal leaves. From Europe.

A. caeruleum (also *A. azureum*), blue globe onion. Midsummer. 20 to 30 inches tall. 1½-inch-deep blue flower heads. This native of Siberia clumps up rapidly and blooms in mid-to late summer. Hardy to zone 3.

A. cernuum, nodding onion, wild onion, lady's leek. 12 to 24 inches tall. Many different cultivars bloom from early June to fall. One of the most ornamental species for the garden, this North American native has dozens of pink, purple, rose, or white blooms. 'Early Dwarf', a lavender variety, grows to only 8 inches and blooms somewhat earlier than the other wild onions. It forms nice clumps and is a good rock garden plant. Hardy to zone 3.

A. christophii (formerly *A. albopilosum*), stars-of-Persia. Late spring to early summer. 1½ to 3 feet. This has the largest flowers of any allium; sometimes the umbels of showy lilac-colored blooms reach nearly a foot in diameter. The blooms become stiff and will eventually spread seeds, so cut them off if you don't want new plants coming up everywhere. The leaves are short-lived, so position among other plants to camouflage the dying foliage in summer. Excellent for drying. Plant the bulbs 6 inches deep for best results. Hardy to zone 4.

A. giganteum, giant allium. Midsummer. The tallest species, with stems up to 4½ feet. Flower heads are 5 inches in diameter, each consisting of hundreds of lilac-colored florets. Plant at least 6 inches deep to help support the tall

BLOOMING SEQUENCE OF HARDY SUMMER-BLOOMING BULBS

EARLY SUMMER

Allium aflatunense
  A. christophii
  A. karataviense
  A. moly
  A. oreophilum
  A. schoenoprasum
  A. senescens (various cultivars)
  A. tricoccum
Anemone x fulgens
Arum
Hypoxis
Iris cristata
  I. pseudacorus
  I. pumila
Ixia
Lapeirousia
Oxalis

EARLY SUMMER TO MIDSUMMER

Allium atropurpureum
  A. giganteum
  A. pulchellum
  A. roseum
  A. senescens (various cultivars)
Anemone coronaria
Iris sibirica
  I. germanica
  I. kaempferi
Lilium canadensis
  L. candidum
  L. martagon
  L. regale
Aurelian and Asiatic hybrid lilies

MIDSUMMER TO LATE SUMMER

Allium caeruleum
  A. rosenbachianum
  A. senescens (various cultivars)
Crocosmia x crocosmiiflora
Eucomis
Hymenocallis
Iris (reblooming)
  I. xiphioides
Lilium henryi
  L. lancifolium (tiger)
Oriental hybrid lilies

stalks. The foliage shrivels before the flowers appear. Good for cutting. Grows in partial shade. Protect with a mulch in cold climates, or dig and store for the winter. Hardy to zone 5.

A. karataviense, Turkestan onion. Late spring. 8 to 10 inches tall. 3-inch, pale grayish pink globular head and attractive wide blue-green leaves. A useful flower both for the border and for cutting. Can be easily grown indoors in pots. From Turkestan. Hardy to zone 5.

A. moly, lily leek, golden garlic. Late spring to early summer. 8 inches to 1 foot tall. Unusual because of its 2- to 3-inch clusters of bright yellow blooms and broad leaves. This native of Europe makes a nice small clump and will tolerate dry shade. Good for naturalizing. Hardy to zone 4.

A. neapolitanum, Naples onion, daffodil garlic. Early summer. 15 inches. Some people call this the finest white-flowered allium. It has rosy stamens in the midst of loose, white 3-inch umbels. Lightly fragrant, a good cut flower, and lovely in the border or rock garden. The cultivar 'Grandiflorum' has larger flowers. A native of southern Europe, it is hardy only to zone 7.

A. oreophilum. Late spring. 6 to 8 inches tall. The 2-inch rose-colored blooms have a pleasant fragrance. Good as an edging plant or in the rock garden. Native to Turkestan and Central Asia. Hardy to zone 3.

A. pulchellum. Summer. 1½ to 2 feet tall. Loose umbels in pink, yellow, or white. Native to southern Europe and western Asia. Hardy to zone 7.

A. rosenbachianum, Rosenbach onion. Mid- to late summer. Up to 3 feet tall. Ball-shaped, rose-colored, 4-inch blooms make this a good plant for the border and for cutting. A native of Turkestan. Hardy to zone 5.

A. roseum, rosy onion. Early summer. 20 inches. Showy 3- to 4-inch pink blooms. Good for cutting or the perennial border. A native of southern Europe and northern Africa. Hardy to zone 5.

A. schoenoprasum, chives. Early to midsummer. Up to 2 feet. This common garden herb has many superior cultivars that are good ornamentals and can be grown from seed. Hardy to zone 3.

A. schubertii. 2 feet. Its large flower head is made up of hundreds of light pink florets of different heights. A native of the Mediterranean region. Hardy to zone 6.

A. senescens (photo, page 114). 1 to 2 feet. Natives of Europe and good ornamentals, these grow from rhizomatous roots; the foliage clumps remain in good condition throughout the season. The different cultivars bloom at various times throughout the season in shades of pink, lilac, and rose. They attract bees and butterflies. The tall cultivars are good for the border; the dwarfs, for rock gardens.

A. sphaerocephalum. Drumsticks, ballhead onion, globe-headed garlic. Mid- to late summer. 2 to 3 feet. Although it is sometimes called a coarse ornamental, the ball-shaped clusters of densely packed bell-like, dark purple flowers make this a good flower for borders, natural plantings, and flower arrangements. Also good for dried bouquets. Hardy to zone 4.

Anemone (a-NEM-o-nee)

COMMON NAME: windflower
TYPE OF ROOT: tuber-like rhizomes
DEPTH TO PLANT: 2 to 3 inches
PLANTING TIME: fall, where hardy; spring, where tender.
BLOOMING SEASON: summer
LIGHT PREFERENCE: partial to full shade

There are many species in this genus, which is part of the Buttercup Family. You'll find *A. blanda*, the Greek anemone, under spring bulbs, in chapter 9. The summer bloomers described below are good for the summer border. They have fernlike foliage and the blooms close at night and on cloudy days.

Anemones do best in partial or full shade, and in soil that is rich and well-drained; they also grow well in pots or large containers. They grow easily from seed sown in early spring, or from divisions of the tubers.

Before planting the tubers, soak them overnight in slightly warm water, and plant them in soil that is rich in humus by laying them on their sides. They are not an easy plant to grow unless you have the right conditions for them, since they need a cool spring and hot summer, as well as some shade at midday and in the afternoon. If they are hardy in your climate, plant them in the fall and mulch them. If not hardy, plant them in the spring, dig the tubers in the fall, and store them over the winter in dry sand or peat moss.

Anemone coronaria, poppy anemone. 10 to 18 inches tall. Brilliant flowers in blues, reds, lavenders, and whites, both single and double, make this plant a favorite, and it is thought by many people to be the "lily of the field" in the Bible. Anemones were favorites of Rembrandt, who used the flowers in some of his paintings. The plants are grown in commercial greenhouses for the cut flower market, and a bouquet of these long-lasting beauties is a luxurious treat in the cold winter months. The species are natives of southern Europe, and hardy only to zone 8, although they can be wintered over in cooler zones with protection. There are many cultivars in a wide range of different colors.

A. × *fulgens*, flame anemone, scarlet windflower (photo, page 112). Late spring to early summer. 1 foot. Bright red flowers with black stamens. Widely grown in greenhouses for floral use, and good for rock gardens. Hardy to zone 5.

Arum (AY-rum or AR-um)

SPECIES AND COMMON NAME: *A. italicum*, Italian arum
TYPE OF ROOT: tuber
DEPTH TO PLANT: 2 to 3 inches
PLANTING TIME: spring or fall
BLOOMING SEASON: early summer; red berries in fall.
LIGHT PREFERENCE: light shade

The small whitish flowers in early summer resemble jack-in-the-pulpits. They grow from thick, fleshy tubers and, though the flowers are not impressive, their attractive arrow-shaped leaves with creamy white markings readily identify this plant. The 1-foot plants are dormant during the summer, and leaves appear in the fall and last through the winter. Bright orange-red berries appear in tight clusters before the new foliage grows and add color to the fall landscape. They like rich, moist soil, and do best in light shade. Good choices for wildflower plantings or rock gardens. Native to southern Europe. Hardy to zone 6.

Asarum (as-AR-um)

SPECIES AND COMMON NAME: *Asarum canadense*, wild ginger, snakeroot
TYPE OF ROOT: rhizome
DEPTH TO PLANT: 1 to 2 inches
PLANTING TIME: spring or fall
BLOOMING SEASON: early summer
LIGHT PREFERENCE: shade

When we were children, we liked to hunt for this native American wildflower plant in the woods, dig it, wash the roots, and chew them for their sweet ginger flavor. The brown, trumpet-shaped flowers that come in early summer are unusual because they consist of three sepals and no petals, and they lie horizontally on the ground. The large, 7-inch-wide heart-shaped leaves that rise above the flower make the plant a good ground cover in moist, shady spots where many other plants don't grow well. It grows 6 to 12 inches high. Hardy to zone 2.

Crocosmia (kro-KAWS-mee-a)

(photo, page 112)

COMMON NAME: montbretia
TYPE OF ROOT: corm
DEPTH TO PLANT: 3 inches
PLANTING TIME: spring
BLOOMING SEASON: late summer
LIGHT PREFERENCE: sun

These interesting natives of South Africa with brightly colored blooms belong to the Iris Family and are related to the gladiolus. There are several species but the hybrids of *Croscosmia × crocosmiiflora*, known as the common montbretia, are most useful in the garden. Popular for years in England, these graceful plants are finally getting a hearty welcome in American gardens.

Plant croscosmia in the spring, in a sunny spot in rich, well-drained soil, protected from the wind. Set the corms 3 inches deep, about 4 inches apart. They grow in various heights, up to 4 feet. Apply a mulch, because they like cool roots. Where the plants are not hardy, dig the corms in the fall, discard the old mother corms, then dry and store the new ones in dry sand, vermiculite or peat over the winter. Plant them in the spring.

The flowers, which bloom in late summer, come in shades of red, orange, or yellow. Good cultivars include the following:

'Aurora' — orange
'Emily MacKenzi' — yellow with red center
'Fiery Cross' — orange-red
'Kathleen' — orange-yellow
'Lucifer' — red

'Norwich' — light yellow
'Venus' — peach-yellow

Most garden books credit crocosmia with being hardy only to zone 7, but we have had no trouble growing them in zone 3 in the shelter of a tall hedge.

Eucomis (YOU-kow-mis)

COMMON NAME: pineapple lily
TYPE OF ROOT: bulb
DEPTH TO PLANT: 3 to 4 inches
PLANTING TIME: fall
BLOOMING SEASON: midsummer
LIGHT PREFERENCE: sun or light shade

Growing up to 2 feet tall and a native of South Africa, eucomis is in the Lily Family. The flowers are a spiky cluster of greenish white starlike flowers, and above them is a circle of ten to thirty bracts resembling leaves, which gives the plant a pineapple shape. The leaves at the base of the stem grow in a rosette form. In cool climates these plants do well in greenhouses and also in large pots or planters on terraces where they can be moved indoors for the winter.

Plant them outdoors in the fall in well-drained soil, in sun or light shade. Leave the bulbs undisturbed for years. Hardy to zone 7.

Hymenocallis (hy-men-o-KAHL-is)

COMMON NAME: Peruvian daffodil, spider-lily, basket flower
TYPE OF ROOT: bulb
DEPTH TO PLANT: 4 inches
PLANTING TIME: spring or fall
BLOOMING SEASON: mid- to late summer
LIGHT PREFERENCE: sun or light shade

Most species of these members of the Amaryllis Family are imports from warm regions of North and South America and some are not hardy outdoors year-round in regions colder than zone 8. (See *Hymenocallis*, chapter 11.) They are an elegant border plant with fragrant white or yellow flowers that grow high above the thick-leaved foliage. They get their name from their long spidery stamens. Some are deciduous and others are evergreen.

Outdoors, plant them 4 inches deep in sun or light shade, in well-drained soil that can be kept moist during their growing season, although deciduous species like dry soil during dormancy. They grow 2 to 3 feet tall. Where they are not hardy, you can dig the bulbs before frost and dry them; then pack them in peat moss for the winter and store at temperatures of 55 to 60°F. The plants also do well in large containers, but plant them only an inch deep.

H. caroliniana, the inland spider-lily, grows wild in wet places from the Midwest to the Gulf of Mexico. It has a large umbel of white flowers on a 2- to 3-foot leafless stalk, and is a good bog plant for wild gardens in zone 5 and warmer.

H. narcissiflora, Peruvian daffodil. 2 feet tall. A native of South America. In cooler zones, treat it as a tender bulb or grow it as a potted plant in the house or greenhouse. It has two to five flower clusters on each stem. Popular cultivars include 'Daphne', 'Festalis', 'Minor', and 'Sulphur Queen', with yellow flowers. Hardy to zone 8.

Hypoxis (hy-POK-sis)

COMMON NAME: star-grass
TYPE OF ROOT: rhizome
DEPTH TO PLANT: 1 to 2 inches
PLANTING TIME: spring or fall
BLOOMING SEASON: late spring, early summer
LIGHT PREFERENCE: sun and light shade

This native American wildflower of the Amaryllis Family grows from short rhizomes, with starlike, bright yellow flowers in June. It natu-ralizes well in both sun and light shade in dry locations. It grows to 1 foot or more. *H. hirsuta* is the common species. Hardy to zone 4.

Iris (EYE-ris)

COMMON NAME: iris
TYPE OF ROOT: rhizomes and bulbs
DEPTH TO PLANT: varies
PLANTING TIME: midsummer to fall
BLOOMING SEASON: late spring and summer
LIGHT PREFERENCE: varies (see individual species)

Among flower lovers there are a great many iris fanatics, and when you see a bed in full bloom in late spring or summer or a catalog filled with iris photos, it is easy to understand their passion. The shape, style, and limitless colors of these elegant flowers makes them the *haute couture* of horticulture. It was probably their colors that gave them the name *Iris*, from the ancient goddess of the rainbow, and breeders have developed many more shades since the 1840s when they first began seriously to hybridize them in France.

Classification of Iris

There are more than 200 iris species, some of which grow from rhizomes and others from bulbs. The spring-flowering iris mentioned previously (chapter 9) grow from bulbs, but most of the popular summer-blooming plants come from rhizomes, including the bearded iris, Siberian iris, Japanese iris, and their numerous cultivars.

There are three horticultural groupings of rhizomatous iris, divided according to the appearance of their falls: bearded, beardless, and crested.

Bearded Iris

These have a "beard," hairs on the base of the falls, seen on such old-time favorites as

IRIS TERMS

BEARD. The fine filaments or hairs that cover the basal half portions of the falls on some iris.

BICOLOR. Top and bottom petals are different colors.

CREST. A central serrated ridge along the basal half of the falls.

FALLS. Petals that hang downward.

PLICATA. Petals of one color with borders of different colors.

STANDARDS. Upright petals of the flower.

"flags" and numerous cultivars once known as "German iris." The true bearded iris are further classified into the following:

> Miniature dwarf
> Standard dwarf
> Intermediate
> Miniature tall (table iris)
> Border
> Standard tall

Beardless Iris

These have smooth falls, including the Siberian and Japanese iris.

Crested Iris

These have a central serrated ridge on the base of the falls, instead of a beard. This small group includes *I. cristata* and *I. japonica*.

Iris Culture

A gardening customer told us once that it was completely unnecessary to have planting directions for irises. "All you need to do is to grab a bunch of roots, stand with your back to the garden, and fling them over your shoulder. Every one will grow," he guaranteed.

We never tried it, being much too fond of our iris to take a chance, but his directions no doubt came from the fact that rhizomatous iris need shallow planting. Most species do best in a spot with plenty of sunlight and soil that is deeply cultivated, fertile, and well-drained. For this reason they thrive in slightly raised beds and light soil. None of them like competition from weeds or other plants, with the exception of Siberian iris, which can easily hold their own. When they have finished blooming, clip off the faded flowers, both so they'll look better and so that they won't form seed pods that weaken the plant.

Fertilize at the beginning of the growing season, either with compost, dried manure, or a sprinkling of a complete organic or chemical fertilizer. Don't be too generous with the nutrients unless you want to increase your supply of iris. Overfeeding will produce lots of plants that will need frequent dividing. We like to spread a mulch consisting of several inches of leaves over the iris in the fall, and rake it between the plants in the spring as they begin to grow. If you don't have leaves, any organic mulch will do. See chapter 4.

Pests and Disease

Some gardeners maintain that dogs, cats, and children are the worst pests in an iris garden, since the stems are brittle and are easily broken over when they get taller than 2 feet. Iris have their share of other pests, but, like many plants, they are less likely to be bothered by insects and diseases when they are interspersed with other plants in the border. Another reason for mixing them is because a bed of all iris can look rather dull after the blooms have faded.

If you buy plants from a reliable firm, they are very likely "clean," but if you move them from another planting to your own, before you replant them, as a precautionary measure dose them with a garden dust containing both a fungicide to control disease and an insecticide to control borers and other root-eating creatures.

The iris borer is one of the most troublesome insect pests and weakens the plant by attacking the rhizomes. If your plants appear sickly, dig one up and inspect the roots. If they are infected, drench the plants, including the roots, with a water-soluble insecticide, and repeat the treatment once a week for two or three weeks.

In warm climates, especially, nematodes may feed on the roots; in the West, bulb whiteflies are often present. In the Northeast, thrips and the iris weevil may appear on the leaves, but usually not in serious numbers. A garden insecticide should control them all if you follow the directions carefully.

Heterosporium leaf spot bothers bearded iris. It is a fungus that discolors the foliage and weakens the plant, preventing good growth and flowering. This disease is often serious enough to cause undedicated gardeners to destroy their iris and give up growing them. To help prevent it, avoid overhead watering, since the fungi develop fastest on wet foliage. Also, cut the leaves to within ½ inch above the ground before winter and destroy them to prevent disease from overwintering there. (Never compost iris plants.) If it becomes an annual problem, treat the plants with a fungicide at two-week intervals early in the season to control it.

Fungus rots — botrytis rot and mustard seed rot — can both damage iris. The first shows as a gray blanket of mold, and the other resembles mustard seeds covering the leaves. Fungicides control both quite effectively.

Bacterial soft rot can be another serious disease for iris. The bacterium lives in soils and enters roots that have been damaged or otherwise weakened. Plants that have been injured by cultivation, by the burrowing of the larvae of the iris borer moth, or by stress from winter temperature extremes are prime candidates. Dig up any infected plants, destroy them, and start over with clean roots in a new spot.

Scorch is another condition that is difficult to control. It destroys all the small roots, and the foliage turns brown. If you suspect that it has infected your plants, destroy them immediately. It apparently is caused by drought conditions, excess fertilizers, or pesticides; it can be of either viral or bacterial origin.

Popular Iris Species

I. cristata, dwarf crested iris. This miniature crested iris, only 1 to 3 inches tall, is native from Maryland to Georgia and west to Missouri. It has a white and yellow crest and dotted lilac purple standards, as well as white, blue, and pink cultivars. It likes woodsy, well-drained soil and light shade and the long thin rhizomes creep rapidly along the surface of the soil. Don't cover the rhizomes with soil, or they will rot.

I. ensata (also listed as *I. kaempferi*), Japanese iris. For many years we didn't raise these aristocratic beauties because we had always heard they were difficult to grow, until one year a friend brought us a a small rhizome of a white-flowering cultivar of unknown name. We planted in our perennial border, and forgot about it. Two years later it burst forth with gorgeous large orchidlike blooms that were worthy of a *House Beautiful* centerpiece. It always attracts attention, and everyone who sees it in bloom covets it. Although we have divided the clump several times, it is still thriving.

The tall (2½ to 4 feet) stalks flower after the Siberians and bearded irises have faded. Their flat blooms may be either single, double, triple or multipetaled. The colors range from white to various shades of lavender, deep violet, and rose, and they are often mottled, veined, or dotted with yellow.

The plants originated in Japan, and Asian gardeners use them freely. They do best in acidic soil with a pH between 5.5 and 6.5, so don't spread lime or wood ashes near them unless the soil is already extremely acidic. They thrive in full sun, but can stand some afternoon shade. Plant each rhizome with its base about 2 inches deep, in either spring or fall. Give the plants extra water during the blooming season but don't grow them in wet soil.

We have learned not to divide them as often as we do the bearded and Siberian irises, although it is usually necessary every three or four years, because they won't bloom well if the clumps become crowded. They grow well in zones 4 and warmer, and we have had no problem raising them in zone 3 under the protection of a winter mulch of leaves. Popular Japanese iris cultivars are

'Apple Blossom Cascade' — pink
'Cobra Dancer' — purple
'Gold Bound' — double blooms are white
    with gold band
'Ise' — pale blue with deep purple veining
    and a heavy bloomer
'Nikko' — purple and blue
'Pink Frost' — double light pink
'Red Titan' — red-purple
'Tinted Cloud' — blue-lavender and violet
'Wine Ruffles' — wine purple

Iris x *germanica,* bearded iris (photos, page 111). Breeders have created many lovely hybrids by crossing *I. germanica,* the German iris, with others, and the resulting list of tall bearded cultivars is enormous. Many are pleasantly fragrant, and one variety, *florentina,* provides orris root, the powdered dry rhizome, used to make perfume. Their colors cover the spectrum, from light pastels to deep velvety shades, as well as blends — those with many colors blended in the falls. All are distinguished by a "beard," an upright moustachelike growth where the upright flower meets the falls.

Most tall bearded iris live up to their name by growing 3 or 4 feet tall, but there are those that are only 2 feet high and, rarely, a cultivar reaches 5 feet. Because the flowers are fragile and some are so tall, they are vulnerable to damage by wind and heavy rainstorms, which we always dread when the iris clumps are in full bloom. If your region is prone to inclement weather you may want to plant, instead, dwarf irises (up to 15 inches) or intermediate irises (15 to 27 inches tall).

Each blossom is relatively short-lived and stays at its prime for only two or three days in warm weather, though somewhat longer when it is cool. Fortunately, the buds open at different times throughout the blooming season, so a clump can last for weeks and a garden filled with bearded iris can be beautiful for well over a month in early summer.

The best time to plant the rhizomes is mid- to late summer when they are dormant. Plant them horizontally 1 to 2 feet apart in a sunny bed. Don't quite bury them, but press the soil firmly around them. A strong clump will have six to ten flowering stalks, but they spread rapidly and become overcrowded. When this happens, they do not flower properly, so you may find it necessary to dig up and divide the clumps, removing the old rhizomes and replanting the healthy ones. Sometimes it is necessary to do it annually after they've finished blooming. Bearded irises are hardy to zone 3, except for the rebloomers, which are hardy only to zone 5 (see page 124).

The following are a few of the many popular cultivars of tall bearded iris available:

'After All' — creamy ivory
'Art Shades' — yellow with lavender pink
'Black Bart' — glossy black
'Blue Luster' — bright blue
'Camelot Rose' — silvery orchid and red-
    orange
'Carnaby' — pink and rose
'Christmas Time' — white with a red beard

'Close Up' — creamy pink and brownish rose
'Desert Song' — cream colored
'Dutch Chocolate' — chocolate and red-brown
'Elysian Fields' — buff and pink
'Gingerbread Castle' — brown
'Glacier Sunset' — white with orchid shades
'Gold Burst' — white with yellow
'Holiday House' — pink and buff blends
'Laced Cotton' — white
'Lemon Mist' — yellow
'Monaco' — lavender with pink and white
'Prosperity' — yellow
'Sable Night' — deep purple

I. pseudacorus, yellow flag. This old species from Europe and Africa has gone wild in North America where it blooms in early summer. It thrives in wet spots, and like the blue flag, *I. versicolor*, can grow even in shallow standing water. The two make good companions for planting around garden pools or farm ponds. 'Alba' is a white cultivar, and 'Gigantea' has larger yellow blooms.

I. pumila, dwarf bearded iris (photo, page 111). One of many dwarf species of iris, these grow only about 5 inches tall and are especially effective in mass plantings, rock gardens, and as a ground cover. They grow well either in sun or light shade and need very little care, but we have found ours bloom better if we divide the rhizomes every few years. In addition to the common dark-blue-flowering species, cultivars with red, white, lilac, and various shades of blue and yellow blooms are available. They bloom in early summer. The species is a native of Asia Minor and Europe, and they are hardy to zone 3 with light winter protection.

I. sibirica (photo, page 57). Most of the garden species that we call Siberian iris are derived from this species (from central Europe and Russia) and from *I. sanguinea* (from Manchuria and Japan). These stately plants are easy to grow and bloom in late spring and early summer, just before most of the bearded iris. Their blooms have narrow, erect standards and hanging falls and come in shades of purple, blue, pink, and white, as well as red tones. They grow from 2 to 3½ feet tall in a tight clump that becomes very large and tenacious because their thick roots go deep into the soil.

Their only fault, we find, is that their blooming time is short; and there are lots of faded blooms that need to be removed, although some gardeners prefer to leave the blooms and later use the attractive seed pods in fall arrangements. Their exceptionally beautiful flowers compensate for their brief life, and they make wonderful arrangements. They are not as formal in appearance as either the bearded or Japanese species and are especially attractive in a natural or wild garden. They don't need division as often as bearded iris, but if you notice that the clump is becoming crowded, it's a good idea to split it up so that it will bloom better.

The Siberians are heavy feeders, so mix compost or dried manure with the soil at planting time. Mulch them and give them extra water during any dry periods, especially when they are blooming. They are reliably hardy to zone 3 without protection. Here are some worthwhile cultivars:

'Amelia Earhart' — blue
'Anniversary' — white
'Blue Moon' — violet-blue
'Dark Circle' — purple
'Harpswell Haze' — light blue
'Mountain Lake' — blue
'Orville Fay' — dark blue, large flowered
'White Swirl' — white
'Wing on Wing' — white

I. xiphioides, English iris. These bulb iris originated in Portugal or Spain, but came to England at an early date and were widely planted. They grow to 20 inches, and do best in moist soil in either sunshine or a semi-shaded location. Plant them 8 inches deep. The flowers bloom in midsummer, and numerous cultivars are available, including 'Isabella', lilac rose; 'Mont Blanc', white with a touch of blue; 'Queen of the Blues', blue with purple falls. The plants are slightly hardier than the Dutch hybrids, and grow well in zones 5-8.

Reblooming Iris

All of us wish our iris bloomed longer, and breeders have developed cultivars to fulfill our wishes. They blossom in spring or early summer and again in late summer or fall. This characteristic means that you can often enjoy the blooms well into the fall, although the second bloom is more sparse than the earlier one.

In their attempt to create rebloomers, hybridizers are working with many different species of iris including the Siberian and Japanese, but they have had the most success with bearded species. The rebloomers are now available at specialty nurseries in many heights and colors.

Since most of this type of hybridizing has taken place in warm zones, the rebloomers are considered hardy only in zones 5 and warmer, although some growers report good results with them in zone 4 as long as they give them winter protection. The plants have not been successful in the regions near the Gulf of Mexico, however, and appear to prefer dry, warm areas; so if your summers are rainy, warm, and humid, these are not the best plants for your border.

Gardeners who are interested in more information are invited to join the Reblooming Iris Society (see Appendix).

Ixia (IK-see-a) (photo, page 114)

COMMON NAME: corn-lily
TYPE OF ROOT: corm
DEPTH TO PLANT FROM BASE: 2 to 3 inches
PLANTING TIME: fall
BLOOMING SEASON: early summer
LIGHT PREFERENCE: sun

From South Africa, this plant is a member of the Iris Family, with cup-shaped flowers that grow on spikes above grasslike leaves. It is hardy enough to grow without protection in zones 7 and warmer, but will grow in cooler zones with protection and adequate snow cover.

Where they are hardy, plant the corms in the fall, 2 to 3 inches deep and at least 1 foot apart in well-drained, rich soil, and in full sun. Fertilize them each fall. In cool climates, plant them in the spring; lift the bulbs after the foliage has died and store them in a dry spot. They are also a good plant to force in a greenhouse for winter blooms.

I. maculata. 1½ to 2 feet tall. Many yellow or white flowers with a dark blotch in the throat. The cultivar 'Rose Emperor' has pink blooms.

I. viridiflora. 1½ feet tall. Greenish flowers with a black spot. Hybrid cultivars include orange 'Afterglow', blue 'Azure', white 'Bridesmaid', copper-red 'Huber', red 'Vulcan', and double pink 'Wonder'.

Lapeirousia (la-pay-ROO-see-a)

COMMON NAME: lapeirousia
TYPE OF ROOT: corm
DEPTH TO PLANT: 3 to 4 inches
PLANTING TIME: fall
BLOOMING SEASON: late spring, early summer
LIGHT PREFERENCE: full sun

A member of the Iris Family, lapeirousia has small, star-shaped pink flowers; it grows to 1 foot. This South African native is reliably hardy in areas cooler than zone 7 only if it has winter protection. Where it grows well, it is a good plant for the border. The plants are often forced in a cool greenhouse.

In the fall, plant the corms 3 to 4 inches deep in rich, light soil and full sun. Give them a complete fertilizer each year in late fall, and divide the corms every few years.

L. laxa, one of the hardiest species, has a red bloom with dark red blotches at the base of the three lower petals. 'Alba' is a pure white cultivar.

Lilium (LIL-ee-um)

COMMON NAME: lily
TYPE OF ROOT: bulb
DEPTH TO PLANT: 5 to 8 inches with exceptions (see individual species)
PLANTING TIME: spring or fall
BLOOMING SEASON: different types bloom throughout the summer
LIGHT PREFERENCE: sun

Without question, lilies, particularly the new strains, are among the most beautiful of flowers. No one is likely to argue with the famous biblical passage from the Sermon on the Mount, referring to the lilies of the field: "Even Solomon in all his glory was not arrayed like one of these." (Most experts believe that the reference was not to *Lilium,* though it could have been to the martagon lily, which grows abundantly near the Sea of Galilee.)

The term "lily" is confusing because so many flowers with lilylike blooms are commonly called lilies even though they do not belong to the genus *Lilium.* Daylilies (*Hemerocallis*), lily-of-the-valley (*Convallaria majalis*), foxtail lily (*Eremurus*), and lily-of-the-Nile (*Agapanthus africanus*) are only a few that are not true lilies.

Lilium species and hybrids are most people's favorites of all the summer flowering bulbs, but this was not always true. Only a half century

ago, the most common lilies in North American gardens were likely to be wild species such as the tiger, the regal, and the Madonna lilies. Some gardeners also grew the coral lily, the Henry, and Turk's-cap, and they transplanted native ones such as the Canada lily into their borders. Garden books barely mentioned lilies as summer-blossoming flowers.

Growing fine lilies wasn't easy in North America before the 1940s. Few horticulturists propagated them, and because lilies, unlike most other bulbs, never settle into a completely dormant period, they were difficult to ship in good condition over the long distance from Europe by the slow ships available. Also, they were often infected with viruses.

Then came Jan de Graaff, who turned the lily world upside down in a few short years. He was born in Holland in 1903 into a flower-raising family. At a young age he became fascinated with lilies and determined to solve the virus problem and breed better kinds. His family didn't share that interest, but he was hired as a consultant to the newly formed Oregon Bulb Farms in 1928 and recognized a chance to work seriously with his favorite plant. In 1934 he bought the company and gradually replaced the hundreds of acres of tulips and daffodils there with lilies.

Working with a collection of species brought from Holland, as well as native lilies, he made thousands of crosses. In the early 1940s he recognized an outstanding flower in his acres of seedlings and named it 'Enchantment'. It was the first of many stunning cultivars and became an instant success. Unlike most plant breeders, de Graaff decided to market his introductions as groups of hybrids rather than to register each one as a separate cultivar. Among the more well-known groups were the Mid-century, Aurelian, Candidum, Hollywood, Imperial, and Oriental hybrids.

In spite of his many later achievements, Jan

de Graaff considered 'Enchantment' his best introduction, and many of us today agree with him. The clump in our garden has survived for over forty years, and it increases so rapidly we have started dozens of new plants from it.

Thanks to de Graaff and other talented hybridizers, gardeners now can choose from hundreds of beautiful, easy-to-raise cultivars in a wide range of colors, forms, sizes, and fragrances. Whatever your taste, there are lilies to supply it, and backyard gardeners can grow the elegant flowers one would expect to find only in expensive urban floral shops. There are dwarfs that are suitable for rock gardens, as well as border types that reach 8 feet tall. It is possible to have one lily or another in bloom in your garden from early summer until mid-fall (see sequence of bloom chart on page 127). Most are hardy to zone 4 and many will survive well in zone 3 if they have a winter mulch or consistent snow cover. The *Lilium* genus consists of over eighty species, and when you add the thousands of hybrids that have appeared in the past half century, the selection available for planting is overwhelming.

The Lifespan of Lilies

In general, the longest-lived lilies tend to be the rugged, old-time native species, and these types are still the best ones to use when landscaping a wildflower bed or cottage garden. Bulbs such as the regal, Henry, and tiger lilies have proven themselves as long-lived garden plants.

One of the discouraging things about modern lilies is their reputation for a short life. This is not planned obsolescence, but many new lily cultivars were developed for size and beauty, and the genes controlling durability were neglected. Their reputed short lifespan can also sometimes be attributed to a gardener's neglect, since some of the new cultivars are demanding. The stunning Oriental lilies, especially, are fussy about soils and drainage, as we will discuss later. Not surprisingly, growers have accepted this shortcoming of their favorite types of lilies, and cheerfully replace them every three or four years, feeling it is a small price for their exceptional beauty. Hopefully, since breeders have, we suspect, reached the peak of perfection on beauty, they will now concentrate on endurance.

Not all modern lilies are short-lived, however. In addition to 'Enchantment,' we have had several other Asiatics bloom in our gardens for many years, including 'Sutter's Gold' and several whose names have been lost.

Lilium: The Basics

Lilies grow from bulbs with fleshy, overlapping scales, and they have two different rooting habits. Some develop roots on the stem between the bulb and the soil surface as well as from the base, and others produce them only from the base of the bulb. Those with stem roots must be planted deeply, but some of the base-rooting types need shallow planting. A few lilies also have stoloniferous bulbs, which means that they have long underground stems that reach out and grow new plants a few inches from the parent.

True lilies grow with an erect stem and spear-shaped leaves, and their flowers always have six tepals (three petals and three sepals) and six stamens. The blooms have been classified in six groupings, according to their form.

Trumpet lilies. Outward-facing, trumpet-shaped blooms. 'Pink Perfection', Madonna, and the regals are good examples.

Chalice lilies. Outward-facing, flaring types. Many Mid-century hybrids are of this type.

Pendant lilies. Bell-shaped blossoms hang down from the stems, as on the Nepal lily.

Reflexed lilies. Petals curve backward so far that they touch the stem. Tigers and Turk's-caps are examples.

Bowl lilies. Blossoms face outward with wide-open blooms.

Sunburst lilies. Blossoms face outward with wide-open blooms that are looser than the bowl types, with a starlike form. Some of the Aurelians such as 'Moonlight' are of the sunburst type.

Getting Started

Buying potted lily plants from a nursery or garden center has some advantages. You can set them out anytime during the spring, summer, or fall, and if you buy them in bloom you can be sure of their color and height. Potted plants are more expensive than bulbs, however, and unless you are dealing with a nursery that specializes in lilies, the choice is likely to be limited.

You can plant dormant bulbs in either spring or fall. Buy them from a reliable grower or catalog outlet because otherwise you can't tell for sure how they've been handled or how long ago they were dug. A bulb that has some of its roots intact when you receive it will grow best the first year. Domestic growers usually ship them with roots, but bulbs from Europe are likely to arrive without them.

Lily bulbs do not reach their near-dormant state until late in the season, so they cannot be dug and shipped as early in the fall as narcissus, tulips, and other spring-flowering bulbs. Sometimes they are not ready for shipping until too late for planting in cold climates, so suppliers store them in ideal conditions and ship them in the spring. Spring-planted bulbs do not always bloom as well the first year as fall-planted bulbs, but should thrive by the second year.

If lilies could have perfect conditions they would be in a bed of very well drained, slightly acid soil enriched with enough humus to hold the moisture they need. The bulbs would get full sun until about noon, then shade such as that from a tight fence or hedge for the hot part of the afternoon. Ideally, a heavy layer of snow

SEQUENCE OF BLOOM FOR VARIOUS HYBRID LILIES

(This sequence is true for zone 5, and may vary slightly in other zones.)

Asiatic	mid-June to mid-July
Martagon	mid-June
Madonna	late June
American	end of June and early July
Canadian	July
Regal	July
Trumpet and Aurelian	July-August (long season)
Henry	early August
Oriental	August
Tiger*	August

*L. Lancifolium

would cover the bulbs from the time the ground froze in early winter until weather warmed in spring. Needless to say, most of us can't provide these perfect conditions, but knowing what they are gives us a head start.

The easiest of the modern lilies to grow are the Asiatic hybrids. Most bloom in early summer, are vigorous, and less fussy than the others about growing in a perfectly drained bed. They clump up fast, live for years, and are very colorful. Since most don't grow too tall, they are ideal plants for the front of the border.

Although lilies need plenty of sunlight, if they get light shade during the hottest part of the day the colors are less likely to fade, and the blooms last longer. A spot with good air circulation helps to keep the plants free of disease. Good soil drainage is necessary for all lily bulbs but especially for the Orientals. When a gardener has trouble growing lilies the first time around, the reason is often lack of drainage.

Lilies do not compete well with other plant

life, so unlike narcissus and crocuses, they are not good choices for naturalizing. But in a cultivated bed they make a spectacular show. They are also nice accent plants in a shrub border, especially when planted along with broad-leaved evergreens, since they enjoy the same acidic, cool living conditions. Or you can also plant them, as we do, in individual clumps in a border among herbaceous perennials. The foliage of other plants helps shade the lily stalks, keeps them cool during the growing season, and hides their unattractive stalks after they've finished blooming.

Preparing the Soil

If you have light fertile soil, the lilies will love it. (See chapter 4.) Till it deeply, to at least 2 feet (although that may not be possible if you garden in rocky earth like ours). The large bulbs of many lilies need plenty of loose earth beneath them for their roots to grow.

We have heard it said many times that it is unwise to add manure to soil where you intend to plant lily bulbs. This statement may be true if the manure is fresh from the farm, but our experience has been that if it is well-aged or composted there is no problem. Our lily bulbs have always thrived in it. If we must use fresh manure we spread it over the surface of the soil in the fall, so it can wash in over the winter.

Most lilies do best in soil that is slightly acidic with a pH of 5.5 to 6.5, so use lime only if your soil tests lower than 5.0. The Madonna lily (*L. candidum*) is an exception and prefers an alkaline soil. If the soil where you intend to plant lilies (particularly the Oriental ones) is heavy, mix in sand, and plant them in raised beds. Since the bulbs must be set deep, raising the bed 8 inches above the surrounding terrain isn't likely to be too much. If the soil is unusually heavy, remove it all and spread a 2-inch layer of sand or gravel in the bottom of the trench. Replace the soil and then plant.

As alternatives to raised beds, a slight slope can also provide good drainage, or you can build individual "hills" for each plant, similar to those that vegetable gardeners make for their melons and pumpkins.

Planting

Lily bulbs deteriorate rapidly when out of the ground, so prepare the bed in advance and plant them as soon as they arrive. If you can't plant immediately, store them in a refrigerator or other cool spot (35° to 40°F), but only for a few days.

If directions come with the bulbs, follow them when planting. If you have no directions, plant them with the base of the bulb from 5 to 8 inches below the soil surface. Deep planting helps them better withstand winter's cold and summer's heat, and they'll require less staking. This variance in depth sounds rather vague, but the smaller bulbs should go to more shallow depths, and the larger ones to the deepest. Exceptions to the rule are the Madonna lily (*L. candidum*) and Chalcedonian or scarlet Turk's-cap (*L. chalcedonicum*), both of which should be set with their tops only about 1 inch deep. Space the small bulbs 8 inches apart and large ones from 12 to 18 inches apart. Lilies look especially nice in a border if planted in groupings of three or five of the same color, but the size and type of planting you have in mind will influence how you set them.

When you plant certain perennials, such as peonies or gas plant (*Dictamnus*), you should choose a spot where you want the plant to remain for many years since they resent being moved. We've found no such problem with lilies, however. It's easy to move them around the garden if you want to try out new color combinations, or if you've planted a tall cultivar too near the front. Even though fall or spring is the best time to move them, you can safely transplant lilies just about any time during the growing season, even when they are in full bloom. Just be careful not to cut into the deeply planted bulb, take a large ball of soil with it to protect the fragile roots, and keep it watered afterwards.

We have found that stalks from the deep-planted bulbs do not always come up perfectly straight, and some kinds may wander around underground a bit before poking through. Don't be surprised if the bulbs you set out in perfectly straight rows the previous fall have different ideas when they emerge in the spring.

If you mixed fertilizer with the soil when you tilled it, there is no need to use more at planting time, but if you added no plant food earlier, mix 2 tablespoons of a complete fertilizer into the soil around the base of each bulb when planting, being careful not to let any fertilizer touch the bulb. Always water the bulbs thoroughly after planting so that no air pockets will remain in the soil around them, and set in a small marker to identify the plant. This can also indicate where to insert a plant stake later, if necessary. Finally, add a mulch of organic matter to help preserve moisture and help prevent heaving from frosts and thaws during the winter. Lilies do not compete well with other plants so a mulch helps to keep them weed-free and lessens the need for cultivation, which could disturb the roots. A mulch also helps delay early growth in the spring, which is often injured by frost. Lilies also do well in large deep pots or planters that provide the drainage that makes them happy (see chapter 2).

Care after Planting

Lilies need a steady supply of moisture during the growing season, so give them extra water during that period if the weather is even slightly dry. The best watering method is with a soaker hose or trickle irrigation so no water will stay on the foliage for long periods to encourage disease.

Lilies need extra nourishment as they grow. After shoots poke through soil in springtime,

give plants some liquid organic fertilizer such as fish emulsion or seaweed, or a chemical fertilizer such as Peter's or Miracle-Gro. After blooms have faded, give them one more feeding to help the bulb replace the energy it has spent blooming. Some lily growers use only chemical fertilizers because they believe that organic ones encourage fungus diseases, but organic gardeners dispute that argument vigorously.

Once planted, our lilies don't receive much additional care, but we grow mostly the tougher kinds. The tall Imperials sometimes need to be tied to a stake to help hold up their many heavy blooms. We have heard that if there is enough potash in the soil, lily stems will be stronger and seldom need staking. If you want to try it, you can use wood ashes to supply the potash, but don't apply more than a sprinkling once a year, because too much will make the soil alkaline, which lilies don't like.

Unless you want to grow some lilies from seed, to save the plant's energy cut off all the blooms as soon as they fade. Always leave the rest of the stalk standing until the foliage has turned brown, then cut it to the ground and apply additional mulch.

Companion Plantings

An underplanting can add interest to a bed of lilies when they are not blooming. It can also help keep their roots cool and camouflage their dying foliage. Whatever plant you use should not be deep-rooted or vigorous enough to deprive them of water and nutrients, however. The well-known gardener Barbara Damrosch uses ferns in her lily bed because lilies and many ferns like the same humus-filled, cool, acidic soils and partial shade. She chooses ferns that are somewhat shorter than the lilies so the flowers stand well above them, and their attractive, textured foliage is an excellent complement. Low-growing annuals also make good underplantings (see chapter 2).

Lily Pests

If you start with healthy bulbs, disease should not seriously affect your lilies as long as there are no diseased plants growing nearby. Inspect all new bulbs for rot before you plant them, and be on the lookout for botrytris. See chapter 5 for how to cope with bulb disease and insect problems.

Viruses are the most serious bulb diseases because there is no cure. Virus may show up as stunted growth and a mottled color on the leaves, and the infection spreads easily to other plants. Tiger lilies (*L. lancifolium* or *L. tigrinum)* are notorious carriers of the disease, even though it doesn't noticeably affect them. Always plant the tigers some distance from other lilies, and carefully control the aphids that spread the disease.

Mice and voles can devastate lily plantings, so take steps to eliminate them and the moles that make the burrows they use (see chapter 5). Other lily-loving pests we have encountered are woodchucks, rabbits, and deer. The family dogs and cats can break over the stems.

Propagation

Propagating your own lilies is fun and an inexpensive way to extend your plantings. You can start new bulbs by seeds, division, scales, bulbils, offsets, and layering. When you plant seeds (sexual propagation), the resulting plant is not likely to be exactly like its parent, but if you produce a new plant by using a portion of the parent (asexual propagation), the new plant will be a duplicate. For details see chapter 14.

Seeds

Some companies sell lily seeds, but if you already have nice cultivars you may want to save and plant their seeds. The resulting plants won't be exactly like the cultivars, but they should be worthwhile. Let the pods ripen on the plant and when they are dry and brown, cut them off and dry them a bit more. Then shell them, dust the seeds with a fungicide to prevent botrytis, and plant them immediately.

You can plant seeds outdoors in a protected cold frame, mulch them, and leave them there to sprout in the spring. Alternatively, you can plant them in flats of a starting media such as Pro-Mix and let them grow indoors during the winter.

Transplant the seedlings to a bed outdoors as soon as freezing weather is over, and let them grow there. When the bulbs are the size of large marbles, move them to wherever you want them to grow. Some should bloom in two years.

Division

There are several ways to divide a lily to start new plants. A mature bulb divides naturally each growing season into two bulbs or more, and they may be of equal size. In either fall or spring, dig, separate, and replant them at a depth of from 4 to 8 inches deep, depending on their size. The largest ones should bloom the first year after planting, but it's likely you will have to wait an extra year for the smaller ones. To get a larger supply of bulbs you can use the bulblets or scales.

Bulblets

Little bulbs grow between the bulb and the surface of the soil on some types of lilies. Dig into the soil around the plant with a spading fork to loosen it, and then carefully break off or cut off the bulblets around the stem with their roots intact. Plant them 1 to 2 inches deep and 3 inches apart in a cultivated bed. Leave them there for a year or so before replanting at the proper depth after they reach a good size. They should bloom that summer.

Scales

Immediately after the flowers have faded, carefully dig the bulb and pull off a few firm, healthy scales. Take those close to the base of the bulb since the new bulblets will form best when you take a bit of the basal plate with the scale. Removal of four to six scales won't damage the bulb and it should continue to bloom well the following year. Some people remove up to half of the scales and find that the plant still blooms, but we haven't tried it. You can also increase your supply of lilies by pulling a few scales from a large bulb you have just purchased. As long as you take only a few and plant the bulb immediately, it will bloom well.

Place the scales in a bag and dust them with a fungicide powder. Then fill a flat that is at least 2 inches deep with a moist starting mix such as Pro-Mix. Plant the scales by sticking them into the mix, pointed side up, leaving part of the pointed end sticking out of the mix. Place the flat in a plastic bag and seal it with a bag tie after punching two or three holes for ventilation. Set it in a warm place where it will get bright light, but no direct sun, and keep it moist.

About six weeks after potting, the scales will turn brown and start to shrivel. Take off the bag and check one or two scales to see if they have rooted. Although there will be no top growth, one or more tiny bulbs should have formed at the base of each scale, along with a cluster of roots. If the bulbs are at least ¼ inch in diameter, pull them carefully from the scales and plant them as you would bulblets or bulbils.

Bulbils

Small bulbils grow on the stems of certain lilies in midsummer, including the tiger (*L. lancifolium*), Sargent (*L. sargentiae*), sulfur (*L. sulphureum*), and bulbil lilies (*L. bulbiferum*). As soon as these separate from the plant easily, pick them off and plant them ½ inch deep in light soil or in flats filled with a growing mix. After they have grown a few inches tall, transplant them and treat them like the bulblets that grew from the scales (above). The lilies that produce bulbils will develop many more of them if you pick off the flower buds before they open. The plants will then concentrate on producing bulbils.

Stem Layers

Although it seems drastic, it is possible to separate the stem of the Madonna and regal lilies from the bulb and grow new bulbils from it. After the blooms fade and the leaves begin to brown, remove the stem with a twisting motion, bury it lengthwise in a sand-soil mixture, and within a few months up to a dozen or more bulbils will have formed along it. Plant these (as under bulbils), and many will bloom the second year.

Modern Hybrid Lilies

There are several classes of modern lily hybrids, and a large number of cultivars in each one. The following are among the best known.

American Hybrids. These are derived from species that are native to North America and consist mostly of crosses between *L. parryi* and *L. pardalinum*. Among them are the Bellingham Hybrids, which are tall-growing — up to 7 feet — with leaves that whorl around the stem. The flowers are spotted and have recurved petals in orange, pink, red, and yellow.

Asiatic Hybrids (photos, pages 112 and 113). These crosses, from Asian species, flower from early to midsummer, and some were formerly sold as Mid-century hybrids. They come in white and a wide range of colors — pinks, reds, golds, oranges, yellows, and various combinations. Most grow from 2 to 5 feet tall and seldom need staking. The blooms may be upward- or outward-facing, and some are pendant. They are not fragrant.

'Apollo' — orange-red with dark spots
'Antarctica' — white
'Chinook' — peach with spots

'Corina' — red
'Connecticut King' — yellow
'Crete' — rose
'Enchantment' — nasturium red
'Geneve' — white overlaid with light pink
'Grand Cru' — yellow with brown center
'Jolanda' — orange-red
'Maria Callas' — white with pink tips
'Orchid Beauty' — yellow with bronze
'Pirate' — deep red
'Roma' — creamy white
'Tiffany' — pink with gold centers

Aurelian Hybrids. These crosses, developed from Asian species, were formerly known as olympic or trumpet hybrids, and they are also called Chinese trumpet lilies. They grow up to 8 feet tall and almost always need staking. They come in white and many colors including gold, orange, pink, and yellow. Some have reddish stripes and purple, brown, or green backs. The blooms are usually fragrant, and come in trumpet, cup, bell, or pendant shapes. They bloom in July and are hardy to zone 4, and to zone 3 with protection.

'African Queen' — yellow with brown outside
'Black Dragon' — white with reddish outside
'Golden Splendor' — golden yellow
'Green Magic' — white with greenish overcast
'Moonlight' — gold
'Pink Perfection' — pink
'Regale Album' — white

Candidum Hybrids. Hybrids of the Madonna lily, these grow 3 to 4 feet tall with lance-shaped leaves and pure white flowers. They bloom in early summer. Plant them so the tops of the bulbs are only an inch below the surface of the soil, and mulch them in cold zones. The Nanking Lily (× *Testaceum*), is a popular yellow cultivar.

Oriental hybrids (photo, page 113). These consist of a collection of crosses originally made between *L. auratum* and *L. speciosum* and others. They range from 30 inches to over 6 feet in height. Most are fragrant, and the large blooms are flat-faced, bowl-shaped, or with backswept petals. They include the beautiful Imperials and others with large showy flowers. The wiry stems sometimes need staking to hold the flowers in an upright position. They are more demanding in their soil drainage requirements than most others but are well worth any effort to please them.

'Casa Blanca' — large, white, flat blooms
'Imperial Crimson' — flat crimson blooms with white edging and darker spots
'Imperial Gold' — white with gold markings
'Imperial Pink' — bright pink with red dots and markings
'Imperial Silver' — silvery white with red dots
'Jamboree' — bright red with darker spots and white edging
'Little Love' — white with gold band
'Mona Lisa' — light pink and white
'Star Gazer' — upward-facing, crimson red, edged white

Lily Species

Of the many wild species, some are useful in the landscape. You will find them listed in specialty lily catalogs.

Native North American Species

It is a thrilling experience to come upon one of the native lily species unexpectedly. Most are hardy enough to grow even in zone 3, but they require conditions that mimic those of their native wild habitats. Those listed below, unless noted otherwise, do best in moist, somewhat acidic soil.

L. canadense, the Canada lily, grows on the East Coast of North America from Quebec and Nova Scotia to Georgia. Flowers are usually yellow or red, in midsummer. It grows to 5 feet tall, with about six flowers on a stem. Hardy to zone 3.

L. columbianum, the Columbian lily, is native to the Pacific Northwest, and has as many as forty small reddish yellow blooms on 4- to 8-foot stalks in late summer. Hardy to zone 6.

L. grayi, Gray's lily, has several red-orange, bell-shaped flowers on 3-foot stalks. A native of Virginia, south to North Carolina and Tennessee. Best for wildflower plantings. Hardy to zone 4.

L. humboldtii, the Humboldt lily, grows in the Sierra Nevada on the Pacific coast. Up to fifteen orange, reflexed lilies grow on 4- to 5-foot stalks in midsummer. Hardy to zone 5.

L. pardalinum, the leopard lily, grows up to 7 feet tall and is a West Coast native. It spreads rapidly and has red flowers with brown spots in midsummer. Cultivars include the sunset lily ('Giganteum'), yellow with red tips, and 'Johnsonii', bright red. Hardy to zone 3.

L. parvum, the Sierra or alpine lily, is a native of the high Sierras. Flowers are bell-shaped, red or yellow, on 3- to 5-foot stems. The plants do best in the shade with plenty of moisture. Hardy to zone 4.

L. philadelphicum, the familar wood lily, grows over a large part of eastern North America. It grows 2 to 3 feet tall, with orange to red flaring, upturned flowers that are often spotted with maroon. Sometimes grows well in wooded, damp areas as its name implies, but mostly it is found in dry, prairielike conditions; it is one of the most drought-tolerant species. Hardy to zone 4.

L. superbum, the true Turk's-cap lily, is a tall grower, up to 10 feet, with large yellow, reddish, or orange flowers that are spotted maroon. Blooms in midsummer. It does best in moist, acidic soils, from southern New England to Florida and into the Midwest. Hardy to zone 5.

L. washingtonianum, the Washington lily, is a native of mountains along the Pacific coast and grows to 4 feet. The numerous white flowers fade to lilac purple. They grow well in the wild, but have proven difficult to cultivate. Unlike most native lilies, it prefers dry soil but needs plenty of moisture before it flowers. Hardy to zone 6.

Lily Species from Other Lands

Foreign species and their cultivars that are beautiful additions to a flower border include the following:

L. auratum, gold-banded lily. The flowers are white, often with spots and stripes of crimson and gold. Blooms in late summer. 'Praecox', the alpine form, is a short cultivar, but the variety *platyphyllum* may grow to 10 feet, with up to forty flowers on a stalk. Natives of Japan, these popular garden flowers are hardy to zone 5 and much of zone 4.

L. brownii, Brown's lily, blooms in late summer with flowers that are white inside and purplish outside. Different varieties grow from 2 to 4 feet tall. Probably a native of China. Hardy to zone 6.

L. bulbiferum, bulbil lily or orange lily, is unusual because of the large number of bulbils that grow along the stem if the flower buds are picked off early. Grows to 4 feet, with orange blooms, and since it is very hardy it is a favorite with hybridizers. Tolerant of lime, this is a native of western and southern Europe. Hardy to zone 3.

L. candidum, Madonna lily, has pure white blooms that have made it a garden favorite for at least a thousand years.

Madonna grows to about 3 feet and sometimes more. It blooms in early summer and is a good plant to grow with delphiniums. Probably a native of the Near East and the Balkans. Plant the bulbs with their tops only an inch deep, unlike those of most other lilies, and mulch it for winter protection in zones 3 and 4.

L. chalcedonicum, scarlet Turk's-cap. This vermillion-scarlet lily with reflexed blooms that grows to 4½ feet is native to Greece. The cultivar 'Maculatum' is spotted with purple. Hardy to zone 6.

L. concolor, star lily. This native of the Orient is a popular garden flower, with 18- to 36-inch stalks, each of which holds ten or more star-shaped scarlet flowers. Some varieties have yellow or multicolored blooms. Hardy to zone 4.

L. davidii, the David lily, has small red, reflexed blooms with black spots that resemble those of the tiger lily. Grows 4 to 5 feet tall; varieties are also available that are taller and have blossoms of other shades of red with purple spots. Hardy to zone 4.

L. formosanum, Formosa lily, is a fine species that was once used far more as a garden flower, but has gone out of favor because it is so susceptible to mosaic. It grows to 5 feet or more with fragrant white flowers that are funnel shaped and wine purple on the outside. It blooms from late summer into the fall. Lily catalogs often list varieties of this species. A native of Formosa, it is hardy to zone 5.

L. hansonii, Japanese Turk's-cap lily, has small, fragrant, orange-yellow, recurved flowers that are spotted brown on 30-inch stems in early summer. An excellent garden plant, this native of Korea and Japan is very hardy — to zone 3.

L. henryi, a long-time garden favorite from China, can grow up to 8 feet tall with numerous, brown-spotted, orange blooms. The *henryi* species and the regals were the first lilies we grew when we began to grow perennials decades ago. We found that their weak stalks often need staking to prevent them from twisting, and it is best to grow them in partial shade, since the blooms fade quickly in sunlight. The cultivar 'Erectum' grows more erect than the others, and 'Citrinum' has pale yellow flowers with brown spots.

L. lancifolium (L. tigrinum), tiger lily, is one of the easiest lilies to grow, and you often see it flowering around abandoned country homes. Brought from China at an early date, the or-

ange-red blooms with dark purple or black spots in midsummer made the plant an instant favorite. The black bulbils that form abundantly along the 3- to 4-foot stalks during the summer fall off and often grow, or you can pick and plant them. In addition to the species, there are cultivars in orange, pink, white, red, and yellow, and some with double blooms. All look best when growing in a clump of a dozen or more of the same color. Tiger lily bulbs are often infected with a virus, which, while it doesn't usually affect them, can spread to other bulbs. Plant them at least a hundred feet from other lilies. Hardy to zone 3.

L. longiflorum var. *eximium,* Easter lily, from the Orient, is well known to everyone as a pot plant, and many cultivars are available. Pure white, fragrant, and trumpet shaped, it would be an exceptional garden flower if only it were more hardy (only to zone 8) and not as susceptible to mosaic. If you want a real gardening challenge, buy a few bulbs in the fall, pot them up, and get them to hit peak bloom a few days before Easter (see chapter 13). Colored hybrids of the familiar white lily have been developed, including the dusty pink 'Casa Rosa', the deep red 'Coral Ace', and the lemon-yellow 'Yellow Ace'.

L. martagon, martagon lily or Turk's-cap, is a hardy species from Europe that has been widely used in breeding many new cultivars. The flowers range from white to purplish pink and black-red and bloom in early summer. The plants are 30 inches tall and hardy to zone 4.

L. medeoloides, wheel lily, a species from the Orient, gets its name from the whorl of leaves on its stems. The flowers come in various shades of red and have no fragrance. Heights vary from 1 to 4 feet, and the shorter ones make good rock garden plants. They bloom in midsummer. Hardy to zone 3.

L. monadelphum, Caucasian lily, is a good garden plant with fragrant, yellow flowers that have a few black spots. This native of the north

Caucasus blooms early, and grows to 5 feet. Hardy to zone 3.

L. pumilum, coral lily, was very popular with gardeners before the modern hybrids became available. It grows to 18 inches with grasslike leaves and many bright red flowers that are pendulous and fragrant. From China and Siberia. 'Golden Gleam' is a yellow cultivar. Hardy to zone 3.

L. regale, regal lily, is often the flower that comes to mind when people think "lily." This very fragrant, trumpet-shaped beauty has blooms that are white inside, lilac or purple outside, and its 6-foot stems produce so many heavy flowers that staking is often necessary. A native of China, it was brought to this country in 1903. Regals do best in full sun and bloom in midsummer. Although it is hardy to zone 3, it sometimes starts to grow too early and is killed by a late frost.

L. rubellum, rubellum lily, grows up to 30 inches tall. It is a Japanese species with dainty pink, fragrant, bell-shaped flowers. Blooms early and is hardy to zone 5.

L. speciosum, the showy or Japanese lily, from Japan, blooms late in the summer with very large flowers in various shades of red, pink, and white. Its 3-foot stalks may support as many as forty blooms. When you cut off the stem and bury it lengthwise, bulblets will form along it. Numerous cultivars are available; the red cultivar 'Rubrum' is one of the most popular of all bulbs. Hardy to zone 4.

Oxalis (ox-AL-is) (photos, pages 110 and 148)

COMMON NAME: wood sorrel, lady's sorrel
TYPE OF ROOT: rhizome, tuber, or bulb
DEPTH TO PLANT: 2 inches
PLANTING TIME: fall
BLOOMING SEASON: summer
LIGHT PREFERENCE: varies (see species)

There are about 850 species of these low-growing bulbous plants, including both annual and perennial kinds with small flowers that are pink, red, yellow, or white. Some are grown as ornamentals and others are vigorous weeds. Their cloverlike leaves usually have three segments and they tend to close up at night and on cloudy days. Florists often sell pots of oxalis around St. Patrick's Day because their foliage resembles that of shamrocks. When they are cultivated outdoors it is chiefly for their foliage, as a ground cover. They are propagated by both seeds or division.

O. adenophylla. Small pink flowers with maroon centers and silver-green foliage make this 6-inch plant good for rock gardens. Hardy to zone 5.

O. braziliensis, Brazil oxalis. Bears deep red flowers, but is too tender for outdoor growing in areas cooler than zone 8. It is a popular pot plant elsewhere and is the species most often sold during March as a shamrock.

O. corniculata, creeping oxalis. Hardy to zone 4 and most of zone 3. This European native has escaped and become weedy in some areas. It has bright yellow flowers all summer, and is a good ground cover or rock garden plant.

O. montana, American wood-sorrel. This North American native has white flowers, veined pink, and blooms from late spring throughout the summer.

O. rubra, window-box oxalis. A tender plant from Brazil, this is used mostly as a pot plant or in window boxes. It has lilac, pink, or white blooms. Hardy to zone 8.

The Tender Summer-Blooming Bulbous Plants

A PROFUSION OF EXOTIC, colorful, fragrant flowers and lush foliage abounds in many areas of the tropics. We would envy it, except that we can grow many of those tropical plants in our very own garden in zone 3. They are not hardy, of course, and can't tolerate frosts or live through our winters outdoors, but that doesn't stop us from growing them. We either plant them as annuals and buy new roots each spring, or dig them in the fall, store them for the winter, and replant them the following spring.

The most popular tender summer bulbs are dahlias, gladioli, and tuberous begonias. They have so many devotees that each has a society for gardeners who love them (see Appendix). There are many other lesser-known bulbs, too, for every kind of personal taste and landscape. A friend of ours who visits Florida each winter always brings back lots of caladium tubers to plant in her shady garden in Massachusetts.

Others enjoy spectacular tropical plants like the elephant's ears, cannas, the elegant calla lilies, or dainty pink fairy lilies for the rock garden.

Most of us feel that it's worth the trouble to plant these bulbs after the danger of spring frost is over and, in the fall, lift their bulbs, corms, rhizomes, or tubers, store them for the winter, and replant them the following spring. We have reserved a corner of a cool upstairs room to keep them, and as we check them occasionally during the winter months, it's fun to know that those odd-shaped, dead-looking roots are dormant living things. They, and we, are awaiting the spring sunshine, showers, and warm temperatures to break dormancy.

Many tender plants are not as readily available in northern nurseries as the hardy specimens. The Appendix will help you locate mail-order sources. For hard-to-find plants we recommend *Gardening by Mail: A Source Book* by Barbara Barton and *Source List of Plants and Seeds*. (See Appendix.)

Achimenes (ak-i-MEE-neez) (photo, page 148)

COMMON NAME: monkey-faced pansy, orchid pansy
TYPE OF ROOT: rhizomes with fibrous roots
DEPTH TO PLANT FROM BASE: 1 inch
PLANTING TIME: spring (fall in frost-free areas)
BLOOMING SEASON: varies throughout summer
LIGHT PREFERENCE: bright light out of direct sun

These natives of tropical America, relatives of African violets, are raised mostly as pot plants or in hanging baskets, but are attractive in a shady summer garden as well. They grow 1 to 2 feet tall, and the blooms resemble pansies.

Plant the rhizomes horizontally in soil that is rich in organic matter and well drained. For container growing, set three or four in a 6-inch pot. Temperatures that do not drop below 60°F at night suit them best. Treat them as annuals in the garden in temperate zones, or, at the end of the summer, dry and save the roots over the winter as you would gladiolus corms. Hardy to zone 10.

A. *grandiflora* has large, reddish purple blooms, sometimes two in an axil. 'Atropurpurea' is lower growing and blooms earlier.

A. *longiflora* has red-purple blooms with a white throat that are about 1½ inches wide. The cultivar 'Blauer Planet' is more compact with large flowers. 'Major', violet and purple, has even larger blooms.

A. *patens*, 12 to 18 inches tall, has many cultivars including violet blue 'Gloria', red 'Million', orchid 'Orchidee', white 'Purity', and lavender 'Lavender Beauty'.

Acidanthera (as-id-AN-the-ra)

(photo, page 152)

SPECIES AND COMMON NAME: A. *bicolor*, Abyssinian gladiolus, peacock orchid
TYPE OF ROOT: corm
DEPTH TO PLANT FROM BASE: 4 inches
PLANTING TIME: spring
BLOOMING SEASON: summer
LIGHT PREFERENCE: full sun

These unusual plants from Africa, in the Iris Family, should be more widely planted. The fragrant, 2-inch-wide, star-shaped creamy white flowers have a dark purple center and grow on 15- to 24-inch stalks. Their sword-shaped leaves and flowers resemble gladioli. They make good cut flowers.

Since they need a long growing season, start the corms indoors in peat pots, and move them outdoors after frosts are over. Set the corms about 5 inches apart. In temperate climates, dig them after the first frost, dry them for two or three weeks, discard the old corms, and store the fresh ones. They need exposure to the air, so store them in a paper bag or an open, uncovered box in a dark cool room at 55° to 60°F. They are hardy to zone 7.

Agapanthus (ag-a-PAN-thus)

(photo, page 148)

SPECIES AND COMMON NAME: A. *africanus*, blue lily-of-the-Nile
TYPE OF ROOT: rhizome
DEPTH TO PLANT FROM BASE: 2 inches
PLANTING TIME: spring
BLOOMING SEASON: midsummer
LIGHT PREFERENCE: full sun or light shade

These members of the Amaryllis Family are natives of Africa. Various cultivars have clusters of florets of blue, violet, or white blooms atop a

20-inch, leafless stalk. Some have variegated foliage. They are usually grown in tubs or large containers in the North, and flower best when pot-bound. The plants are heavy feeders, so replenish the fertilizer frequently. In the fall, move the pots indoors to a cool, frost-free spot. Water them sparingly during their dormant period. Every three years, divide the rhizomes and repot them. Most are hardy to zone 9, but the deciduous Headbourne hybrids can be grown in zone 6 with winter protection.

Alstroemeria (al-stree-MEER-ia)

COMMON NAME: Peruvian lily, lily-of-the-Incas

This tender plant from South America is sometimes listed incorrectly as bulbous, though it actually has thick fibrous roots.

Begonia (tuberous) (photos, page 152) (be-GOH-nee-ah)

SPECIES AND COMMON NAME: *Begonia* x
    tuberhybrida, tuberous begonia
TYPE OF ROOT: tuber-corm
DEPTH TO PLANT: cover with 3 inches of soil
PLANTING TIME: spring
BLOOMING SEASON: throughout summer
LIGHT PREFERENCE: light shade

This group of hybrids is a wonderful example of the extraordinary creations modern horticulturists can develop when they seriously set out to improve a plant. The small-flowered native begonia of the tropics has been transformed, by crossing several species, into an easy-to-grow garden beauty that produces sensational blooms from early summer until freezing weather.

The flowers are both single (female) and double (male). Both sexes are arranged on one plant in pairs or in groups of three, with one male between two females. The blooms have a velvety, rich texture, and come in brilliant shades of red, pink, rose, yellow, and orange, as well as white. Some are fragrant.

The plants have a front and a back since the flowers and leaves grow outward from only one side of the plant. Some types are low-growing and ideal for a border in groups of three to five. Others are pendulous, perfect for hanging baskets or window boxes. They are divided into groupings according to their habit of growth and flower forms, and the following are among the popular types available.

Camellia-Flowered Begonias. Large-flowering doubles in bright colors, these are favorites for partially shady borders, pots, window boxes, or other planters.

Carnation (Fimbriata) Begonias. Double flowers that resemble carnations.

Cascade Begonias. Hanging begonias with large flowers that are ideal for window boxes and hanging pots. They come in a variety of sizes and colors in both single and double forms.

Miniature Begonias. Small-flowering, heavy-blooming types that are becoming increasingly popular.

Non-Stop Begonias. Small double flowers throughout the summer. The plants are more resistant to heat than other begonias. The **Pastel Begonias** are part of this group.

Novelty Begonias. White or yellow flowers with red edges.

Patio Begonias. Heavy blooming, 2 to 3 feet tall, these are excellent for container culture.

Picotee Begonias. Large, usually double blooms in a variety of colors with contrasting edges.

When choosing a plant, keep in mind that the size and quality of the flower is determined genetically and does not depend on the size of the tuber, although a larger tuber is likely to produce a larger plant and more blooms.

Since their native habitat is at high altitudes in the Andes, tuberous begonias do best when they have temperatures that are moderate in the day and cool at night. They thrive in light or medium shade and in spots that get sunlight only in the morning or late afternoon, which makes them good choices for containers or window boxes on the northeast side of a building, or on terraces with little sunlight. None are suitable, however, for growing under trees with heavy leaf growth, since there is not enough light or moisture in such a spot.

Culture

It takes about five months from planting to full bloom to get the longest season of summer color from tuberous begonias. Start them during January and February in pots or flats filled with either a starting mix or potting soil with a mixture of ⅓ vermiculite, ⅓ peat, and ⅓ sand. Add a slow-acting fertilizer such as dried manure. A bulb pan works well since their root systems are shallow.

Set each tuber-corm on the soil mix with its concave side upward and the rounded side downward. Once it has sprouted, cover the tuber-corm with about ½ inch of soil and place the flat in a warm, bright, east-facing window. Keep it watered, but not soggy wet. Roots will form all over the tuber. If you start them in flats, after they have grown 2 inches, move them into pots. Plant one tuber in a 6-inch pot if it is to remain there, or one in a 3- or 4-inch pot if you intend to set it in the ground after frosts are over. Give them a watering of liquid fertilizer every two weeks throughout the growing season. Keep them in strong light, but out of afternoon sun.

Pruning and Disbudding

If you don't prune at all, a large begonia tuber-corm will produce ten to twelve stems plus several branches, and the flowers are likely to be small, tangled, and look messy. To get the strongest plant, remove all but the most vigorous stem. As side branches develop, prune off all but one or two so the plant will have a strong shape. Then, to get the largest blooms, pick off the small single female flowers as soon as they form, so they won't crowd the large double male flowers. Each bloom lasts about two weeks. Pick them as soon as they fade, and stake the plants to keep them upright.

Possible Problems

When people have trouble growing tuberous begonias, usually the cause is either overwatering or underwatering. Bud dropping can result from either extreme. When the plants are too wet, or the air is too humid, stem rot or powdery mildew may attack them. Mealybugs, aphids, whiteflies, slugs, and snails are attracted to this plant. To prevent damage from diseases and insects, water them carefully and, if insects or diseases appear, ask at your garden store for an appropriate control (see chapter 5).

Storage

Except in the frost-free areas of zone 7 and warmer, dig the tubers in the late fall, or remove them from the containers, shake off the soil,

Start tuberous begonias in midwinter by planting tuber-corms in potting soil with concave sides up. When sprouts show, cover the tuber-corms with about ½ inch of soil and keep watered.

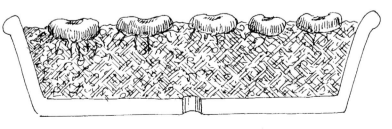

and dry them further for a few days with their tops still on. Then cut off all but 1 inch of the top and dry them further. Finally, remove the remaining stems, spread them out in shallow trays, and cover with dry peat moss, dry sand, or vermiculite. Store at a cool temperature of 40° to 50°F.

If you prefer, it is possible to leave the tubers in their pots and let them dry there. Then turn the pots on their sides in a closet, shed, or basement that stays at 40° to 50°F. We had many more losses with this method, however, than when we dried them without soil.

Before frost, the plants can be potted and brought inside for a winter houseplant, or dried, stored, and replanted in the spring. The corms keep growing larger each year and can be replanted ten times or more. When they become very large you can double your supply of begonias by cutting them in two pieces, leaving a bud on each half when you plant it. You can also start tuberous begonias from seed, but since the seed is so tiny, the process takes a lot of patience.

Caladium (ka-LAY-dee-um)

COMMON NAME: elephant's-ear, angel-wings
TYPE OF ROOT: tuber
DEPTH TO PLANT: near soil level
PLANTING TIME: spring
BLOOMING SEASON: colored foliage throughout summer
LIGHT PREFERENCE: light to dense shade

No one grows caladiums for their tiny flowers. It is their bright-colored foliage that makes them special, and the fact that they grow well in shady spots. They can tolerate early morning and late afternoon sunlight, and need a sheltered spot with moist, acidic soil. Their large, heart-shaped green leaves are variegated with red, white, or pink markings, and the different cultivars range from a dwarf 6 inches to 2 feet tall.

C. bicolor are tropical plants from South America, and the species from which the modern hybrids, *C.* x *hortulanum*, fancy-leaved caladiums, were developed. They are hardy year-round only in the frost-free regions of the Deep South and Southwest (zones 10 and 11),

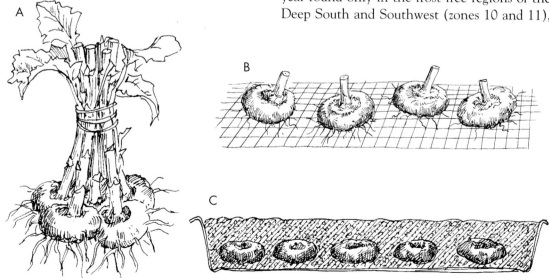

(A) Dry begonia tubers with the tops still on, then (B) cut off all but 1 inch of top and dry further. Finally, (C) remove remaining stems, spread in a shallow tray and cover with dry peat moss.

where you can plant them outdoors in the shade and they will survive throughout the year. In cooler climates caladiums make nice container plants either outdoors or indoors, as long as they get the shade and humidity they need. They are also good landscape plants, either used as annuals or by storing the tubers indoors for the winter. Northern gardeners must give the plants a head start by planting the tubers in flats in January or February. Bury them 2 to 3 inches deep in peat moss and place them in a warm spot out of direct sunlight until they start to grow. After freezing weather ends, plant them outdoors in a shady spot from 12 to 18 inches apart, depending on the size of the cultivar, and give them plenty of moisture throughout the growing season. They combine well with hostas, since they like the same conditions.

To overwinter the tubers, do not water the plants after the leaves begin to die at the end of the season. Before the first frost, dig them and dry them, and remove the tops after they are dry. Dust with a fungicide and insecticide and store them in vermiculite in a cool, dry spot (40 to 50°F). In late winter or spring, divide the tuber clumps to start more plants.

'Blaze' — red-splashed foliage
'Pink Beauty' — pink tones
'White Christmas' — white and green leaves

Canna (KANN-a)

COMMON NAME: canna
TYPE OF ROOT: rhizome
DEPTH TO PLANT FROM BASE: 2 inches
PLANTING TIME: spring
BLOOMING SEASON: mid- to late summer
LIGHT PREFERENCE: sun

These spectacular tropical plants with colorful flowers and giant green or bronze leaves were once a staple in public parks and large estates, where their overwhelming size (up to 8 feet) made a huge splash of color. They are not as common today but are effective in certain landscapes, and the dwarf varieties are fine border plants. The massive size of cannas is too coarse for small beds, so choose only the smaller cultivars for most gardens. Plant them in fertile, moist, well-drained soil. Treat them as tender perennials in areas cooler than zone 8. In regions where frosts come early, start them indoors since they are very sensitive to frost and difficult to cover.

To save the rhizomes over the winter, cut off their tops about 6 inches above the ground just after they have been killed by a frost. Dig them, dry them for a few days, and store them in a cool, dry spot for the winter.

You can also grow canna from seeds if you are patient. The seeds are so hard it is said that natives of the West Indies used them for shot, hence the common name of an indigenous species C. indica — Indian shot (photo, page 149). Soak these seeds in warm water for two days previous to planting to get them to germinate well.

Canna x generalis, common garden canna includes many large-flowered hybrids in many colors and sizes from 2 to 8 feet. Canna x 'Omega' grows to a giant 14 feet tall.

Tall-Growing Cultivars
'Ambassador' — red with bronze leaves
'America' — dark red with bronze leaves
'Apricot' — apricot with bronze leaves
'City of Portland' — pink with green leaves
'Eureka' — white with bronze leaves
'Gaiety' — orange with yellow margins and green leaves
'King Humbert' — scarlet with bronze leaves
'La Boheme' — rose-red
'The President' — red with green leaves
'Pretoria' — orange with green and gold variegated leaves

'Tyrol' — pink with bronze leaves
'Wyoming' — orange with bronze leaves

Dwarf Cannas (2'–3')
'Chinese Coral' — brilliant red
'Cleopatra' — red with yellow
'Firebird' — red
'Picasso' — golden yellow with red spots

Colocasia (ko-lo-KAY-see-a)

COMMON NAME: elephant's-ear
TYPE OF ROOT: tuber
DEPTH TO PLANT FROM BASE: 6 inches
PLANTING TIME: spring
BLOOMING SEASON: grown for summer
   foliage
LIGHT PREFERENCE: light shade

These Asian foliage plants are similar to the *Caladiums*, which are also sometimes called elephant's-ears. Colocasias grow from 4 to 7 feet tall, with leaves 2 feet long. If you want a plant in your garden that has a tropical ambience, this is the plant for you. They also grow well in a shady spot outdoors in a large container and can be taken indoors for the winter months.

C. esculenta, known as the taro plant, has edible, starchy roots and is cultivated extensively in Hawaii and tropical Asia. When dug like potatoes, cooked, and pounded, the roots become poi, one of the staple native foods, although tourists often compare it to glue. The huge, arrow-shaped leaves are the plant's main feature rather than its small yellow flowers. The foliage of different varieties varies from rich green to those with markings of purple or dark blue.

They are hardy to zone 9. Where growing seasons are short, start the bulbs indoors in late winter. When spring frosts are over, plant them outdoors 6 inches deep, about 3 feet apart, in moist, fertile, deep soil in light shade. Choose a spot where the massive plants won't be damaged by strong winds. Dig the tubers immedi-

ately after frost has killed the tops, and dry and store them in dry peat in a cool, frost-free place over the winter.

Crinum. See chapter 13.

Dahlia (DAL-ia) (photos, pages 150 and 151)

COMMON NAME: dahlia
TYPE OF ROOT: tuber
DEPTH TO PLANT: varies
PLANTING TIME: spring
BLOOMING SEASON: throughout summer
LIGHT PREFERENCE: sun to light shade

Few garden plants offer such a variety of flower shapes, sizes, and colors, and such a long season of bloom. Although dahlias no longer enjoy the great popularity that they had during the 1920s and 1930s, there are ideal kinds for the border, cutting garden, and even to use for flowering hedges and foundation plants. A member of the Daisy Family, it is native to Mexico and was imported to Spain probably as early as the seventeenth century. From there the plants reached other European countries. After Swedish botanist Anders Dahl developed several hybrids, the plant was named for him in 1789.

The numerous cultivars range in height from a few inches to over 5 feet, in shapes classified as spiders, pompoms, cacti, anemones, and even dinner plates. The American Dahlia Society has established official classifications, which you will find in many catalogs. (See Appendix for the society's address.) Among the many categories are the following:

Anemone Dahlias. One or more rows of flat petals surrounding clusters of short tubular petals.
Ball Dahlias. Perfectly round, ball-shaped blooms of 4 inches or more in diameter.
Cactus Dahlias. The petals are rolled tight or quill shaped (photo, page 151).

Collarette Dahlias. Single row of petals surrounding a row of petals of a different color.

Dinner Plate Dahlias. Very large, decorative dahlias.

Dwarf Dahlias. 2- to 4-inch flowers on plants up to 30 inches tall.

Formal Decorative Dahlias. Fully double flowers with long symmetrical petals of equal length.

Informal Decorative Dahlias. Long petals that are twisted and irregularly spaced.

Mignon Dahlias. Single dahlias growing about 18 inches tall.

Miniature Dahlias. Plants with ball-shaped blooms, less than 4 inches in diameter. This class does not include the pompoms.

Orchid-Flowering Dahlias. Star-shaped blooms with open centers.

Peony Dahlias. Open-centered flowers with several rows of outer petals.

Pompon Dahlias. Flowers 2 inches in diameter or less.

Single Dahlias. Open-centered flowers with a single row of petals.

Semicactus Dahlias. Petals are tubelike for part of their length.

Dahlias fit well into any landscape. We often see them used in the perennial border, as a flowering hedge along a roadside where plowed snow would ruin a woody hedge, or surrounding a garage or barn foundation. Since they have a long season of flowering, they can provide cut flowers for much of the summer and also make excellent outdoor container plants.

The secret to creating a beautiful dahlia planting is to mass them in groups of at least three to five plants of the same cultivar and color. Every year one of our neighbors creates a very effective display by growing a long row of deep red cultivars against her white garage.

Culture

Dahlias thrive in rich, deeply tilled, loamy garden soil and full sun, in a sheltered spot that is protected from strong winds. Keep them away from trees or shrubs with roots that might compete for nutrients and moisture, and plant them

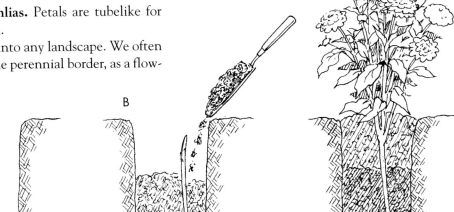

(A) Some growers plant large-flowering dahlias in a 1-foot-deep hole (with sprouts and buds up) and cover with 3–4 inches of soil . As stem grows, (B) they cover it with more soil. (C) The resultant plant is upright and sturdy and usually does not require staking.

only after all danger of frost is past.

When planting the large dahlias (4 or more feet tall), dig a hole for each one 6 to 8 inches deep and mix ¼ cup of bulb fertilizer (9–9–6) into the soil at the bottom. Then set the tuber about 6 inches deep with the sprouts and buds facing upward. Space the bulbs from 3 to 4 feet apart. Plant the short dahlias in a similar manner but only 2 to 3 inches deep and 8 to 12 inches apart. If you buy dahlias in pots, set them in the ground or planters at least 2 inches deeper than they grew in the pots.

Some growers plant their tall dahlias as they do gladioli, by digging a hole about 1 foot deep, setting the tuber at the base of it, and covering it with 3 or 4 inches of soil. As the stem grows taller, they fill in the hole with soil. This deep planting helps the plant stand upright with less staking.

Dahlias over 4 feet tall must be staked because their stems are brittle and hollow. Insert a stake into the base of the hole before planting the tuber, so you won't damage it later. If you don't like the appearance of a tall stake before the plant grows, use a short one to mark the spot, and exchange it for a taller stake later, when the foliage can camouflage it.

Dahlias need plenty of water and nourishment to produce the most spectacular blooms, so be sure the soil is well supplied with compost or manure. Encourage fast growth with weekly additions of a liquid fertilizer until the plants produce flower buds. Apply a mulch to conserve moisture, and give them additional water during dry spells. Unlike some plants, if they become dry, they usually don't recover enough to bloom.

To encourage a more bushy plant, as soon as the tall-growing dahlias are 1 foot high, pinch off their terminal buds. Continue to do this from time to time as the plants grow to stimulate side-branching.

If large flowers are your goal, give the plant plenty of room to grow. Plant it in rich soil, keep it especially well supplied with moisture and liquid fertilizer, and pick off all the flower buds on each branch as soon as they form except the one at the end. Stake it carefully.

Even if you aren't growing large exhibition dahlias, it's a good idea to snip off some of the flower buds if they are so crowded that the flowers can't open properly. Remove all faded blooms before they go to seed, too, to encourage continuous blooming.

Dahlias are sensitive to cold, so if you live where frosts come early you can often extend the season by covering them at the first threat. In our climate a few weeks of warm weather tend to follow the first early cold snap.

Storing Tubers

Dahlia tubers are biennial. They die during their second summer and are replaced by a clump of new tubers that same year. Each fall before the first frost, dig the clump carefully so you don't cut into the tubers, and shake off the loose soil. Hang the entire plant in a ventilated greenhouse or garage to dry slightly, so plant nutrients can return to the roots. Then cut off the top, a foot from the bulb, and dry it a bit more.

Leave the clump intact, but check each tuber for rot and insect damage before storing it. Cut off any shrunken or dead ones, and dust them with a fungicide to guard against rot, making sure all cut surfaces are covered (see chapter 5). Label them if you want to keep the different cultivars separate in the garden. We use metal or wooden labels and tie them on with wires, since after the tubers shrivel, it is easy to lose the markers.

Storage conditions are critical and the tubers will die if you don't handle them properly. The roots should never dry out completely, but still never become moist enough to rot. Pack each clump upside down, one layer thick, in a tray, box, or basket that's not airtight, and cover them with vermiculite, perlite, dry sand, peat moss, or dry leaves. Store them in a dry room that is no warmer than 45°F, and inspect them from time to time during the winter to see that they are not becoming too dry or beginning to rot. If they are over-dry, moisten the packing material slightly; if any show signs of rot, discard them promptly.

Propagating

You can grow dahlias from tubers, seeds, or stem cuttings. Among the nice things about dahlia plants is their tendency to multiply quickly. The easiest way to start a large number of plants is to cut apart the tubers in the spring at planting time. Be sure there is at least one eye on each, because, like potatoes, the new sprouts grow from the eyes. Of course, there is no reason to cut a clump into lots of pieces if you don't need that many. If you want only a few, pull the tubers apart gently and plant the sections that separate easily. The resulting plants will be larger than those you have cut with only one or two eyes.

If you'd like to start plants from scratch, buy a package of dahlia seeds and grow your own tubers. Dwarf dahlias are usually grown this way and treated as bedding plants. If your growing season is long enough, plant the seed directly in the garden. In cool zones plant the seeds indoors in late winter if you want blooms by midsummer. Because dwarfs grow so well from seed, we don't bother to overwinter their tubers.

Some catalogs sell seeds of the large-flowering exhibition dahlias. These are nearly as easy to grow as the dwarfs, although they usually don't bloom the first year. Though you're never sure exactly what the flowers will be like when you plant seed, the time we tried it, some of the plants were excellent.

To start plants from stem cuttings, see chapter 14.

Insects and Diseases

Check all tubers at planting time, whether you purchased them new or stored them over the winter, and discard any that look as if they might be harboring insects or diseases. The most common dahlia pests are borers that live in the stalks and deform them. Cut out any spots in the stalk that indicate borer activity.

During the growing season, dust or spray the plants with an insecticide to control aphids, leaf hoppers, or tarnished plant bugs if you spot the creatures doing serious damage.

Stem rot and wilts sometimes attack dahlias, as do virus diseases such as stunt, ring spot, and mosaic. All are difficult to control, so it is best to destroy all infected plants, and plant new ones in a different area. If you must replant dahlias in the same bed, sterilize the soil first.

Galtonia (gawl-TOE-nee-a) (photo, page 149)

SPECIES AND COMMON NAME: *Galtonia candicans*, summer hyacinth
TYPE OF ROOT: bulb
DEPTH TO PLANT: 6 inches
PLANTING TIME: spring, after frosts are over
BLOOMING SEASON: summer
LIGHT PREFERENCE: sun

Sometimes also sold as *Hyacinthus candicans*, this hyacinth, a member of the Lily Family from South Africa, bears little resemblance to the spring-blooming hyacinths. It produces many 2-inch, fragrant, white, bell-shaped flowers on a 2- to 4-foot spike above low, fleshy, sword-shaped foliage. Plant the bulbs 6 inches deep in well-prepared, humus-rich, moist soil in the spring. Propagate with bulb offsets or from seed. Hardy to zone 6, and to zone 5 if heavily mulched. In cooler zones dig up the bulbs in the fall, dry them, and store them in a cool place that stays above freezing.

Gladiolus (glad-ee-OH-lus) (photos, pages 112 and 147)

COMMON NAME: gladiolus
TYPE OF ROOT: corm
DEPTH TO PLANT FROM BASE: varies from 3 to 8 inches
PLANTING TIME: spring
BLOOMING SEASON: midsummer to fall
LIGHT PREFERENCE: sun

Gladioli are members of the Iris Family and most of the 250 to 300 species are natives of Africa. Their colorful stemless flowers are borne on spikes that range from 1 to 5 feet in height. Their swordlike foliage gives them both their common name, sword lily, and their Latin name, *Gladiolus*, which is derived from the word *gladius*, meaning sword. Use whichever plural of gladiolus you prefer: gladiolus, gladioluses, and gladioli are all technically correct, according to the dictionary. The Gladiolus Society, however, has chosen to use gladioli as the plural, and so do we.

Very few people we know are lukewarm about glads. They either love them or dislike them intensely and don't hesitate to say so. When we first became interested in gardening many years ago, the gladiolus was a leading flower. Breeders offered new corms at outrageous prices, and growers planted hundreds of acres, both for cut flowers and to produce new corms. Nearly every catalog featured many pages of different cultivars.

Before we got around to planting our farm with glads, the fad had dwindled. Breeders concentrated on developing gigantic blooms on tall stems that would win awards rather than creating smaller kinds that gardeners wanted. Florists found the flowers suitable only for massive arrangements, and commercial flower growers soon switched to growing lilies, herbaceous perennials, and annuals that were more

financially rewarding.

As hybridizers began to develop shorter, smaller-flowering plants, gladioli regained some of their popularity, and there are now numerous cultivars in a wide range of colors, sizes, and forms. The new kinds are more disease resistant than the earlier ones, and they last longer in the garden and in arrangements. If picked while the buds are just beginning to show color, they can be shipped safely to distant flower markets.

Since most gladioli are tropical plants, gardeners in climates other than zone 8 or warmer must dig the corms each fall after the tops have frozen and dry and store them for replanting in the spring. The plants are sensitive to frosts at both ends of the season and, like other tall-growing plants, they are difficult to protect. Since it takes about three months for most kinds to bloom, for earlier flowers we sometimes start some corms indoors in small pots and set them out after the risk of spring frost has passed.

Choosing Glads

The bargain assortments of a hundred or more gladioli sometimes offered in Sunday newspapers usually consist of corms much smaller than reliable nurseries ever sell, and few are likely to bloom the first year. You'll be much happier with fewer but larger corms that will produce excellent flowers the same year you plant them. The largest corms are relatively inexpensive when compared with lily bulbs, iris rhizomes, and many other bulbous plants.

Before you buy corms, study the plant descriptions. Many catalogs indicate the ultimate heights of the different cultivars, the size of the flowers, and their blooming season. The latter is important if your growing season is short. We have bought glads in the past that hadn't started to bud before our first frost. Check the sizes of the corms listed to be sure you get what you want. Glad corms are classified as Jumbo, No. 1, No. 2, and No. 3, which is the smallest.

Gladiolus tubergenii 'Charm'

Gladiolus *sp.*

Jumbo bulbs often produce two heavy stalks per bulb. The height of the plants is described as low (2 to 3 feet), medium (3 to 4 feet), or giant (over 4 feet). The flowers, too, are rated according to size, with miniatures measuring smaller than 2½ inches in diameter, and giants larger than 5½ inches.

Planting and Culture

Glads need a spot in full sun. In a mixed border, groupings of six to twelve of the same color and size are more striking than either individual plants alone or groups of mixed colors. In a row we always plant in our vegetable garden for cut flowers, however, the different cultivars and colors intermingle happily.

Since gladioli thrive in rich, well-drained soil, mix compost or dried manure with the soil

Bugle-lily (Watsonia *sp.*)

Monkey-faced pansy, orchid pansy
(Achimenes *sp.*)

at planting time. One of the time-honored ways to prepare soil for glads is to dig a trench or large hole about 2 inches deeper than you intend to plant the bulbs and spread a complete fertilizer at the base. Then cover it with about 2 inches of soil. Plant the corms at a depth that corresponds to their size: large corms (over 1 inch) about 6 inches deep and small ones (under 1 inch) 3 to 4 inches deep. Cover the corms with 2 to 3 inches of soil at first, and, as they grow, fill in the trench or hole until it is level with the ground. Then the shoots don't have to force themselves up through 6 inches of soil. With deep planting they won't be as likely to tip over when they bloom. Because the plants grow tall rather than bushy, you can grow a lot of them in a small space, like high-rise buildings. Set them from 5 to 8 inches apart, depending upon their

Container-grown calla lily (Zantedeschia *sp.*)
and blue lily-of-the-Nile (Agapanthus *sp.*)

Calla lily (Zantedeschia *sp.*) *and* Oxalis
'Iron Cross'

Indian shot (Canna indica)

Canna (Canna aranyalon)

Summer hyacinth (Galtonia candicans)

size. Give the plants additional feedings of liquid fertilizer after they are 1 foot or so tall to help them develop a strong stalk and husky flower buds. Water them during dry periods. It's best to plant them in a new location each year to reduce the risk of disease.

The blooms open gradually from bottom to top, and the flowers at the base of the stalk tend to fade before the top buds open. Consequently, whether in a border or in a bouquet, it is often necessary to do some deadheading if you want them to look their best.

Never cut glads to the ground when gathering them for bouquets, but leave at least three lower leaves to replenish the corm if you plan to save it for another year. Water the plants throughout the season if necessary.

Overwintering the Corms

Dig the corms in the fall four to six weeks after blooming or after the foliage starts to brown. They can survive a light frost or two. The old corm will be withered, but on top of it will be a brand-new one and probably some little cormels between the two. Leave them all attached, and don't cut off the tops immediately.

To dry glads for winter storage, tie the tops

Dahlias offer a wide variety of flower shapes, sizes, and colors, and a long season of bloom.

Dahlia *'Crichton Honey'*

together in bunches of the same color and heights and label them. Then hang them in a warm, dry place, until both tops and roots are thoroughly dry. If you prefer, you can dry them in a warm, airy place on screens, instead. After they are dry, cut off the tops, leaving about an inch of stem. Remove the old corms and discard them. Dust the new corms and cormels with a garden fungicide to prevent disease (see chapter 5), and store them in a paper bag in a dark, dry, cool but frost-free space such as a closet until spring.

In spring, peel the papery covering from the corms and plant them in a thoroughly prepared bed. If you want more plants, grow the tiny cormels in a separate bed for the summer. They should bloom the second year. You can also grow gladioli from seed, but it takes a year or two before the corms will bloom.

Cactus Dahlia

Dahlia 'White Aster'

Cultivars and Species

There are many kinds of gladioli, and you will find a different assortment in each catalog. Recommended early-blooming cultivars include the following:

'Applause' — salmon pink
'Blue Conqueror' — deep violet blue
'Bonnie' — ruffled white miniature
'Golden Glove' — yellow
'Hunting Song' — orange
'Little Fox' — red and yellow miniature
'Milestone' — light blue
'Miss America' — lavender miniature with
    orange markings
'Morning Bride' — white
'Nova Lux' — yellow
'Pink Friendship' — pink
'Priscilla' — white with pink edge
'Red Bantam' — red miniature
'Starburst' — pale yellow miniature
'White Friendship' — white

If you'd like to experiment with species glads, there are some that are winter hardy to zone 7. G. *carneus* (G. *blandus*) has pink flowers, G. *byzantinus* has red flowers, G. × *colvillei* is red with yellow markings, and G. *tristis* is white. All grow from 12 to 18 inches in height.

Dahlia *sp.*

Tuberous begonias in a shady border

Abyssinian gladiolus, peacock orchid
(Acidanthera sp.)

C. N. MCFARLAND

Tuberous begonia (B. x tuberhybrida)

Gloriosa-lily, climbing-lily (Gloriosa sp.)

Aztec lily, Jacobean lily, orchid amaryllis (Sprekelia formosissima)

Gloriosa (glow-ri-O-sa) (photo above)

COMMON NAME: gloriosa-lily, climbing-lily
TYPE OF ROOT: tuber
DEPTH TO PLANT FROM BASE: 4 inches
PLANTING TIME: spring
BLOOMING SEASON: midsummer
LIGHT PREFERENCE: full sun or light shade

This African vine is probably not as widely planted as it should be, since it bears an abundance of attractive, exotic, lilylike blooms in midsummer. Using tendrils at the ends of its leaves, it climbs over a trellis or shrub. It can be grown in containers on porches or in greenhouses, but will do well outdoors if the growing season is long enough. Plant the tubers 8 inches apart. Keep the plant well watered throughout

Tiger flower, Mexican shell flower, flame flower (Tigridia pavonia)

the growing season and, as it grows, give it support. Hardy to zone 8. In cooler zones, dig the tubers before frost and store them over the winter.

G. *rothschildiana*, Rothschild gloriosa-lily. This species has blooms that are yellow in the center and red at the tips, many of which are downward facing. It can grow up to 6 feet in length.

G. *superba*, Malabar gloriosa-lily. Yellow blooms change to red, with petals that are rather twisted. It is often grown in conservatories and can extend up to 10 feet.

Spider-lily, Peruvian daffodil, basket flower (Hymenocallis × festalis)

Rain lily, fairy lily, zephyr lily (Zephyranthes *sp.*)

Buttercup (Ranunculus *sp.*)

Hymenocallis (hy-men-o-KAL-lis)

(photo, page 154)

COMMON NAME: spider-lily, Peruvian daffodil, basket flower
TYPE OF ROOT: bulb
DEPTH TO PLANT FROM BASE: 3 to 4 inches
PLANTING TIME: spring
BLOOMING TIME: summer
LIGHT PREFERENCE: sun or light shade

These bulbs, members of the Amaryllis Family, originate in North and South America. Some species are relatively hardy (see chapter 10, Hymenocallis) but most are tender bulbs. They have clusters of spectacular blooms on sturdy 1- to 2-foot stalks above thick strap-shaped foliage. Each flower has a cupped center surrounded by six narrow petal-like lobes that curve outward from the base of the cup, giving the bloom a spiderlike appearance.

They grow well either in sun or light shade. Plant the bulbs 3 to 4 inches deep. In the fall, dig and dry the bulbs, and store them packed in dry peat at a temperature between 55° and 60°F. It is easy to start additional plants from the offsets that form readily.

Some species are often grown as indoor pot plants. Treat them like amaryllis (*Hippeastrum*), but plant them deeper, with the top of the bulb about 1 inch above the surface of the soil.

H. caribaea is a native of the West Indies and grows to 3 feet with long, shiny, thick evergreen leaves. Hardy to zone 9 and cooler zones with protection. The white flowers are fragrant.

H. speciosa, winter spice, spider-lily. This species is used mostly as a potted plant. The huge white flowers, sometimes 8 inches long, with ten or more on each stalk, are fragrant and hold their fragrance after they are dried.

Polianthes (po-li-ANTH-ees)

SPECIES AND COMMON NAME: *Polianthes tuberosa*, tuberose
TYPE OF ROOT: rhizome
DEPTH TO PLANT FROM BASE: 3 inches
PLANTING TIME: spring
BLOOMING SEASON: midsummer to fall
LIGHT PREFERENCE: full sun or light shade

This native of Mexico is best known for its white waxlike flowers that are so fragrant they are cultivated in France to make perfume. The flowers grow loosely on spikes that are 1½ to 4 feet tall, depending on the species and variety. They need a long season to bloom well, so in temperate climates it is best to start them indoors as early as March. Plant them outdoors after frost danger is over, 2 to 3 inches deep and from 4 to 6 inches apart in fertile, well-drained soil. Mulch them and during their blooming period, keep them watered. In the fall, before a frost, dig and dry the rhizomes, and store them in vermiculite at a warm temperature (at least 55°F).

Many gardeners treat the tuberoses as annuals since they usually don't bloom well the second year. The bulbs multiply rapidly, and the resulting bulblets are too small to flower and must be grown a year or two to get them to blooming size. They are hardy outdoors in zone 9.

Ranunculus (ra-NUN-kew-lus)

(photo, page 154)

COMMON NAME: buttercup
TYPE OF ROOT: tuber
DEPTH TO PLANT: 2 inches
PLANTING TIME: spring
BLOOMING SEASON: mid- to late summer
LIGHT PREFERENCE: sun

The botanical name for buttercups comes from the Latin for "tadpole," perhaps because certain species grow in bogs and around the perimeter of ponds. There are over 250 species that vary in hardiness, although the cultivated, florist types are too tender for year-round growing in all but zones 8 to 11. Most species are yellow, but the hybrids come in a variety of colors and color combinations.

Ranunculus asiaticus, Persian buttercup. These attractive flowers resemble camellias with very tightly packed petals and are often sold in mixtures of all colors except blue and green. The flowers range from 1 to 4 inches in diameter and grow on stems from 1½ to 2 feet tall over fern-like foliage. The Tecelote Giant hybrids have large flowers in gold, orange, pink, red, yellow, and white, as well as bicolors. They make good container plants and excellent cut flowers.

After frosts are over, soak the tubers for three or four hours before planting. Then set them with their crowfoot roots downward in sandy loam, and water them thoroughly. Don't water them again until top growth appears unless the soil has become extremely dry. In ideal conditions the crowns should remain dry and the roots damp, which makes it easier to care for them in pots than in the ground.

They look best when planted in groups of ten or more, about 6 inches apart. Each tuber produces six or more flowers at intervals of about a week, making a succession of bloom throughout July and August.

In the fall, in zone 7 and cooler, dig the tubers after the foliage wilts, and dry and store them in single layers in peat moss or vermiculite at about 50°F for the winter. To get more plants, cut the tubers apart in the spring before replanting.

Sprekelia (sprek-EE-lia) (photo, page 153)

SPECIES AND COMMON NAME: *Sprekelia formosissima*, Aztec lily, Jacobean lily, orchid amaryllis
TYPE OF ROOT: bulb
DEPTH TO PLANT FROM BASE: 1 to 2 inches
PLANTING TIME: spring
BLOOMING SEASON: summer
LIGHT PREFERENCE: sun

These Mexican natives are members of the Amaryllis Family. The flowers, at the top of 12-inch stems, are bright red, each with three upright upper segments and three lower ones rolled into a cylindrical form for part of their length. The stem appears before the foliage. They are hardy outdoors only to zone 9. In other areas, plant them in sandy, fertile, well-drained soil in the spring, and either treat them as annuals or dig the bulbs in the fall and store them.

For winter blooms, plant the bulbs with the top third above the soil surface in 6-inch pots in late fall, and treat them like amaryllis. Once the growth appears, keep the soil moist because it needs plenty of humidity to thrive. If you want more plants, they start readily from the small bulblets (see chapter 14).

Tigridia (ty-GRID-ee-a) (photo, page 153)

SPECIES AND COMMON NAME: *Tigridia pavonia*, tiger flower, Mexican shell flower, flame flower
TYPE OF ROOT: bulb
DEPTH TO PLANT FROM BASE: 4 inches
PLANTING TIME: spring
BLOOMING SEASON: summer
LIGHT PREFERENCE: sun

Natives of South and Central America and members of the Iris Family, these exotic plants with many cultivars come in white, yellow, red, pink, or orange blooms, 3 to 6 inches in diameter, on stems that are 1½ to 2 feet tall. Though each flower lasts only one day, a succession of bloom ensures up to six weeks of flowers. The name "tiger flower" comes from the tigerlike spots in the bloom's cup-shaped interior.

Plant them in full sun 4 inches deep, 6 inches apart, in soil to which compost or dried manure has been added. Protect them from strong winds. If you start the bulbs indoors to get blooms earlier in the summer, plant them in pots, since they are not easy to transplant from flats.

Tigridia are hardy to zone 7. In zone 6 and cooler, dig and store the bulbs over the winter in an airy cool place, as you would gladioli. To propagate them, save the small bulblets and plant them in the spring. They should bloom in two years.

Triteleia (try-TEL-ee-a) (photo, page 54)

COMMON NAME: triteleia
TYPE OF ROOT: corm
DEPTH TO PLANT FROM BASE: 3 to 5 inches
PLANTING TIME: spring
BLOOMING SEASON: summer
LIGHT PREFERENCE: see below

This genus (*Triteleia* is also known as *Brodiaea*) of the Amaryllis Family has about fourteen species, all native to western North America. *Triteleia* are good plants for borders. Their small flowers come in blue and white atop tall stems. They are most happy in Pacific and southern states, zones 7 to 10 where summers are dry, and in those conditions they can live undisturbed for years. The only time they need extra moisture is during their blooming time in early summer. In the moist Northeast they are likely to do poorly, except in dry rock gardens. Plant the corms 3 to 5 inches deep and 3 inches apart in light, sandy soil and full sun. Where winters are severe, mulch them heavily, or dig the corms after frost kills the foliage, and store them in a dry place over the winter.

T. hyacinthina (*Brodiaea hyacinthina*), wild hyacinth. Umbels of ½-inch bowl-shaped flowers in blue, lilac, or white cluster at the top of 2½-foot stems.

T. laxa (*Brodiaea laxa*), grass nut, triplet lily. This species grows to 2½ feet with large, trumpet-shaped blooms that are usually blue, but sometimes violet-purple or white. 'Queen Fabiola', a dark blue cultivar 12 inches tall, is one of the best garden varieties.

Watsonia (wat-SO-nee-a) (photo, page 147)

COMMON NAME: bugle-lily
TYPE OF ROOT: corm
DEPTH TO PLANT FROM BASE: 3 to 4 inches
PLANTING TIME: spring
BLOOMING SEASON: summer
LIGHT PREFERENCE: sun

Natives of South Africa, these members of the Iris Family have tubular flowers on tall spikes in white or various shades of rose, pink, and red, with lower-growing, swordlike foliage.

Plant the corms 4 inches apart and 3 to 4 inches deep, depending on their size. They are hardy outdoors to zone 8, but in cooler zones, dig, dry, and store them for the winter like gladioli.

W. beatricis blooms in late summer, producing an unusually large number of flowers.

W. marginata grows 4 to 5 feet tall with spikes of fragrant, rose-colored flowers. Blooms in early summer.

W. pyramidata has pinkish rose blooms on spikes that reach 4 to 5½ feet tall. Blooms early summer.

Zantedeschia (zan-tee-DESH-ee-a) (photo, page 148)

COMMON NAME: calla lily
TYPE OF ROOT: rhizome
DEPTH TO PLANT FROM BASE: 3 inches

PLANTING TIME: spring
BLOOMING SEASON: throughout summer
LIGHT PREFERENCE: sun or light shade

The calla lily is an eye-catching tropical plant from South Africa. Its tiny flowers are borne on a fleshy spadix, enclosed in an unusual large, waxy, funnel-like white, yellow, or pink spathe (modified leaf).

Calla lilies are hardy outdoors to zone 8. They are tender plants, so in order to get blooms before fall frosts in areas with short growing seasons, start rhizomes in pots in late winter and set them out after all frost danger is past in the spring. In longer growing seasons, plant rhizomes directly in the ground.

Before planting, enrich the soil with manure or compost. Set rhizomes 3 inches deep, 8 to 12 inches apart. Make sure they never dry out completely; a mulch is very helpful. Dig the rhizomes in the fall and dry and store them for the winter in a cool spot (40 to 45°F). Then repot them in fresh soil in the spring and take them outdoors. Or if you wish, pot them in large containers and continue to grow them as houseplants or in a greenhouse. Start new plants by dividing the rhizomes in early spring before repotting or planting outdoors.

Several species are familiar to gardeners:

Z. aethiopica, calla lily. The most common of the callas, this is also called the florist's calla. It grows about 3 feet tall, with a fragrant, large, cup-shaped, waxy white spathe with an outward flare and long arrow-shaped leaves. Dwarf cultivars are available, and some cultivars have smaller blooms.

Z. albomaculata, spotted calla. The spathes come in white, pale yellow, and light pink, with purple markings on the throat of the interior. 24 inches tall. The deciduous leaves are spotted with white markings.

Z. elliottiana, golden calla. Grows to 2½ feet with recurved yellow spathes that are 6 inches long and swordlike deciduous leaves with white spots.

Z. rehmannii, pink calla, red calla. Small rosy red or pink spathes, gets only 1 to 2 feet tall. Its narrow deciduous leaves are sometimes dotted with white spots.

Zephyranthes (zef-i-RAN-theez)
(photo, page 154)

COMMON NAME: rain lily, fairy lily, zephyr lily
TYPE OF ROOT: bulb
DEPTH TO PLANT: 2 to 3 inches
PLANTING TIME: spring
BLOOMING SEASON: varies
LIGHT PREFERENCE: sun

These short, 6- to 12-inch plants produce flowers that resemble crocuses in pink, red, white, and yellow above grasslike foliage.

They need full sun and are good choices for a rock garden or the front of a border. Plant the bulbs 3 inches apart in fertile soil and water them during dry seasons. Most are natives of South America and Mexico and are hardy only to zone 8. In cooler climates, plant the bulbs in spring rather than fall, as you would where they are hardy. Start the late-blooming varieties indoors in late winter and transplant them outdoors after threat of frost is over, so they will flower before freezing weather arrives. Dig them in the fall before frost, and dry and store them in dry peat moss in a frost-free place.

Z. atamasco, Atamasco Lily, grows 8 to 12 inches tall. Unlike the others, it is native to the southeastern United States. The white flowers are occasionally tinged with purple.

Z. candida has white flowers with yellow anthers and blooms in late summer.

Z. grandiflora has large rosy pink blooms. It grows 12 inches tall and blooms in early summer. One of the showiest species.

Late Bloomers

EACH YEAR THE FALL-BLOOMING bulbs surprise us. In the spring we wait for the snowdrops and crocuses to appear because we don't want to miss the first sprouts and flowers. We happily anticipate the first summer lilies and irises, too, as they bud and then bloom, but the lycoris, colchicums, and fall crocuses always seem to appear full-grown in our garden, just like cluster flies and pigeons, though much more welcome. One day, or so it seems, there is an empty spot in the border, and the next, a display of beautiful flowers. They continue blooming for several weeks, and even light frosts don't seem to deter them.

Most nurseries that specialize in bulbs sell some of these fall-blooming gems in a wide range of colors and forms. They ship them at the right time, with directions that advise planting immediately. When you plant, be sure to mark the spot since the foliage they show in the spring dies for the summer. More than once we've planted annuals or perennials in such a "hole" in the garden, forgetting about the bulbs that are taking a nap there in anticipation of their upcoming moment in the sun.

Colchicum and fall crocus are often confused with each other because both are commonly called autumn crocus and their blooms are a similar pink-lavender color. There are several differences, however, the first of which you're likely to notice is that one *Colchicum* bulb usually costs more than a dozen *Crocus sativus* or *Crocus speciosus*. They also differ in height. The crocuses are small plants, usually from 3 to 6 inches tall. Although some species of *Colchicum* are short too, the most commonly planted, *C. speciosum* and its hybrids, grow from 8 to 12 inches. Another difference between them is that the crocus corm isn't toxic, but the corm of the colchicum, if eaten, can be deadly.

LATE SUMMER AND EARLY FALL FLOWERING BULBOUS PLANTS

BOTANICAL NAME	COMMON NAME	SEASON OF BLOOM
Colchicum	autumn crocus meadow saffron	fall
Crocus	autumn crocus	fall
Cyclamen	cyclamen	fall
Leucojum	autumn snowflake	fall
Lycoris	magic lily	late summer

Colchicum (KOL-chik-um)

COMMON NAME: autumn crocus, meadow saffron
TYPE OF ROOT: corm
DEPTH TO PLANT FROM BASE: 3 to 4 inches
PLANTING TIME: August
BLOOMING SEASON: fall
LIGHT PREFERENCE: sun

Although a yellow species, *C. luteum*, blooms in the spring, most colchicums emerge from the ground in the fall on 6- to 12-inch stalks with star-shaped lavender-toned or white blossoms.

A gardening friend gave us some colchicum plants when they were in full bloom many years ago. We planted them and completely forgot about them until they bloomed the following fall, crowded in with some daylilies. We promptly moved the daylily clump and marked the spot so we wouldn't make the same mistake again. Few other flowers bloom so late, and sometimes they are still boldly, or foolishly, blossoming in our garden during an early snowstorm.

Plant experimenters are familiar with *Colchicum autumnale* because it contains the poisonous alkaloid colchicine. This substance is used to produce new plant cultivars by altering the number of chromosomes. Usually the chemical is used to convert seeds or small seedlings, but sometimes the sprouting buds of older plants are treated with it in the spring. The spectacular tetraploid iris and daylily cultivars of recent years are among the successful results of these treatments.

But don't let the toxicity of the *Colchicum* scare you into not planting it and missing out on its beautiful fall blooms. No one is likely to come into your garden and eat the corms, not even the rodents.

Culture

Plant the corms 3 to 4 inches deep and about 8 inches apart in August. They should produce blooms the same fall. Put them in the ground as soon as you get them, in late summer, for they are one of the few bulbs that can bloom when seemingly dormant. Bulbs bursting into bloom while still in bags, buckets, or wheelbarrows are not uncommon, though it isn't good for the bulbs.

The fall-blooming colchicums begin to grow in early spring, but the foliage is not attractive and it dies in the summer, so gardeners often plant them among shrubs or other perennials where the leaves are not conspicuous. Don't cut back the foliage when it starts to die in midsummer. It must die naturally if the nutrients are to reach the bulb. After the leaves are completely dead, the bulbs are dormant. This is a good time to divide and separate them if they have become overcrowded, as is likely after three or four years. When handling them, protect your hands from the toxins by wearing gloves.

Among the common species are the following:

C. autumnale, autumn crocus, meadow saffron. This native of Europe and North Africa is hardy to zone 4 with protection, and grows in sheltered parts of zone 3. Different varieties and cultivars have pink, lavender, or white blooms, sometimes four to a stem, and grow about 8 inches high. 'Album' is a low-growing (4 inches), very hardy cultivar that produces many white blooms, and is ideal in a rock garden.

C. 'Autumn Queen' has deep purple markings on light purple, and is very unusual. A hybrid between C. *giganteum* and C. *speciosum* var. Bornmuelleri, it grows to 6 inches and is hardy to zone 3.

C. *byzantinum* grows to 6 inches and produces many large rosy lilac blooms for several weeks. Native to southeast Europe. Hardy to zone 5.

C. *cilicicum*, from Asia Minor, has star-shaped, deep rosy lavender blooms.

C. *speciosum*, showy autumn crocus. These have large, rosy purple, tulip-shaped blooms up to 4 inches in diameter. Outstanding cultivars that are hybrids of this and other species include the following:

'The Giant' — 8 to 12 inches tall with lavender-pink flowers and a white base

'Violet Queen' — 7 inches tall, rich purple with a white throat, somewhat checkered, hardy to zone 3

'Waterlily' — 6 inches tall, an outstanding double with large mauve-pink flowers that resemble waterlilies

Hardy to zone 5, they all make excellent cut flowers.

Crocus (autumn-blooming) (KRO-kus)

COMMON NAME: autumn crocus
TYPE OF ROOT: corm
DEPTH TO PLANT: 3 to 4 inches
PLANTING TIME: early spring or late fall
BLOOMING SEASON: fall
LIGHT PREFERENCE: sun

This is a good choice for planting at the front of the fall border, tucking among shrubs and foun-

dation evergreens, and using for naturalizing. The 3- to 6-inch plants have flowers that resemble the spring crocuses in white, blue, lavender, and rose.

Plant the corms in the springtime or late summer, 3 inches apart, in light loamy soil. Just as the spring-blooming kinds need sun in the spring when their foliage shows, the fall bloomers need it when their leaves appear. Each species produces foliage at different times. On some, it comes with the flowers; on others it pops up after the flowers; and on still others, it waits until spring. Whenever it arrives, never mow it until it has withered naturally.

Give the plants a sprinkling of a balanced plant food in early spring. New corms form over the old ones each year and sometimes may push the plant out of the soil. If this happens, dig and replant them after their leaves die down. Divide them every three or four years, or they will stop blooming.

Most are hardy to zones 5 and 6 but can be grown in colder areas if mulched for the winter.

C. *cancellatus*, latticed crocus, is native to Iran and regions of southeast Europe, and grows only 3 inches tall. The "lattice" refers to the netted appearance of the corm. Blooms range from near-white to silvery lilac. It does best in poor, rocky, slightly alkaline soil with a hot, dry summer during its dormant season. Hardy to zone 5.

C. *cartwrightianus*, native to Greece, has small lilac-colored flowers that come late. Hardy to zone 5.

C. *kotschyanus* (C. *zonatus*). Native to Turkey and Lebanon, this species is hardy to zone 5 and grows about 4 inches tall. Flowers are pale lilac with dark veins and a yellow throat.

C. *medius* has deep lavender purple blooms with showy scarlet stigmas. This vigorous species grows from 3 to 6 inches tall and spreads rapidly. It blooms late and heavily. Native to

Italy and southern France, and hardy to zone 6.

C. *ochroleucus* has white to pale cream flowers tinged with yellow or orange. Grows to 3 inches. Blooms very late, too late for most northern gardens, and needs a dry summer dormancy season. A native of Syria, it is hardy to zone 5.

C. *pulchellus* has lilac-colored flowers with a deep yellow-orange throat and honeylike fragrance. Grows to 4 inches. A native of the Balkans, it is hardy to zone 5.

C. *sativus*, saffron crocus, is a native of Asia Minor with large, fragrant flowers that are purple or white and from 4 to 6 inches in height. The plants may need support to keep their large flowers erect. Hardy to zone 6.

The orange-red stigmas of the *sativus* flowers are the source of saffron, the expensive spice formerly used for flavoring and coloring butter, cheese, preserves, and other foods. Not everyone appreciates the flavor of saffron in food, but some people prize it highly in dishes such as paella and bouillabaisse. In case you are thinking about raising them for culinary purposes, consider the fact that thousands of stigmas are necessary to yield only one ounce of spice!

Most gardeners do not regard the flowers as great ornamentals, but the plants are of interest historically.

Saffron was much valued by ancient civilizations around the Mediterranean as a dye and a source of perfume, and it was used for religious rituals. In the Song of Solomon we find: "Thy plants . . . are spikenard and saffron," and ancient temples were filled with its fragrance. Legend has it that C. *sativus* was offered to the gods in the ceremonies at the Oracle of Delphi in Greece.

C. *speciosus*. Native to southeast Europe, Iran, and Turkey, this easy-to-grow species has violet-blue flowers and is one of the earliest fall crocuses to bloom. Grows 4 inches tall. Hardy to zone 5.

Cyclamen (SIK-la-men)

COMMON NAME: cyclamen
TYPE OF ROOT: tuber
DEPTH TO PLANT: just under soil surface
PLANTING TIME: early spring or midsummer
BLOOMING SEASON: most peak in fall
LIGHT PREFERENCE: light shade

Every gardener knows the florist's cyclamen, C. *persicum*, an attractive houseplant (see chapter 13). Of the fifteen or so *Cyclamen* species, there are also several excellent garden types hardy enough for year-round growing in areas with mild climates. Some will grow even in zone 5 with winter protection. The miniature butterfly-shaped pink, red, rose, and white blooms are only about 1 inch in diameter and grow on 4- to 5-inch leafless stalks. Their round or kidney-shaped foliage often doesn't appear until after the flowers.

They grow best in light shade, in fertile soil. It is essential that the soil be well drained, so build a raised bed if necessary. They are also good plants for a rock garden. Plant the corms just under the soil surface, space them about 6 inches apart, mark the spot, and cover them with a mulch. Keep them watered after the leaves appear.

You can grow cyclamens from seed, but they take two to three years to bloom. This is a good way to grow them, however, since the genus is endangered worldwide. Although some species are abundant, collectors often can't distinguish them from the rare ones that are nearly extinct. Buy them from nurseries, like Montrose Nursery, that propagate their own. See Appendix for a list of bulb suppliers (see chapter 3 for endangered bulbs).

To grow cyclamens from seed, soak them for six hours and then plant them in a flat filled with a plant-starting mix. Cover them with ¼ inch of mix, and cover flats with newspapers, since the seeds germinate best in darkness. It takes a long time for most to start, and although some will begin to grow in two months, others can take years.

C. *cilicium*, Sicily cyclamen. These dainty 3-inch-tall plants have pink flowers, although some cultivars have white blooms with a red center. Their large leaves have a heart-shaped, silver blotch in the center. They bloom heavily in late summer and fall. Hardy to zone 7.

C. *hederifolium* (*C. neapolitanum*), Neapolitan cyclamen, ivy-leaved cyclamen, baby cyclamen. Elegant, small pink or white flowers with a dark red blotch appear on 4- to 6-inch stems. They have attractive silver-marked leaves, and many flowers are fragrant. A native of southern Europe, it is hardier than most cyclamens, and grows in zone 5 with protection. It is at its prime in the very late summer and fall, but growers in zone 7 report that it begins to bloom as early as May and sometimes continues throughout the summer until the peak bloom, from August through October.

Leucojum (Autumn-Blooming) (lew-KO-jum)

SPECIES AND COMMON NAME: *L. autumnale*, autumn snowflake
TYPE OF ROOT: bulb
DEPTH TO PLANT FROM BASE: 2 to 3 inches
PLANTING TIME: spring or late summer
BLOOMING SEASON: fall
LIGHT PREFERENCE: sun or light shade

Leucojum is Greek for white violet. This genus also includes two spring-blooming species — *L. vernum*, the spring snowflake, and *L. aestivum*, commonly called the summer snowflake. The genus is part of the Amaryllis Family and is native to Europe. Hardy to zone 6, and cooler zones with protection.

The autumn snowflake has small, bell-like blooms that are white with green or red tips, in clusters on hollow stems from 6 to 8 inches tall. Both flowers and leaves appear in early fall. They need perfect drainage and are good for naturalizing, for the front of the border, and for rock and wildflower gardens.

Plant the bulbs in light shade in late summer, 2 inches deep and about 3 inches apart, in soil rich in compost or other organic matter. Provide water when the plants are growing if the weather is dry, and divide them only if you want to start more plants.

Most species are endangered, so buy them only from dealers who sell cultivated plants.

Lycoris (ly-KOR-is)

COMMON NAME: lycoris
TYPE OF ROOT: bulb
DEPTH TO PLANT: 3 to 5 inches
PLANTING TIME: midsummer
BLOOMING SEASON: fall
LIGHT PREFERENCE: sun, light shade

Members of the Amaryllis Family, these interesting bulbs have daffodil-like leaves in spring, and in early summer the foliage disappears completely. In late summer or early fall, a single scape (leafless stalk) shoots up and within a few days a cluster of blooms appears at its top. Lycoris are not fussy about soil, and grow well in sun or light shade. They seldom have disease or insect problems and don't usually need staking.

To get more plants, dig the bulbs and divide them after the leaves die, but before the flower stalk appears. Replant them right away and mark the spot, so you don't inadvertently plant something else there during the summer.

The first three species listed are hardy only in zone 7 and warmer, although they are worth trying in the cooler zones in a sheltered spot with protection.

L. africana (*L. aurea*), golden lycoris, golden spider lily, golden hurricane lily. This 1½- to 2-foot plant has yellow flowers, and the interesting long lobes of the petals curve backward, making it appear spidery and exotic. It is native to China, Taiwan, and Burma, but was once thought to be of African origin, hence its Latin name.

L. incarnata, from China, has fragrant flowers that are salmon or rosy pink. Height 1¾ feet tall.

L. radiata, red spider lily. This native of Japan and China is the most unusual lycoris. It has scarlet flowers in early summer, but sometimes blooms again in the fall. Its lobes and stamens are recurved, making it look like a spider. 1½ feet tall. It has been sold in error as *Nerine sarniensis*.

L. squamigera, magic lily, autumn-amaryllis. This fragrant trumpet-shaped flower is lilac-pink tinged with blue, on a 1½- to 2-foot stalk. Most garden books describe this species as hardy only in zone 5 or warmer, but we grow it successfully in zone 3, possibly because we plant the bulbs 5 inches deep and grow them in a protected place.

Bulbs for Indoor Beauty

ONCE YOU HAVE FILLED your gardens with bulbs, you will want to enjoy them indoors as well as out, and during all months of the year. One way to do this, of course, is by cutting blooms to bring indoors. Or, during the time of year when you can't garden outside, you may want to grow some beautiful flowering bulbs indoors.

Cutting and Arranging Bulbs

Nothing lifts our spirits after a long, cold winter like a bouquet of fresh daffodils and pussy willows; and a massive arrangement of fragrant lilies on the table for a summertime party makes us feel extremely wealthy. Bringing bulb blooms indoors is a treat most gardeners enjoy to the hilt.

The best time to cut flowers is in the morning when sunlight and heat won't wilt them and transpiration is at a minimum. Choose fresh blooms that are in full bud or just beginning to open. When picking bulb plants, remember not to cut all the foliage if you want the bulbs to thrive the following year. Ferns or leaves from other plants will work just as well for greenery.

Using a clean, sharp knife or sharp scissors, cut the stems on a slant so they'll absorb more water, and plunge them directly into a pail of tepid water that you've carried to the garden. If you're cutting lilies or tulips, snip off the pollen-bearing tips of their stamens to avoid spreading pollen stains over other flowers and your tablecloth.

Keeping Cut Flowers Fresh

The cut flowers you buy from a florist have already been well conditioned, and those you pick from your own garden will last longer, too, if you condition them before arranging. Most bulb flowers need only a few hours in cool water, though a few need some special attention (see page 166).

It's essential that water can flow through the stems of cut flowers at all times. To help ensure that it does, follow these steps:

❖ Cut the stems while holding them under water, if possible, to prevent air bubbles from forming that might keep water from flowing through the stems.

❖ Strip from the stems any foliage that will be under water, because it will quickly decay and bacteria will proliferate that can clog the flower stems. Likewise, remove from an arrangement any flowers that are past their prime.

❖ Hollow-stemmed bulbs such as narcissus, tulips, and hyacinths often have beads of moisture at the base of their cut stems that can seal the stem and prevent water absorption. Remove the moisture, by wiping it away or by re-cutting the stem and submerging it in water right away.

There are several ways to prolong the life of an arrangement:

❖ Mix a preservative, available from a florist, with the water; or add a homemade potion — a spoonful of sugar and a few drops (about ¼ teaspoon) of household bleach that will suppress bacteria.

❖ Keep flowers cool and out of drafts.

❖ Spring blooms, especially, like springlike conditions, so keep their water cool and set them out of direct sunlight.

❖ Change the water in arrangements frequently.

❖ Drooping flowers may indicate that something is clogging the stem; recut them to try to correct the problem.

If you want to keep a bouquet of narcissus fresh for a special occasion, by cutting them in bud you can usually store them for up to two weeks in the refrigerator at about 36°F. Place a damp towel at the bottom of the refrigerator and set the container on it. Twice a day, spray the buds with a mister to keep them slightly moist.

Creating the Arrangement

In a well-proportioned arrangement or even a simple bouquet, the flowers should stand considerably taller than the container. It's an insult to the blooms to see only their pretty heads peeking over the top of a tall vase! A good rule of thumb is to position them from 1 to 1½ times above the height of the container.

The easiest way we've found to make sure the flowers stay where we put them is to use a floral foam, such as Oasis. In some containers you can cut the foam to fit snugly within the sides, but in others it works better to fasten it to a metal pinholder device that you've secured to the base with florist's clay or another adhesive. (Before putting the the foam in place, stretch a piece of old panty hose over the pinholder for easy removal of the foam.) Be sure to water foam regularly because if the flower stems dry out they won't absorb water again.

Not all bulb flowers lend themselves to formal arrangements, and soft-stemmed flowers, particularly, are ideal for informal bouquets. Wildflowers and tiny spring blooms such as grape hyacinths or snowdrops can be bunched together beautifully in a glass salt shaker, wine glass, jelly jar, or other small container. Large blooms, such as velvety tuberous begonias, are ideal for floating, singly or in a group, in a shallow dessert bowl.

Conditioning Certain Bulb Flowers

Narcissus. Our first warning about narcissus came from the local florist: "Don't mix daffodils with tulips in an arrangement because the daffodils produce a clear toxic sap that kills the tulips." It made sense. The same toxins that repel mice and rabbits in the garden can harm other flowers that are placed in the same container.

Fortunately, with a simple procedure you can condition narcissus to make them harmless to their neighbors: Cut them, place the stems in a container of clean, cool water, and hold them there for four hours or overnight. Then discard the water and don't recut the stems. Your narcissus will no longer damage other types of blooms.

Tulips. Tulips are among the most difficult flowers to arrange, because their curving stems seem unmanageable. Certain tricks of the trade can help you control them, however. If you want straight stems, pick blooms in tight bud and trim the end off each stem to ensure that water will flow freely. Then wrap the bunch carefully, with lower stems exposed, in a tube formed by a newspaper or other non-absorbent paper, fastening it with rubber bands, so that it will stand upright in a container. Place stems in cool water in a cool spot for a couple of hours or overnight. After a long stiff drink, the stems will no longer droop. On the other hand, you may prefer curved stems that hang over the side of the container.

Then, move the tulips to a vase filled only one-third full of water, and refill it to that level with fresh water each day. You'll notice that tulips, like anemones, grow up to 1 inch taller in water. Repeat the conditioning procedure if the stems you want to be straight become droopy after a few days.

Dahlias. Most people condition dahlias like other flowers, by simply placing them in cool water for a few hours. Experts have found, however, that they can prolong the life of the blooms by dipping the stems into about 2 inches of very hot water for a brief time (about 10 seconds). Then they put them in a container filled with cool water and leave them for several hours before arranging.

Indoor Growing Requirements

Many tropical and semitropical bulbs are ideal for adding greenery, color, fragrance, and even fresh air to the winter homescape. You don't need to be a gardener to use potted plants from a florist in the winter to brighten up your home. "It's cheaper than traveling to Mexico," our neighbors explained last February when we admired their living room full of fragrant, colorful flowers.

Most people buy their tender, bulbous plants already in containers and sometimes in bloom from a florist, garden outlet, or even supermarket. Amaryllis bulbs appear potted, in boxes, each fall in time for us to grow them for Christmas blooms, and, in the late winter, pots of Easter lilies blossom in shops and stores. Throughout the fall and winter we see calla lilies, clivias, gloxinias, and other exotic bulb plants for sale. Those that are already potted and growing are tempting because you can see exactly what you're getting.

We don't often find unpotted tropical bulbs available locally or in general bulb catalogs, but specialty catalogs sell those you can pot up yourself for winter blooms. They are less expensive than potted plants, and some are no more difficult to grow than geraniums or fibrous begonias.

Like other houseplants, each tender bulb has its own light, heat, and humidity requirements. They vary in the length of time they bloom, too: Some produce flowers for many weeks each year, and others blossom for only a short period. Most bloom best indoors in the winter when we need them most, but a few can dress up a terrace or poolside outdoors by producing flowers in the summer months.

Most bulbous plants need a rest period after flowering, before they can bloom again. Some lose their leaves and appear to die, but others stay lush all year if you keep them indoors. They vary in the treatment they need during their "nap time," and in the way they revive. (See individual bulbs described on pages 170-75 for cultural requirements.)

We describe only fairly common bulbous plants that are not difficult to grow at home without a greenhouse. Other intriguing indoor bulb plants are available if you have a particularly green thumb, a greenhouse, and the time and desire to fuss and provide the conditions they need. The Amazon lily (*Eucharis*) and the blood lily (*Haemanthus*), for example, need more humidity and heat than most homes supply. The butterfly iris (*Moraea*) grows too tall for most homes. The lovely red-flowering Guernsey lily (*Nerine sarniensis*) and the sea daffodil (*Pancratium*) also need the conditions only a greenhouse can supply.

Increasing Humidity

Not every tropical bulb plant needs lots of moisture to grow well, but some need higher humidity than the average home provides during the winter months. We know of one creative family that vents a clothes dryer into their small greenhouse to add moisture. We sometimes wash laundry in the evening and hang it on racks near the plants to dry overnight, but we must admit it isn't a very attractive way to provide moisture.

To provide "spot" humidity for dry plants, use one or more of the following methods:

❖ A humidifier with automatic controls is one of the most effective ways to add moisture. Some are compact and inexpensive.

❖ Spray plant foliage frequently with a mister, and wash off the leaves from time to time (unless the leaves are the type that shouldn't be wet, such as those of gloxinias).

❖ Set the plants on deep saucers or trays covered with small stones and water. The pots should be above, not touching, the water.

❖ Group plants loving high humidity together in an empty aquarium or plastic tent. As you water them, the moisture will be concentrated in that area.

❖ Place pans of water on registers, radiators, or stoves. If you keep a woodstove going during the winter, place a steaming kettle on it. These provide ideal humidity for raising plants.

Containers

Whether to use terra-cotta or plastic pots can always get a discussion going among gardeners. Aesthetically, both kinds have their champions now that plastic is being fashioned more tastefully. Although we have never seen any great difference in how most plants grow in either one, some bulbs — those that need especially well-drained environments — do best in clay pots because the clay "breathes" better than plastic, and water evaporates faster. We use mostly plastic containers for many reasons: They are much easier to clean and sterilize after use than clay pots, and they weigh far less. Also, they are less inviting to fungus and mold growth. Finally, plants in plastic pots require less frequent watering.

Whatever containers you use should have drainage holes that are large enough so they don't plug up easily. Cover the bottoms with a layer of pebbles or pieces of broken clay pots to prevent wet soil from sealing the holes.

Problems of Indoor Bulb Plants

Although it might seem that indoor plants grow in a protected environment, anyone with houseplants knows that diseases and insects attack them, just as they do those outdoors. Certain natural controls are missing indoors, such as beneficial insects and wind to control humidity; and bugs and diseases slip in on dirty pots, in unsterilized soil, and on plants that were already infected when you bought them.

To help avoid problems, buy only potting soil that has been sterilized. Always wash pots as soon as you empty them, too, and sterilize both them and the tools you work with in a solution of 1 part household bleach and 5 parts water.

Whenever you buy potted plants or bulbs, look them over carefully before taking them home. Whiteflies, aphids, and other sucking creatures often infect plants in commercial greenhouses, and some, such as mites and scale, are difficult to spot. Discolored or misshapen foliage may be caused by sucking insects or diseases that are difficult to identify without a magnifying glass. As we've mentioned before, when you buy bulbs, check them carefully, too, before potting them. If there is any rot or other unusual condition, either discard the bulbs or plant them in an isolated room where they can't infect other plants.

When you're trying to identify a plant malady, first check for possible physiological stress. It can be devastating to a bulbous plant to cope with problems such as overcrowding, a pot that is too small, overwatering or underwatering (very common!), temperatures that are too warm or too cool (especially at night), or an excess or lack of fertilizer. Most plants suffer when placed near fans, cold windows, registers, or radiators.

Certain species, especially those in the Iris Family, are susceptible to fluoride damage. If you notice a burned appearance on the margins of the leaves, test the fluoride level of your water. A high level may be causing fluoride-toxicity.

If none of these problems seems apparent, and removing the damaged leaves or stems doesn't halt the symptoms, it may be necessary to spray or dust the plant for disease or insects. We often use soap (not detergent) and water for this purpose, but you may need to resort to something stronger. Choose a fungicide to treat disease, an insecticide for insect control, or an all-purpose garden dust to combat both. Read the manufacturer's label to be sure the product was developed to cure the problem that afflicts your plants, and be certain it is safe to use indoors. Follow directions carefully and repeat treatment as recommended to deter further outbreaks.

STANDARD SOIL RECIPE FOR POTS

YIELD: 1 QUART

Thoroughly mix the following:

- ⅓ quart commercial potting soil
- ⅓ quart peat moss
- ⅓ quart perlite or vermiculite
- 1 teaspoon lime
- 1 tablespoon complete fertilizer (either organic or other slow-release type)

Potting

Most bulbous plants are not particularly fussy about soils and do well with the standard mix described in the box above. Different brands of commercial potting soils on the market vary widely and some are not well sterilized. We have purchased bargain soils that were so riddled with weed seeds, grass roots, and soil diseases that they appeared to be scooped off worn-out pastures.

When potting a bulb, fill the pot with soil to about 1 inch from the top. Be sure to leave enough room for watering. (See individual bulbs on pages 170-75 for planting depths.)

It is more important to be precise when watering indoor plants than those planted in the ground because nature can't help correct any excesses of too much or too little moisture. Overwatering prevents good root growth, causing weak plants that easily pick up diseases. A tough plant such as amaryllis can stand some neglect, but it, too, will never recover if it dries out too much.

Check the soil frequently to decide on your watering schedule, and adjust it according to the amount of sunlight and temperature. During short winter days, plants need less fertilizer and water than they do late in the winter when the days lengthen. If your home is dry, plants in a sunny window may require daily watering, yet those in a shady corner may need it less than once a week. Always water bulbs sparingly during the time they are going dormant.

The fertilizer you mixed in your potting soil should keep the plant going for most of the growing season, but during its budding periods give it a shot of liquid fertilizer to help it bloom better and build up the nutrients in the bulb before becomes dormant. Don't fertilize it after the blooms have faded, unless otherwise stated for a particular bulb.

Flowering Bulbs Indoors

The following bulbs are natives of South Africa and the tropics and semitropics of North and South America, and are hardy outdoors only in similar regions (zones 9, 10, and 11). Unless stated otherwise under the individual species, they are suitable for growing indoors rather than outdoors in the temperate zones.

Clivia (KLY-vi-a)

COMMON NAME: Kaffir lily
TYPE OF ROOT: tuber
HEIGHT: 2 feet
BLOOMING SEASON: midwinter
LIGHT PREFERENCE: light, but no direct
   sunlight

Clivias, native to South Africa, were popular houseplants a century ago, and subsequently were not much grown until recent years when more gardeners have become enthusiastic about them. And no wonder! Clivias burst forth with numerous spectacular fragrant blooms in midwinter, just when their clusters of 2-inch-wide orange, red, salmon pink, or yellow blooms are more than welcome. As a bonus, when the flowers fade, red berries form on 2-foot stalks above the evergreen, straplike foliage.

Clivia does best when somewhat pot-bound and crowded into a window box or planter. It needs a light soil, so use a mixture of 4 parts vermiculite, 1 part commercial potting soil, and 1 part peat moss. Plant the tuber with the top barely covered with soil, and water it thoroughly. Water sparingly until the buds appear, and then water normally. Once a month feed it a solution of liquid fertilizer. Clivias do not need either high temperatures or high humidity, so the conditions in most homes are ideal. In fact, they bloom much better in cool temperatures and do best with plenty of light, but no direct sun.

After they finish blooming, let them dry out somewhat between waterings, but never let them dry out completely. At this point, fertilize them only once every two months. After they become semidormant in the fall, give them even less water and discontinue feeding until new buds form.

Although you can propagate clivia by division of the tubers, for the best flowering, don't divide it. When it becomes too large for the pot, move it to a bigger container.

Crinum (KRY-num)

COMMON NAME: crinum lily, spider lily
TYPE OF ROOT: bulb
HEIGHT: 2 to 3 feet tall
BLOOMING SEASON: summer
LIGHT PREFERENCE: Direct sunlight, at least
   a half day

This plant is an easy-to-grow member of the Amaryllis Family with small pink, red, and white lilylike blooms in clusters on tall stalks above the foliage. It is a native of South Africa. It becomes much too large for growing on a windowsill, but its exotic, tropical appearance is

GROWING CRINUM OUTDOORS

Crinums are hardy outdoors to zone 8, but in cooler zones you can grow them in the ground if you dig, dry, and store them indoors over the winter, treating them like dahlias. Plant them after threat of frost has passed in a fertile, fairly moist spot in full sun for plenty of flowers, or in light shade for more lush foliage. Set them 2 to 3 feet apart, because they become large.

ideal for certain spacious areas. Since it blooms in summer, the pot can be moved outdoors if you wish.

Plant the bulb in a pot that is only slightly larger than it is, since it prefers being pot-bound. Set it half in and half out of the soil, using the standard soil mix, page 169. Place it in a spot where it receives at least a half day of direct sunlight. Keep it moist during its growing season, from April to September.

After it blooms, water it sparingly, and allow the soil to dry between waterings as it becomes dormant. Increase watering in the spring as it begins new growth. Each month during the growing season, provide a weak solution of liquid fertilizer.

Although it prefers to be pot-bound, every three or four years it will need repotting, because the roots become too crowded. In early fall, after the foliage has died, remove it from the pot, wash away the old soil, and repot in new fertile soil. Plant the offsets if you want additional plants.

Specialist bulb catalogs usually list several species of crinums, as well as cultivars. *Crinum* x *powellii* cultivars include pink 'Rose' and white 'Album'. 'Ellen Bosanquet' is a well-known hybrid with wine red flowers.

Cyclamen (SIK-la-men)

SPECIES AND COMMON NAME: *C. persicum*, florist's cyclamen
TYPE OF ROOT: tuber
HEIGHT: 12 to 18 inches
BLOOMING SEASON: winter
LIGHT PREFERENCE: bright light, no direct sunlight

This tender, larger version of the miniature hardy cyclamen described in chapter 11 blooms for a long season in the winter months with delicate pink, purple, red, or white butterfly-shaped blooms on 1- to 1½-foot stalks above variegated heart-shaped leaves. It is native to central Europe and the Mediterranean region to Iran.

It is much easier to buy these plants already potted from a florist, but specialty firms sometimes sell the tubers. If you buy them by mail, pot them as soon as they arrive, one tuber to an 8-inch pot, using the standard soil mixture (page 169). Fill the pot about half full, set the tuber on top of the soil, then fill the pot and arrange the tuber so ⅓ of it rests above the soil and ⅔ below.

Cyclamens need bright light but shouldn't be in direct sunlight. They do best in cool temperatures and may not flower if temperatures are too high. They also like high humidity, which you can provide by misting the plants each day and watering them regularly when they are growing and blooming. Be careful not to overwater them, however. Continue to water them, but less frequently, after the blooms fade. After the leaves have dried, store the dormant bulbs in a cool spot, such as a dark basement and don't water them at all for eight to twelve weeks in late spring and summer.

Instead of storing them indoors in the summer, you may wish to remove them from the pots and plant them outdoors in a lightly shaded spot; but be sure to bring them indoors before frost.

After their dormant period, keep them barely moist in a cool spot until the new buds start. When the sprouts appear, begin regular watering again and feed them each week with a weak solution of liquid fertilizer during the growing and blooming season.

Freesia (FREE-si-a)

COMMON NAME: freesia
TYPE OF ROOT: corm
HEIGHT: 18 inches
BLOOMING SEASON: winter
LIGHT PREFERENCE: full sunlight after they
    start to grow

These members of the Iris Family have very fragrant 2-inch blossoms in white, blue, purple, pink, lavender, gold, and orange, both single and double. They are native to South Africa. They grow on slender, long stalks that are difficult to shape and stake. Florists use growth retardants such as A-rest to make them stay compact, but such products are tricky for home gardeners to use. Instead, gardeners put up with the freesia's sprawling growth habits so they can enjoy its fragrant, attractive blossoms.

For winter flowers, pot the corms in the fall in a standard soil mix (page 169), ten to twelve weeks before you want the plants to bloom. Plant several of the same kind together in a container, setting them about 2 inches apart barely under the soil surface. Place them initially in a cool spot that isn't sunny but has bright light. Then, when they begin to grow, set them where they get full sunlight for at least half the day. If the location is too warm, the stems will be weak. Keep them watered lightly as they form roots, and feed them monthly with a weak solution of liquid fertilizer. Stake them with unobtrusive plant stakes and twine when

they are about 6 inches tall. The blooming season lasts about two weeks.

Remove the flowers as soon as they fade, and stop the watering so the corms can become dormant. As soon as the leaves have died, remove the corms from their pots, dry them in a warm place, and store them in open trays at a cool temperature until the next planting season.

By starting the corms in late winter or spring you can use them for window boxes or patio plants during the summer. Divide the corms for more plants.

Hippeastrum (hip-e-AST-rum)

COMMON NAME: amaryllis
TYPE OF ROOT: bulb
HEIGHT: 1 to 2 feet
BLOOMING SEASON: winter
LIGHT PREFERENCE: full sun

Though our friends in Florida enjoy their amaryllis in the garden in early spring, we depend upon these spectacular bulbs from tropical America to brighten up our home during the dark days of late December and early January. We usually buy potted plants, so about all we need to do to get blooms is unpack them from their boxes and add water. Directions for care are always included. You can also purchase bulbs in bulk from specialty bulb companies.

We are always astonished at how fast the plants and their gorgeous flowers grow. The period from bulb to bloom is surprisingly short, usually only five to seven weeks in a warm room, and each tall sturdy stalk holds two to four huge lilylike flowers in red, pink, or white tones. Doubles and dwarf cultivars are available, as well as miniatures that produce flowers one-third the diameter of the large hybrids. The miniature stalks grow to 1½ feet, however.

If you buy unpotted bulbs, you can get excellent results by following a few simple directions.

Choose the largest bulbs available because those will not only produce large flowers, but also additional stalks for a longer season of bloom.

Use a pot only about 2 inches wider than the bulb itself, because amaryllis do best when they are comfortably pot-bound. The standard soil mix (page 169) works well for them.

First, cut off any dead or unhealthy roots emerging from the base of the bulb, leaving only those that look strong. Fill pot half full of potting mix, set bulb in it, and add enough soil so that nearly half of the bulb will be above the surface of the soil. Place pot in a room where it gets full sun or at least a minimum half day of sunlight. Water it thoroughly after planting and about once a week thereafter, or more often if the soil is dry. Rotate the pot occasionally so the stalk will grow straight. The flowers do not last a long time, but by keeping them cool and out of direct sunlight they last longer.

Some people discard the bulb after enjoying its blooms, but we frequently save them and get even better flowers the following winter. After the blooms have faded, it is necessary to rebuild the bulb's energy if you want it to produce flowers the following year. Cut down the flower stalks but don't remove the foliage or take the bulb from its pot (unless you want to propagate some of the tiny bulblets that are attached to it; see chapter 14). Remove part of the soil from around the bulb, however, and replace it with new soil, working in a teaspoon of a slow-acting fertilizer such as Osmocote. If you don't add a slow-release fertilizer, give it additional liquid fertilizer once a month. Water it only enough to keep it from getting too dry.

If you keep the plant in a cool place in the house or greenhouse, the leaves should stay green until spring. Then, either keep it indoors as a houseplant, or after frosts are over, set the pot outdoors on a porch or deck. You can also, if you prefer, sink it in the garden where it will need only a minimum of care.

At the end of the summer or early fall, move the pot into a cool, dark room and let the leaves wilt. Then cut them off and let the bulb remain in a semidormant state for five to eight weeks. Don't water it during this period. Six to eight weeks before you want the blooms, move the plant to a spot where it will receive light and room temperatures for a few days to further cure the bulb. Then, water it. For Christmas blooms, bring it into the light in mid-November.

Some gardeners have good luck saving the bulbs by treating them somewhat differently. They add a slow-acting fertilizer to the pot after blooming, then withdraw water in late spring and early summer to induce dormancy. During the summer they store the bulb dry in its pot in a cool cellar. In early fall they move it to a warmer spot (about 60°F). About November they begin to water it again, and the plant springs to life. We have used this method successfully and find it much easier than planting it out in the garden.

If you continue to save the bulb for additional years of bloom, after three years repot it with completely new soil. With the high price of amaryllis bulbs in mind, you may also want to separate and plant the bulblets and offsets that form around the main bulb. They will make welcome gifts when they bloom in two or three years.

Hymenocallis. See chapter 11.

Lachenalia (lak-en-AY-lia)

COMMON NAME: Cape cowslip, leopard lily
TYPE OF ROOT: bulb
HEIGHT: 1 foot
BLOOMING SEASON: late winter
LIGHT PREFERENCE: full sun

This compact, easy-to-grow plant has red, orange, or yellow bell-shaped blooms 1 inch long on stems that reach a total height of a foot or less. Its leaves, which are often spotted, give it the name "leopard lily." It is native to South Africa.

In early fall, plant six bulbs in a 6-inch pot or bulb pan using the standard soil mix (page 169). Set the bulbs with their tops just below the soil surface, then soak them with water and leave them alone until they begin to grow. Place the pot in a sunny window where it gets at least a half day of sunlight, and keep it well watered during the growing period. After the plants begin to bloom, place them in a cool spot each night so that the flowers will last longer.

After they blossom, remove the faded flowers and stop watering the plant. When the leaves have died back, remove the bulbs, dry them, and store them in a ventilated bag in a dark, dry place until you replant them in the fall. If you want more plants, separate the small bulblets from the large bulbs, and plant them.

Lilium (LIL-e-um)

SPECIES AND COMMON NAME: *Lilium longiflorum*, Easter lily
TYPE OF ROOT: bulb
HEIGHT: 2 to 3 feet
BLOOMING SEASON: early spring
LIGHT PREFERENCE: full sun

Because of the special care needed to get Easter lilies to bloom on schedule, it is usually best to buy them in bud or bloom. Often people have asked us what to do with them after they have stopped blooming, however, and whether it is possible to plant them outdoors as a garden lily.

Although they are hardy in zone 8, they are not suitable as outdoor bulbs for cooler areas. If you want to save them and try for Easter blooms in successive years, however, take them from the pot, plant them in the ground for the summer, and fertilize them. Repot them in the fall in the standard soil mix (page 169) and place

them in a cool, frost-free (36° to 40°F) place to store for five weeks or more. Then give them a warm location to start growth, keeping the nighttime temperature at 60°F. Give the new shoots bright light but not direct sunlight. After they reach 1 inch tall, place them in direct sunlight. Water them and fertilize them. Within 3 to 4 months, if all goes well, you'll have an Easter lily in bloom.

Professionals who grow Easter lilies in a greenhouse carefully control the lighting and temperatures as they grow. We have found it is difficult to duplicate those conditions at home and get them to bloom heavily at a precise time. After urging many of them to rebloom, we have concluded that recycling them isn't worth the effort.

Narcissus Tazetta. See chapter 7.

Sinningia (sin-IN-jia)

SPECIES AND COMMON NAME: *Sinningia speciosa*, gloxinia
TYPE OF ROOT: tuber
HEIGHT: to 1 foot, usually shorter
BLOOMING SEASON: winter
LIGHT PREFERENCE: bright, indirect light

This showy houseplant, the florist's gloxinia, is a member of the Gesneria Family, as is the African violet. It is native to Brazil. Its velvety foliage resembles that of the African violet, and its luxuriant trumpet-shaped flowers, up to 5 inches in diameter, range from solid blues, purples, and reds in various combinations to pastels. Some cultivars have double blooms.

It is far less trouble to buy the plants in bloom, but if you want to grow your own, plant the tuber in a 5- or 6-inch pot at a depth that leaves the top just under the soil level. Water it thoroughly after planting and place it in a warm spot. Then water it only sparingly until the leaves begin to show, but keep it moist, because gloxinias like plenty of humidity. Always use room-temperature water and water it from the bottom so you don't spill it on the leaves. Gloxinias prefer bright indirect lighting, so keep them out of strong sunlight. (Fluorescent lights work well in the winter.) Feed them a weak solution of liquid fertilizer once a month. It will take two to three months to flower, from the time it begins to grow, but it blooms over a long period.

If the plant is struggling, check to be sure that it is getting as much light as it needs and enough humidity. You may need to enclose it temporarily in a tent of clear plastic to increase the humidity level if your home is dry.

After it stops blooming, gradually decrease watering and when it is nearly dry, cut off the foliage and store the tuber in its pot in a dark cool spot (50° to 60°F) for about two months, lightly moistening the soil occasionally. When you see small new leaves, repot the bulb in fresh soil so it will be ready for its next blooming cycle.

It is easy to start new plants by cutting off a leaf and rooting the stem in a glass of water placed in the light, but not full sun. You can also start them from seed.

Sprekelia. See chapter 11.

Vallota (val-LO-ta)

SPECIES AND COMMON NAME: *Vallota speciosa,* Scarborough lily
TYPE OF ROOT: bulb
HEIGHT: 2 feet
BLOOMING SEASON: late summer and fall
LIGHT PREFERENCE: full sun

These members of the Amaryllis Family bloom in the late summer with attractive trumpet-shaped blooms arranged in clusters of five to ten at the top of a tall stalk above handsome straplike leaves. They are usually a bright scarlet color, but cultivars also come in pink and white. They are native to South Africa.

Plant them in the spring, one bulb in a 6-inch pot, or three in a 12-inch pot. They enjoy being pot-bound. Use the standard soil mix (page 169) but double the amount of lime since they prefer a pH of about 6. Set the bulb so that nearly half of it is above the soil line. Keep it in a warm, dark place until it begins to grow, lightly watering it. Once growth begins, feed it once a month with liquid fertilizer. It needs at least a half day of sunlight each day and fairly high humidity, with room temperature in the daytime and 50° to 60°F at night.

Remove the flowers as they fade, and cut off the stalk after it stops flowering. After the leaves begin to turn yellow, stop watering and feeding and keep it dry until the sprouts start to grow again, although the soil should never dry out completely. After three or four years repot the bulbs during a dormant period, and remove the bulblets that grow around the bulb. Plant these, too, if you want more Scarborough lilies.

Zantedeschia. See chapter 11.

Extending Your Bulb Plantings

WHEN WE WERE YOUNG, the half-century-old patch of daffodils in front of our home had stopped blooming well. Aunt Abbie suggested that the bulbs were probably overcrowded because they were so old, so one spring day when they were in bloom we dug up the entire patch. Then we spaded up another bed and replanted them further apart, not having the faintest idea of how to do it properly.

If we had ever read a book on bulbs, we would have known better than to break up a clump when they were at their peak of growth, and would have waited until they were dormant. But though we didn't even bother to water them, they didn't wilt in the moist spring soil and they are still blooming every spring, many years later. We don't need any other proof of how tough some bulbs are and how easy it is to divide them, although these days we are much more careful about how we do it.

When it comes to bulb propagation, most of us visualize magnificent fields of red, orange, yellow, and white tulips in the Netherlands that stretch as far as the eye can see, or rows and rows of perfect lilies in Oregon. No one does it better than the skillful specialists who live in ideal climates and grow millions of bulbs for our pleasure.

We backyard gardeners, wherever we live, however, can also propagate bulbs on a modest scale to expand our own plantings, give them to friends, or even sell them. It isn't difficult. Most of us have already done it as we did when we lifted a spade and divided and replanted that clump of daffodils. We've also broken up clumps of lilies, cut apart dahlia tubers, or separated gladiolus corms. Some of us have even pulled off a few scales to start more bulbs of our favorite lilies, or planted seeds of alliums, anemones, or dwarf dahlias.

Natural Reproduction

Bulbous plants vary in the way they reproduce naturally. All produce seeds, and some, such as certain anemones, *Chionodoxa*, and *Eranthis*, spread readily in this manner.

Some bulbs and corms replace themselves each year. The original bulb or corm can be considered an annual since it shrivels up and in its place leaves a new large bulb or corm, and often a cluster of smaller ones. Those that reproduce in this way include *Allium*, *Crocus*, *Erythronium*, *Galanthus*, *Gladiolus*, *Iris*, *Scilla*, and *Tulipa*.

Other bulbous plants produce small bulbs (bulblets) each year. Amaryllis *(Hippeastrum)*, Hyacinth, *Muscari*, and *Narcissus* are popular garden plants that reproduce in this manner. Still others produce underground stem bulblets (certain lilies); bulbils, little bulblets that form in the leaf axils or other parts of the plant above ground (certain lilies and species tulips); or offsets, small plants that grow away from the bulb.

Tuberous and rhizomatous plants reproduce from their roots or stolons (including lily-of-the-valley and most iris).

Propagation Methods

Gardeners can take advantage of the natural reproduction methods of bulbs to increase plantings more quickly.

Division

Digging, separating, and replanting bulbs is not only one of the easiest ways to enlarge your gardens, it is difficult to do badly. By dividing clumps of bulbs you can be certain that your new plants will be exactly like the parent. It is necessary to separate most bulb clumps from time to time anyway, or they become too crowded. The bonus of the job is that you increase your plants, usually by many times.

If you want the bulbs to multiply even faster than they do naturally, don't plant them as deep as the charts recommend. There is less resistance to expansion at a shallow depth, but as they devote their energy to making more bulbs, they will have less vigor, so don't expect the flowers to be as spectacular. Use more fertilizer than normal, too, if you want to increase bulb production.

There is no one right way to divide bulbs. It is best to do it when they are dormant, but you can do it successfully directly after they bloom if you plant them quickly after digging the clumps and separating them, and water them promptly. We have divided lily clumps, spring bulbs, and irises even when they were in bloom, but if you must do it then, choose a rainy week, and always plant your new divisions at the recommended depth.

Bulblets

Carefully dig up the entire clump of bulbs that you wish to divide after they have become dormant, and separate them according to size. Replant the large parent bulbs immediately so they won't dry out, and plant any medium-sized bulbs where you want them to grow, at the proper depth. The small bulblets need special

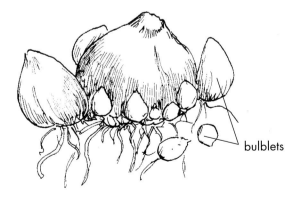

Separate small and medium-sized bulblets from the parent bulb.

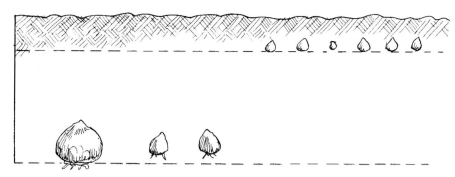

After dividing bulblets from parent bulb, plant large and medium-sized bulbs at the proper depth for that species; plant small bulblets 1 inch deep and 1 inch apart.

treatment, however, and would not amount to much if planted deep. Set them only 1 inch deep and 1 inch apart in a thoroughly prepared bed where they can grow without competition from grass and weeds. A sunny spot is best, but they will do well even if they get some light shade during the afternoon. Let them grow there for two summers. Then, in early fall, dig them from the bed and plant the largest ones just as you'd plant bulbs you buy, at the proper depth, in the location where you want them to grow. They probably won't bloom the following year, but should have flowers the second spring after planting. Leave any bulblets that are still tiny in the bed to grow for another year, and plant them the following fall.

Cormels

Plants such as freesias, gladioli, and montebretia, as well as several small spring flowers including crocuses, grow from corms, which are actually solid stems. During the growing season the old corm gradually disappears as a new one grows on top of it. Small corms (cormels) subsequently grow around the base of the new corm.

In the fall, dig the corms of the tender bulbs (freesia and gladiolus) for winter storage and treat them as described in chapter 11. In the spring, pick off their cormels and after threat of frost is past, plant them outdoors ½ inch deep in a bed of thoroughly tilled soil. In the fall, dig them again, and store them for the winter. When you plant them the following spring, set

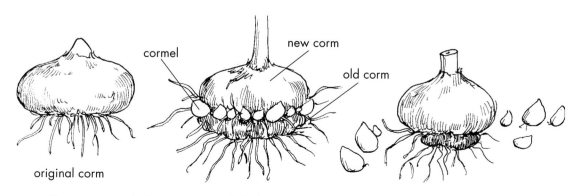

Separate cormels that grow around the base of the new corm and plant them ½ inch deep.

the ones that have made good growth at the proper depth, and they should bloom that year. Grow the smaller ones for another year.

When hardy corm-producing plants have formed a clump, if you wish to divide them, dig them after they have become dormant and carefully pick apart the corm and cormels. Treat them as you do bulblets, growing them in a bed for a year or two until they are large enough to bloom.

Bulbils

Visitors often ask if they can have some of the little black seeds growing along the stem of

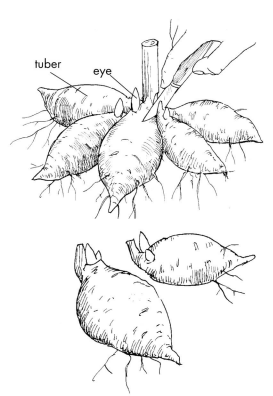

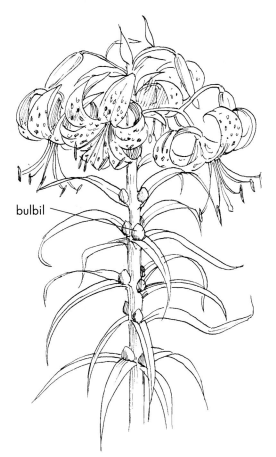

Pick bulbils from tiger and bulbil lilies and plant them as described for bulblets and hardy cormels.

Cut off the tubers that have at least one eye, dust the cuts with fungicide, and plant.

our tiger lilies (*Lilium lancifolium*) and the bulbil lily (*L. bulbiferum*). They aren't seeds at all, but small bulbs called bulbils. They grow above ground in midsummer about the time the lilies bloom. These bulbils fall to the ground and often grow by themselves, but their chances for survival are much better if you help them out. Grow them in a cultivated bed for a year or two just as you do bulblets and hardy cormels. For more information about the many ways of propagating lilies see chapter 10.

Tubers and Tuber-corms

Tuberous roots are enlarged stems, like corms, but unlike bulbs and corms they have no tunic or outer skin. Dahlias and cannas are good examples of tubers. Each has several buds, called eyes, on the exterior surface, which will eventually sprout. On tubers such as dahlias, the eyes form near the base of the old stem, but on tuber-corms they grow near the middle.

To start more plants, in early spring, as soon as the eyes are noticeable, cut apart the tubers with a sharp, sterilized knife, being sure there is at least one eye on each section. Dust the cut surface with a fungicide to prevent disease. Plant them in pots indoors for early summer blooms, or outdoors after danger of frost is over. Unless the divisions are very small, they should bloom the same year.

Tunicate Bulbs

The tunicate bulbs, including narcissus, tulips, squills, alliums, and belladonna lilies, are covered with a tunic or membrane, and their scales are so tight that there is no way you can pull them off to plant. These bulbs produce bulblets naturally, but if you want to propagate

STERILIZING TOOLS

Unless the knives used in dividing bulbs and taking cuttings are sterilized, there is a good chance that a rot, fungus, or virus from one bulb could be spread to others. Make a solution combining 1 part chlorine bleach with 5 parts water, and dip the knife into it between each bulb operation.

them more quickly, dig them in late summer and cut them apart. Since the spring- blooming bulbs have no foliage at that time of year, you must plan ahead and mark where they are growing so you can find them easily at the right time. It is possible, too, to cut apart the dormant bulbs you've just bought, if reproduction is more important to you than blooms.

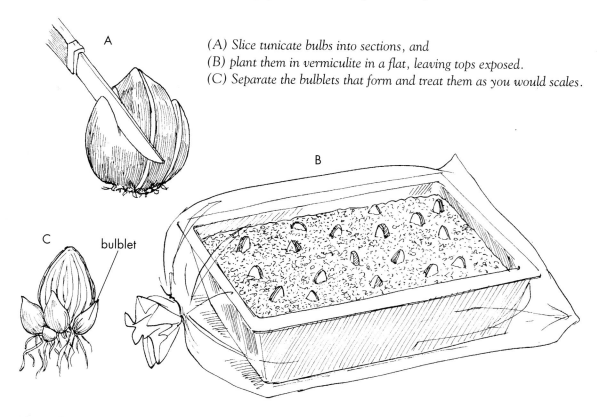

(A) Slice tunicate bulbs into sections, and
(B) plant them in vermiculite in a flat, leaving tops exposed.
(C) Separate the bulblets that form and treat them as you would scales.

bulblet

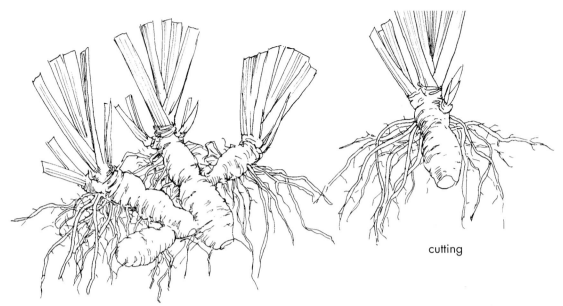

Divide iris rhizomes by cutting them apart, leaving one or more leaf stalks on each.

The cutting method seems drastic, but it works, even though you sacrifice the bulb in the process. Before you start, sterilize a sharp knife (see box on page 180) and slice each bulb into equal sections from top to bottom, as you would slice bread. Divide a normal-sized tulip bulb into four sections, and a larger bulb, such as a top-sized narcissus, into six. Plant each section in moist vermiculite or seed-starting mix in a deep flat, and leave the tops slightly exposed above the surface. Seal the flat in a clear plastic bag, treating the sections the same as you would scales (see chapter 10). Bulblets should form in two months or less. Dig the sections, pick off the bulblets, and follow the same procedure as you would for scales (see pages 130-131).

In addition to the bulbs already mentioned, *Hippeastrum*, *Hymenocallis*, *Lycoris*, and *Sprekelia* can be divided in this way.

Rhizomes

To start new plants from the rhizomes of hardy plants such as iris and lily-of-the-valley,

dig up a portion of the clump just after they have stopped blooming. Cut apart the sections, leaving one or more leaf stalks on each. Then cut back their tops to about 1 inch from the ground and replant them, barely covering the fleshy rhizomes. Unless you've made the divisions quite small, most should bloom the following year. Even if you do not need more plants, it's important to separate iris clumps frequently to preserve their vigor: Siberian iris nearly every year, and Japanese and bearded iris every three years or so.

To divide the rhizomes of a tender plant such as the calla lily, split the rhizomes apart carefully, and pot up each section. If you are growing it outdoors during the summer, divide it just before moving it outside. If you grow it in the house or greenhouse, divide it anytime when it's not in bloom.

Stem Cuttings

It's possible to start bulbs from some of the vigorous kinds of lilies such as the regals and

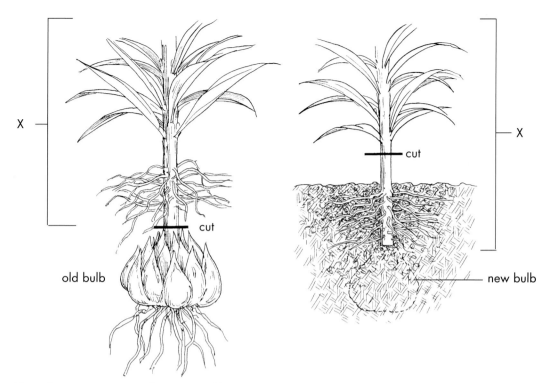

To make a stem cutting of an Asiatic lily, just after bloom cut stem below root cluster that formed above bulb. Reset this new "plant" (X) at the same depth it grew before; a new bulb will form below roots. Replant old bulb.

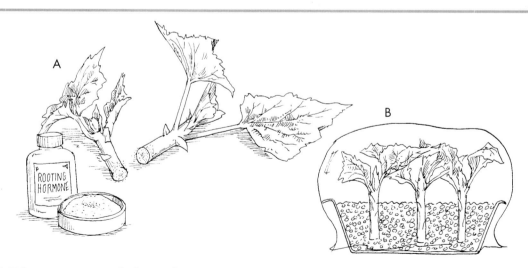

(A) Take stem cuttings of tuberous begonias with at least two leaves in early summer, dip cuttings in rooting powder, and set 2 to 3 inches deep in flat.

(B) Cover with plastic and keep moist in a well-lit location.

most Asiatic hybrids by using cuttings made from the flower stalk. Dig up the bulb in late summer after the flower has bloomed but before the leaves turn brown, shake off the dirt, and cut off the stalk just below the cluster of roots that form above the bulb. Replant the stalk and root mass to the same depth as it grew before. Then cut back the stalk to about 4 inches above the soil level mark. A new bulb will grow below the roots, although it may not bloom for a year or two. Replant the old bulb to the depth it grew before. Although removing the stalk from the bulb will deprive it of some of its vitality, it should still bloom the following year.

This technique is possible on lilies because they are among the few bulbs that form clusters of roots at the base of the stem as well as below the bulb. We have had great success starting regal, tiger, and native lilies in this way, but it will work only with deeply planted bulbs, so don't try it with Madonna lilies and others that grow just below the surface.

It's also possible to start other bulbous plants from stem cuttings. If you want more plants from an extra-special tuberous begonia or dahlia, its soft new growth will form roots readily in early summer. Cut off a few stems with two or more leaves on them, dip the cut surfaces in a rooting powder such as Rootone, and stick them, base down, 2 or 3 inches deep into a flat filled with a mixture of moist perlite and vermiculite. Cover the flat with a sheet of clear plastic and keep it in a warm, well-lighted place, but out of direct sunlight. Mist the leaves daily and pot them up as soon as the roots develop, in three or four weeks.

Tissue Culture

Some nurseries propagate bulbs in laboratories rather than in fields, using tissue culture. Under conditions that are so sterile that even the water used and the air that enters the building is sterilized, a tiny piece of bud tissue is cultured. Thousands of plants can be produced in a short period of time from a single parent plant in a medium-sized room. Another advantage is that the new bulbs are completely virus-free.

Growing Bulbs from Seed

Although we don't usually think of bulbs as originating from seeds, it's possible to grow many bulbous plants in this way. *Alliums*, certain *Anemones*, *Ranunculus*, tuberous begonias, and *Chionodoxas* are among those often grown from seeds. This kind of propagation takes more time and patience than growing plants from bulbs, but it is worthwhile and you may end up with some beautiful flowers of a type that never existed before.

Species plants nearly always come true from seed. Seedlings of species irises, snowdrops, and tiger and regal lilies reliably grow into plants that are replicas of their parent. But when you plant seeds from a cultivar, such as a 'King Alfred' daffodil or an 'Imperial Silver' lily, the

Place flat of seed-starting mix in a shallow pan of water to soak before planting seeds.

resulting plant is unlikely to be a copy of the parent. It could become a gorgeous beauty, or, quite possibly, a candidate for the compost pile. You never know, and for some folks, the fun of doing it is that gamble.

You may have noticed seed pods forming on some of your own bulbous plants when you haven't picked the flowers. Lilies, dahlias, gladioli, irises, and other summer bloomers set seeds readily, as do narcissus, lily-of-the-valley, and many of the low-growing spring bulbs we use for naturalizing.

Your own plants are good seed sources because you can plant the seeds fresh as soon as they ripen, just as nature does. Seeds also cost far less than bulbs; if you save your own, the price is only your labor. Some catalogs offer seed packets of both species plants and cultivars. Bulb societies sometimes furnish sources of seeds in their newsletters, as well as listings of members who would like to exchange them.

We prefer to plant seeds in outdoor seed beds as soon as they ripen, because they usually start to grow much faster than they would otherwise. Also, certain species need a cold period to stimulate germination. Most, however, will germinate if you dry them for a few days and store them in paper envelopes for later planting. Seeds planted at once germinate best, but some kinds still take several months to sprout, even if they were fresh when you planted them. More than once we have become discouraged and tossed out flats of unsprouted seeds, only to find them happily growing later in the compost pile.

When you're ready to plant, fill some flats nearly full of a seed-starting mix (**not** potting soil). Be careful not to fill them too full or water will run over the edge. Soak the mix thoroughly by setting the flat in a pan of water or by sprinkling it several times. Let it drain, and then spread the seeds thinly over the top. Cover them lightly with more of the same mix, or with a thin layer of fine perlite. Cover the flat with a sheet of plastic, and keep it in a warm place where it will get lots of light, but out of direct sunlight. Remove the plastic as soon as small green leaves appear.

After the seedlings sprout, water them in the morning so the foliage will be dry during the day and they'll be less likely to become infected by a damping-off disease. Once a week, mix a weak solution of liquid fertilizer with the water to encourage faster growth. Use an organic plant food such as liquid seaweed or fish emulsion, or a chemical plant food such as Miracle-Gro.

Thin the seedlings if you planted them too thick, so you can separate them easily later. After they are an inch or so tall, fill individual pots or flats with potting soil and transplant the seedlings into them. If you prefer to transplant them into large flats, space the seedlings an inch or more apart. Keep the containers watered and fertilized until fall. When the seedlings become

Transplant 1-inch-tall seedlings into individual pots.

dormant, dig up the tender plants such as gladioli, tuberous begonias, and dahlias. Dry their bulbs and store them indoors for the winter as described in chapter 11. The hardy bulbous plants — lilies, narcissus, and crocuses — will survive in a protected cold frame.

When you pick seed pods from bulb plants, they have been pollinated willy-nilly by insects. If you pollinate the flowers yourself, you can make choices about which plants give and receive the pollen, and thereby increase the chances of getting an outstanding new hybrid. Narcissus, gladioli, irises, and lilies are particu-

larly good plants for hybridizing. Detailed instructions are given in the following chapter.

As we said, you'll need patience while waiting for seedlings to produce bulbs and bloom. Although it may be several years before some produce their first blossoms, from experience we assure you that the excitement of seeing them is well worth the long wait. If the very first blooms are disappointing, however, do not despair and throw them away, because it often takes another year or so before they reach their peak.

15

Hybridizing Bulbous Plants

THE BIGGEST THRILL of bulb-growing for some gardeners comes when they produce a brand-new cultivar. It might compare in excitement with the pride of becoming a parent or the creation of a best-selling novel. Each year bulb lovers officially register and "introduce" many new lilies, irises, narcissus, tulips, cyclamens, and other bulbs that they have hybridized over a period of years. Breeders strive to develop plants that are better or more unusual in some way than previous cultivars in color, shape, size, length of bloom, plant vigor, disease resistance, hardiness, or other worthwhile attributes. Although we see expensive new cultivars with intriguing names listed in catalogs each year, only a few will eventually become bulb "classics." Most are destined to quietly disappear. Nevertheless, even those plants that are never registered bring a great deal of pleasure to the people who work with them.

Anyone can hybridize bulbs simply by moving pollen between two different flowers of the same genus of bulb, and collecting and planting the resulting seeds. Pollen is usually transmitted by insects, primarily bees, but it can also be carried a short distance by wind. Until horticulturists thoroughly understood the biological reproduction process of plants, most bulb cultivars were the results of this random pollination by nature. When an alert gardener spotted a plant that stood out as better than the others, he or she watched it for several years, then named and propagated it. Although some cultivars introduced today are still the results of nature's accidents, most now come from planned parenthood.

Choosing Parent Bulbs

It is easier to work with some plants than with others. Narcissus, tulips, crocuses, irises, gladioli, and lilies are good plants for beginners to hybridize. Bulbs that produce double blooms and those with tiny flowers are somewhat difficult to pollinate because their reproductive parts are hard to locate. Keep in mind that pollination takes place only within the same genus, with rare exceptions, so you must work with the various species and cultivars of a single genus. In other words, you can successfully hybridize the various species and cultivars of tulips, but it is a waste of time to try to cross a tulip with a narcissus. Crosses made between cultivars or varieties within the same species have the greatest chance of success.

Generally it is more worthwhile to work with named cultivars than with botanicals (species bulbs), because a great deal of hybridizing has already been done between different species and most of the possibilities are likely to have been exhausted.

When selecting the parents for your cross, look carefully at their attributes. If a prize-winning, blue-ribbon bloom is your goal, obviously you should start with attractive parents. You might aim for qualities such as unusual colors or color combinations, huge size, unique shape, many blooms on a stalk, fragrance, or a long blooming time, and choose parents that have tendencies in those directions. Most breeders also seek to add special qualities to the plant as well as the flower, and try, for example, to create a tulip that will bloom well for many years, a crocus that flowers over a long season, or a hyacinth that is hardy in most zones. You may want to search for qualities that enable a plant to do well in dry locations or in shade, to naturalize quickly, or to produce attractive foliage.

To get the qualities you want in a new plant, it may be necessary to choose one parent that may have an undesirable characteristic, such as a weak stem. You can lessen the chances of having that trait show up in the offspring by making certain that only one of the parents has the problem. For instance, if you are seeking a fragrant red lily, avoid choosing two parents with weak stems even if they both rate high in fragrance and color.

Hybridizers often work with many different generations of plants in their quest for an outstanding cultivar. In biology class most of us learned Mendel's law about dominant and recessive traits in animal and plant life. An understanding of this law helps breeders find those elusive combinations that produce winners. If, for example, a desired quality is missing in a new bulb grown from a seedling, the experts don't always throw it away immediately. Instead, they may make more crosses with it, hoping that properties of its less dominant genes show up in the second or third generation.

The number of possible combinations of genes of different cultivars is astronomical and bulb breeders frequently make thousands of crosses and plant thousands of resulting seeds, hoping to get one or two special bulbs. In spite of the most careful planning, hybridizing success still depends to a great extent on luck. Before you collect parent plants and begin to hybridize in a serious way, learn all you can about the process. Visit other breeders and view display gardens that feature new introductions; join the plant society that specializes in the kind of plant you are working with (see Appendix). The expertise of the members and their publications will help you take advantage of the progress that has already been made and give you information about the characteristics of the cultivars you want to improve.

Making the Cross

Once you have determined which parent plants you want to use, the fun begins. Before you start moving pollen around, review the way pollination works. For cross-pollination to take place, the yellow, reddish, or brown powdery *pollen* must be moved from the *anthers* at the tops of the *stamens* (male organs) of one flower to the tip of the *pistil* (female organ) of another flower. (The pistil is the long green stem that sticks out a bit beyond the cluster of pollen-covered stamens.) These organs are readily visible on such plants as tulips, crocuses, narcissus, irises, and lilies. Once moved, the pollen adheres to the sticky *stigma* at the top of the pistil and travels down the pistil's hollow tube to the *ovary* where it "mates" with the female ova. If all goes well, within three or four days after it has been fertilized, the seeds begin to develop.

When you cross-pollinate, it's important to work with pollen that is uncontaminated. Try to pollinate a flower immediately after it opens to prevent the bees from beating you to it. To be absolutely certain they don't, cover the bud on the flower that is to receive the pollen with a

The day before you plan to cross-pollinate, cover both donor and receiver buds with a bag to avoid contamination.

bag just before it opens; and cover in the same way the bud of the flower donating the pollen before it opens, since bees can easily mix the pollen on the stamens of one plant with that of another as they gather honey. Some hybridizers force open the buds a bit before nature does, so they can be sure the pollen will be uncontaminated. Bagging both flowers the day before you need them will also keep the pollen dry in case of rain or a heavy dew during the night. We like to make all crosses early in the day because the pollen of many plants is more viable then.

There are many ways to transfer pollen from one flower to another. You can use a small brush, but because brushes are difficult to clean between uses, hybridizers often favor Q-tips; by using a new one for each cross, they avoid mixing pollen. We like to pick one of the stamens from the male parent, and using the stem (filament) as a handle, dust the pollen onto the top of the pistil of the mother plant. This is possible only if both flowers open the same day, so if you want to pollinate a later-blooming bulb with an

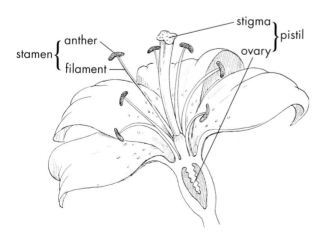

Parts of a flower

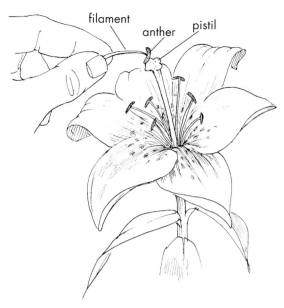

Pick a stamen from the donor plant and brush pollen from it onto the pistil of the receiver.

early-flowering one, you must store the pollen for a few days or weeks.

After dusting the pollen onto the pistil, replace the bag over the newly pollinated flower for a day to prevent any unwanted pollen from entering the pistil before yours has had a chance to work.

Seed production consumes a great deal of a plant's energy, so if you are working with bulbs such as lilies that produce several flowers on a stalk, it's best not to pollinate more than two or three flowers on each plant, and to allow only one of those to make seeds. Pick off all the remaining buds and flowers on the stalk after one seed pod has started to form, so that all the bulb's strength will go into developing seeds rather than producing more blossoms. It is a good idea to make crosses on more than one plant, however, for insurance, because few of us ever get 100-percent success when cross-pollinating. With some kinds of bulbs even experts feel lucky if pods form on more than half of their crosses.

Fasten a label on the stalk with its "pedigree," indicating date of cross, name of the mother plant (the one receiving the pollen), followed by an × and then the name of the father plant (the one donating the pollen). A typical notation on a narcissus might read, "7–2–94, 'King Alfred' × 'Arctic Gold'." If you make more than one cross between the same parents, indicate also the number of that cross.

Record all the information in a breeding program notebook. After the seeds have formed, make sure that their records follow them, from the time you place them in containers through the seedling and transplant stage, and all the years while you are evaluating their good and bad characteristics. The data will help you better calculate the consequence of each cross in working toward whatever goals you are seeking.

It takes several weeks for most seeds to fully mature. If you are working with tulips, narcissus, or irises, they will have plenty of time to

Plant label records a cross between the mother plant 'Enchantment' and the father plant 'Golden Showers'.

mature because they bloom early in the season, but with plants that bloom late such as lycoris and gladioli, pollinate some of the first blooms that open on the cultivars you want to cross. Because their growing season is so short, hybridizers in the North sometimes either work in a greenhouse or grow their plants in pots. Then they can move their work indoors after the weather cools, and the seeds can continue to mature.

Don't let the pod dry completely on the plant, or it may open and the seeds will scatter and be lost. Usually a pod first cracks open at the top — a good signal that you should harvest the seeds. If you plant them immediately there is no need for further drying, but if you must store them for a few weeks or more, spread the seeds on a tight mesh screen for additional drying after removing them from the pod. Knowing just how dry is dry enough for storage is difficult to guess. Any excess moisture will cause them to rot, but if they dry for too long, they won't germinate. Fortunately, unless you forget them for several weeks, they should germinate. For further directions about planting and growing seeds, see chapter 14.

Handling the Seedlings

Since it may take from two to four years from the planting of a bulb seed until the bulb is large enough to flower, this is not a hobby for the impatient. It also helps explain why new cultivars are expensive. Although sometimes you know right away that a plant is not worth further attention, a new bulb seldom shows great promise the first year it flowers, and you can't usually be certain for several more years whether or not you have something worth growing. Many times we have written detailed descriptions of a flower, only to find that in future years the plant got quite different ratings. Some showed improvement, but others peaked early and never

managed to provide a worthy encore. Some professional hybridizers feel that it is important to evaluate a new bulb for fifteen to twenty years before registering it.

When a quality bulb appears in your collection, assign it a number so it can be identified for possible registration or for use in hybridizing more promising seedlings. If you select any of your first generation seedlings (called F1 for first filial generation) for future breeding you can *line cross* them with some of the most promising of the new plants that originated from the seeds of the same parents, *backcross* them with one of their parents, or *outcross* them with completely unrelated cultivars of the same genus. The second generation of seedlings resulting from these crosses is referred to as F2.

Storing Pollen

At some time you will probably want to cross-pollinate two cultivars that do not blossom at the same time, or select pollen from a spectacular bulb belonging to a friend far away. If you keep it cool and dry, you can store pollen safely for some time. Hybridizers sometimes use empty gelatin capsules for storage, because they can seal them tight. Others dust Q-tips with pollen and cut them to a size that fits nicely into the tight plastic 35-millimeter film containers. Still others pick and store the pollen-covered anthers (the tips of the stamens). If you do this, don't include any of the filament (stem portion) because it contains moisture that can cause the pollen to spoil in a short time.

Label each container with the bulb's name and the date. The pollen should last for a week unrefrigerated. Refrigerated, it can stay viable for the entire hybridizing season; if frozen, it should be good for a year. To use the stored pollen, dust it on with a Q-tip, and keep the storage container out of the sun at all times.

Registering New Cultivars

You can get information about how to register and introduce a new plant cultivar from the plant society that deals with your particular bulb (see Appendix). Unless you are positive that you have a plant that is truly superior and unusual, however, it isn't doing the world's plant registry a favor to introduce it. Also, if you have a good seedling plant but don't plan to register it, be sure not to give it a name. Chances are that the name you choose will be one already in use, and if you give bulbs away, your friends may pass their misnamed plants on to others, and you will have added to the confusion of plant nomenclature that already exists.

Even if, like most of us, you never introduce an 'Enchantment' lily, or a 'Thalia' narcissus, you can still have a lot of fun moving the pollen from flower to flower. It is exciting to watch the first buds develop on a new bulb and be on hand for the "grand opening." You'll enjoy the many surprises that appear in your seedling bed, and even though you may not decide to take your originations to flower shows, you'll no doubt create quite a few that look smashing in your flower border.

APPENDICES

Metric Conversions

Dimension

1 inch = 25.4 millimeters
or
1 inch = 2.54 centimeters

1 foot = .305 meter

1 yard = .915 meter

1 square foot = .0929 square meter

1 square yard = .8361 square meter

Weight

1 pound = 454 grams
or
1 pound = .454 kilogram

Volume

1 pint (dry) = .55 liter

1 pint (liquid) = .47 liter

1 quart (liquid) = .95 liter

1 bushel = 35.24 liters

Bulb-Growers' Calendar

January

✓ Cut down on watering your Christmas amaryllis after the blooms have faded.

✓ Care for the paper-white narcissus Aunt Betty gives you every year.

✓ Check the bulbs you potted last fall for forcing to see if any sprouts have started. Bring one or two pots out of storage, put them in a sunny window, and begin watering.

✓ Order seeds and summer-flowering bulbs and plants.

February

✓ Plant seeds of tuberous begonias.

✓ Move any potted forced bulbs that are blooming out of the sun so the flowers will last longer. Bring more out of storage for continuous blooms.

March

✓ Start seeds of bedding dahlias, lilies, and others.

✓ Plant tuberous begonia tuber-corms in flats indoors.

✓ Pot up some dahlia tubers and canna rhizomes for early blooms.

✓ Check early-sprouting plants for winter and rodent damage.

✓ Fertilize summer-flowering bulbs as soon as the ground thaws.

✓ Remove the mulch put on solely for winter protection. Renew mulch on permanent plantings.

✓ Watch for disease on newly sprouted seeds.

April

✓ Take time to enjoy the garden at the height of its spring bloom. Cut off faded blooms, and make a list of bulbs to order for fall planting.

✓ Till land as soon as it dries out for later planting of summer bulbs, small bulblets, bulbils, and cormels.

✓ Label narcissus and any other spring-flowering bulbs that you plan to dig later so you can find them.

May

✓ Dig tulips after blooms have faded. Lay the bulbs on the ground in an unused part of the garden. Cover the bulbs with soil, but leave the green tops sticking out. Leave them there until the tops die completely, then dig them up, cut off the tops, dry the bulbs for a few days, and store them in paper bags in a cool, dry place for early fall planting.

✓ Set out annuals over deeply planted narcissus and other bulbs. They will help hide the dying foliage and will furnish summer color.

✓ Plant tender summer-flowering bulbous plants such as gladioli, dahlias, and tuberous begonias in spots where the tulips were removed.

✓ Set out bulblets, cormels, and so on in well-prepared beds to grow for future planting.

✓ Begin regular spraying with a fungicide if botrytis or powdery mildew is a problem.

✓ Water everything if necessary.

✓ Add liquid fertilizers to plants making slow growth.

June

✓ Check plantings for insects and diseases. Start control measures if necessary.
✓ Remove faded blooms.
✓ Stake tall-growing plants.
✓ Order spring-blooming bulbs for fall planting.
✓ Keep up any necessary watering.

July–August

✓ Remove side branches of exhibition-type dahlias so blooms will be bigger.
✓ Take cuttings from tuberous begonias and dahlias to start more plants.
✓ Continue watering and pest control when necessary.
✓ Gather bulbils from lilies you want to propagate.
✓ Remove faded blooms and any diseased leaves.

September–October

✓ Get beds ready for planting bulbs.
✓ Protect them from rodents.
✓ Make charts of all new plantings.
✓ Pot spring bulbs and put them into storage for winter blooms.
✓ Fertilize established beds of bulbs.
✓ Place leaves or other mulch over all bulb plantings for winter protection.

November–December

✓ Buy tender bulbs such as amaryllis, calla lilies, and paper-white narcissus to pot up for indoor winter blooms.
✓ Consider sharing some of the plants potted for forcing with friends who are shut-in at home or in nursing homes or hospitals. They will enjoy watching them come to life and bloom.
✓ Take a well-deserved rest from your gardening chores, but keep an eye out for early-arriving bulb and seed catalogs.

Bulb Organizations

The addresses of plant societies may change frequently as different officers are elected. If you have difficulty locating a society, please contact the American Horticultural Society for the current address.

American Begonia Society
P.O. Box 5
Bio Dell, CA 95562-0056

American Daffodil Society
1686 Grey Fox Trails
Milford, OH, 45150
(513-248-9137)

American Dahlia Society
10 Roland Place
Wayne, NJ 07470-3421
(201-694-4864)

American Horticultural Society
Box 7931 East Boulevard Drive
Alexandria, VA 22308

American Iris Society
8426 Vine Valley Road
Sun Valley, CA 91352
(818-767-5512)

Indoor Gardening Society of America
5305 SW Hamilton Street
Portland, OR 97221

New England Wild Flower Society
Garden in the Woods
180 Hemenway Road
Framingham, MA 01701-2699
(508-877-7630)

North American Lily Society
Box 272, Owatonna
MN 55060
(507-451-2170)

North American Gladiolus Council
Salt Lake City, UT
(801-277-9576)

National Wildflower Research Center
2600 FM973
North, Austin, TX 78725-4201
(512-929-3600)

Bulb Books for Gardeners

Anderson, Eric, and Ron Park. *Growing Gladioli*. Portland, OR: Timber Press, 1990.

Art, Henry. *A Garden of Wildflowers*. Pownal, VT: Storey Communications, 1986.

Barnes, Don. *Daffodils: For Home, Garden and Show*. Portland, OR: Timber Press, 1987.

Catterall, Eric. *Growing Begonias*. Portland, OR: Timber Press, 1984.

Catterini, Robert (editor), trans. by J.M. Vasser and A. A. de Hertogh. *Spring-Flowering Bulbs*. Venissieux, France: Horticolor, 1985.

Damp, Philip. *Growing Lilies*. Croom Helm.

deWolfe, Jr., Gordon(editor) *Taylor's Guide to Bulbs*. Boston: Houghton Mifflin, 1986.

duPlessis, Niel, and Duncan Graham. *Bulbous Plants of Southern Africa: A Guide to Their Cultivation and Propagation*. Cape Town, South Africa: Tafelberg Pub., Ltd., 1989.

Hill, Lewis. *Secrets of Plant Propagation*. Pownal, VT: Storey Communications, 1985.

Jefferson-Brown, Michael. *Narcissus*. Portland, OR: Timber Press, 1991.

Kohlein, Fritz. *Iris*. Portland, OR: Timber Press, 1987.

Lodewijk, T. *The Book of Tulips*. Portland, OR: Timber Press, 1987.

Nightingale, Gay. *Growing Cyclamen*. Portland OR:T imber Press, 1987.

Phillips, Roger, and Martyn Rix. *The Random House Book of Bulbs*. New York: Random House, 1989.

Price, Molly. *The Iris Book*. New York: Dover Publications, 1973.

Rix, E. Martyn. *Growing Bulbs*. Portland OR: Timber Press, 1983.

Time-Life Gardeners Guide: Bulbs. Alexandria, VA: Time-Life Books.

Wells, J.S. *Modern Miniature Daffodils*. Portland, OR: Timber Press, 1989.

Wilder, Lucy Beebe. *Adventures with Hardy Bulbs*. New York: Macmillan, 1990. Reprint of 1936 classic.

Mail-Order Suppliers

Be sure that your supplier sells only bulbs that have been propagated commercially, not collected in the wild. For further information, write Faith Campbell, Natural Resources Defense Council, 1350 New York Avenue, NW, Washington, DC 20005.

Amaryllis, Inc.
P.O. Box 318
Baton Rouge, LA 70821
  Catalog $1.00, refundable, amaryllis

B and D Lilies
330 "P" Street
Port Townsend, WA 98368
206-385-1738
  Catalog $3.00, refundable, lilies

Bonnie Brae Gardens
1105 S.E. Christensen Road
Corbett, OR 97019
  Catalog free, narcissus

Borbeleta Gardens, Inc.
15980 Canby Avenue
Faribault, MN 55021–7652
507-334-2807
  Lilies, Siberian iris, daylilies, bearded and dwarf iris

Breck's of Holland
6523 North Galena Road
Peoria, IL 61632
309-689-3850
  Catalog free, spring bulbs

The Bulb Crate
2560 Deerfield Road
Riverwoods, IL 60015
708-317-1414
  Catalog free, lilies

Bundles of Bulbs
112 Greenspring Valley Road
Owings Mills, MD 21117
401-581-2188
  Catalog $2.00, spring bulbs

W. Atlee Burpee and Co.
300 Park Avenue
Warminster, PA 18974
800-888-1447
  Catalog free, spring bulbs

Cascade Daffodils
P.O. Box 10626
White Bear Lake, MN 55110
  Catalog $2.00, narcissus

Cooley's Gardens
11553 Silverton Road N.E.
P.O. Box 126
Silverton, OR 97381–0126
503-873-5463
  Catalog $4.00 (refundable with order), iris

The Daffodil Mart
Rt. 3, Box 794
Gloucester, VA 23061
804-693-3966
  Catalog free, fall bulbs

Dutch Gardens
P.O. Box 200
Adelphia, NJ 07710-0200
908-780-2713
  Catalog free, bulbs

French's Bulb Importer
Box 565
Pittsfield, VT 05762-0565
  Catalog free, imported bulbs

Russell Graham
4030 Eagle Crest Road N.W.
Salem, OR 97304
503-362-1135
  Catalog $2.00, refundable, cyclamens and others

Holland Bulb Co.
14071 Arndt Road, NE
Aurora, OR 97002
503-678-3200
  Catalog 2.00, lilies

Jackson and Perkins
2518 S. Pacific Highway
P.O. Box 1028
Medford, OR 97501-9813
503-776-2000
  Catalog free, spring bulbs

J.W. Jung Seed Co.
335 South High Street
Randolph, WI 53957
414-326-3121
  Catalog free, bulbs and seeds

McClure and Zimmerman
P.O. Box 368
Friesland, WI 53935–0368
  Catalog free, wide variety of bulbous plants

Messelaar Bulb Co., Inc.
P.O. Box 269
Ipswich, MA 01938
508-356-3737
Catalog free, spring bulbs

Michigan Bulb Co.
1950 Waldorf NW
Grand Rapids, MI 49550-0500
616-771-9500
Catalog free, bulbs

Grant E. Mitsch Novelty
Daffodils
P.O. Box 218
Hubbard, OR 97032
*Catalog $3.00, refundable,
daffodils*

Charles H. Mueller Co.
7091 River Road
New Hope, PA 18938
215-862-2033
Catalog free, bulbs

The Onion Man
30 Mt. Lebanon Street
Pepperell, MA 01463
*Seedlist, Allium species and
cultivars.*

Oregon Trail Daffodils
41905 SE Louden Road
Corbett, OR 97019
Catalog free, spring bulbs

Park Seed Co.
Cokesbury Road
Highway 254 N
Greenwood, SC 29648–0046
803-223-8555
Catalog free, seeds and bulbs

Pinetree Garden Seeds
Route 100, Box 300
New Gloucester, ME 04260
Catalog free, bulbs and seeds

Prairie Nursery
P.O. Box 306
Westfield, WI 53964
608-296-3679
*Catalog $3 for 2-year subscrip-
tion, bulbs for all seasons, wild
lilies, iris*

John Scheepers, Inc.
P.O. Box 700
Bantam, CT 06750
203-567-0838
*Catalog free, bulbs for all
seasons*

Schriners Iris Gardens
3625 Quinaby Rd. N.E.
Salem, OR 97303
503-393-3232
*Catalog $4 (refundable with
order), iris*

Smith and Hawken
35 Corte Madera
Mill Valley, CA 94941
415-381-1800
*Catalog free, potted bulb plants,
bulbs for forcing*

Sunlight Gardens
174 Golden Lane
Andersonville, TN 37705
615-494-8237
*Catalog $3.00 for 2-year
subscription, wildflowers*

Swan Island Dahlias
P.O. Box 700
Canby, OR 97013
503-266-7711
Catalog $3.00, dahlias

Territorial Seed Company
P.O. Box 157
Cottage Grove, OR 97424
503-942-9547
Catalog free, bulbs.

Thompson & Morgan
P.O. Box 1308
Jackson, NJ 08527
908-363-2225
*Catalog free, seeds, bulbs, and
plants*

Tranquil Lake Nursery, Inc.
45 River Street
Rehoboth, MA 02769–1395
508-252-4002
*Catalog free, Japanese,
Siberian, and species iris*

Van Bourgondien Bros.
245 Farmingdale Road
P.O. Box 1000
Babylon, NY 11702
516-669-3500
*Catalog free, spring and
summer bulbs*

Van Engelen, Inc.
313 Maple Street
Litchfield, CT 06759
203-567-8734
Catalog free, spring bulbs

Mary Mattison van Schaik
Dutch Bulbs
Cavendish, VT 05142
Catalog, imported bulbs

Veldheer Tulip Garden
12755 Quincy Street
Holland, MI 49424
616-399-1900
*Catalog free, spring and other
bulbs*

Wayside Gardens
1 Garden Lane
Hodges, SC 29695–0001
800-845-1124
  *Catalog free, spring and
  summer bulbs*

White Flower Farm
Route 63
Litchfield, CT 06759–0050
203-496-9600
  *Catalog free, wide range of
  bulbs*

Nancy R. Wilson
6525 Briceland-Thorn Road
Garberville, CA 95542
707-923-2407
  *Catalog $1, miniature and
  species narcissus*

Nurseries Offering Reblooming Iris Rhizomes

Amberway Gardens
5803 Amberway Drive
St. Louis, MO 63128
  *Catalog $1.00, refundable,
  minimum order $15.00*

Mid-America Iris Garden
3409 N. Geraldine
Oklahoma City, OK 73112
  *Catalog $2.00, minimum order
  $10.00*

Nicholis Gardens
4724 Angus Drive
Gainesville, VA 22065
  *Catalog $1.00, minimum order
  $10.00*

Rialto Gardens
1146 W. Rialto Avenue
Fresno, CA 93705
  Catalog free

Canadian and English Nurseries Selling Bulbous Plants and Seeds

Chiltern Seeds
Bortree Stile
Ulverston, Cumbria, LA127PB
England
  Catalog $3.00, seeds

C. A. Cruickshank, Ltd.
1015 Mt. Pleasant Road
Toronto, Ontario M4P 2M1
Canada
  Catalog $2.00, bulbs

Ferncliff Gardens
8394 McTaggart Street
Mission, BC V2V 6S6
Canada
604-826-2447
  Catalog free, iris, dahlias

McMath's Daffodils
6340 Francis Road
Richmond, BC V7C 1K5
Canada
  Catalog, daffodils and narcissus

McMillen's Iris Garden
RR1
Norwich, Ontario N0J 1P0
519-468-6508
  Catalog $2.00, iris

Sheppard's Bulb Farm
6707 Bradner Road, RR1
Mount Lehman, BC V4X 2C9
Canada
604-857-0915

Beneficial Insects and Other Pest Controls

Bob Bauer
311 Ford Road
Howell, NJ 07731
908-370-8351

Gardener's Supply Co.
128 Intervale Road
Burlington, VT 05401
802-863-1700
  Catalog free

Gardens Alive!
5100 Schenley Place
Lawrenceburg, IN 47025
812-537-8650
  *Catalog free, source of espe-
  cially refined oil spray*

Growing Naturally
P.O. Box 54
149 Pine Lane
Pineville, PA 18946

Harmony Farm Supply and
  Nursery
P.O. Box 460
Graton, CA 95444
  *Catalog of supplies, including
  especially refined oil spray*

Mantis Eddy
R.D. 1, Box 224
Newpark, PA 17352

Necessary Trading Co.
One Nature's Way
New Castle, VA 24127–0305
703-864-5103
  Catalog free

Ringer Corp.
9959 Valley View Road
Eden Prairie, MN 55344–3585
612-941-4180

Garden Supplies and Equipment

Gardeners Eden
P.O. Box 7307
San Francisco, CA 94120
800-922-5507
Catalog free

Johnny's Selected Seeds
Foss Hill Road
Albion, ME 04910–9731
207-437-9294
Catalog free

A.M. Leonard, Inc.
P.O. Box 816
Piqua, OH 45356
513-773-2694
Catalog free

Park Seed Co.
P.O. Box 31
Cokesbury Road
Greenwood, SC 29647
803-223-8555
Catalog free

Pinetree Garden Seeds
Box 300
New Gloucester, ME 04260
207-926-4112
Catalog free, organic pesticides, fertilizers, soil conditioners; garden equipment, books

Smith and Hawken
35 Corte Madera
Mill Valley, CA 94941
415-381-1800
Catalog free

Other Supplies

Gardener's Supply Co.
128 Intervale Road
Burlington, VT 05401
802-863-1700
Catalog free, earthworms

Travel and Flower Show Information

Netherlands Board of
Tourism
355 Lexington Avenue
New York, NY 10017
312-819-0300
(Travel to Holland Information Line)

For "Tulip Time Festival" in Holland, Michigan, call the Holland Visitors Bureau, 800-822-2770 (outside Michigan).

For the bulbs festival in Orange City, Iowa, write to the Chamber of Commerce, P.O. Box 36, Orange City, Iowa 51041.

Glossary

Acid soil. Soil with a pH of less than 7.

Alkaline soil. Soil that has a pH greater than 7.

Annual plant. One that blooms, produces seeds, and dies the same year.

Anther. The top of a stamen; it contains the pollen.

Asexual reproduction. The propagation of a plant by cuttings, division, grafts, layers, tissue culture, or other vegetative means, rather than by seeds.

Axil. The angle formed by a petiole and the stem from which it is growing.

Axis. The main stalk of a compound leaf or flower cluster. The stem of a plant.

Bare-rooted. A plant that is transplanted without soil attached to its roots.

Basal. Describing the bottom or base of a plant. A basal shoot is a sprout or branch that grows near the ground. A basal cut is made near the bottom of a cutting.

Beard. Fine filaments or hair that cover the basal half portion of the falls on certain iris.

Bicolored. Two-colored blossoms.

Bract. Leaves growing close to and often surrounding a flower, so that they appear to be part of the bloom.

Border. A flower bed, usually consisting of a variety of plants.

Bud. A young shoot that can develop into a leaf or a flower.

Bulb. The fleshy root of plants such as lilies, tulips, and similar plants.

Bulbil. Small bulbs that form in the axils along the stems of certain plants such as tiger lilies.

Bulblet. Baby bulbs that develop around the larger bulbs below the ground.

Callus. A fleshy tissue growth that forms on a plant while a wound is healing. On cuttings it often, but not always, precedes the development of roots.

Calyx. The collective term for the sepals of a flower.

Clone. New plant that is started asexually, especially one started by tissue culture.

Cold frame. An outside seed bed or plant bed enclosed by a frame with a removable transparent cover, intended for growing plants in a protected environment with no artificial heat.

Compost. Rich, porous soil made of thoroughly decomposed organic matter. Excellent for building up worn-out soil.

Corm. Fleshy root similar to a bulb, but consisting of a solid stem. Gladiolus plants grow from corms.

Cormel. Small corms that form around the parent. These can be removed to plant and grow into new plants.

Corolla. The collective term for the petals of a flower.

Corona. A tubular structure at the center of flowers such as narcissus. Long coronas are called trumpets; short ones are cups.

Crest. The ridge on a petal, a cluster of flowers, or leaves.

Cross-pollination. The transfer of pollen from the anther of one plant to the pistil of a flower on another plant.

Crown. The base of a plant stem, usually at ground level.

Cultivar. Named variety of a plant that is usually an improvement from the species and different from other cultivars. It is usually, but not always, necessary to propagate cultivars by asexual means. A cultivar is indicated by single quotes, as in 'Roseum'.

Cup. A short corona.

Cutting. A piece of branch, leaf, or root that is separated from a plant and rooted to create a new plant of the same variety.

Deadheading. The removal of faded blooms.

Deciduous. Plants that lose their leaves at the end of their growing season and are not evergreen.

Division. The propagation of a plant by dividing it into two or more pieces, with roots and leaves or buds on each one.

Dormancy. The rest period of a plant during which it is not growing or showing signs of life. Also refers to seeds before they sprout.

Double flower. Having more than the normal number of petals.

Edging plants. Dwarf, compact plants that are used for the front of a border, or for planting along paths or steps.

Escape. A plant that has escaped from cultivation and is growing successfully in the wild.

Evergreen. Plants that retain their foliage for more than one growing season.

Eye. A bud. With perennials, it usually refers to a dormant bud growing on the root.

Fall. A sepal of an iris flower, usually hanging downward.

Floret. An individual flower in a cluster.

Germination. The sprouting of seeds.

Ground cover. A low-growing plant that spreads rapidly either through seeds, by underground stems that form new plants, or by horizontal top growth that layers into new plants.

Harden off. The process whereby perennials and annuals that have been started indoors are gradually exposed to outdoor conditions.

Herbaceous plant. A plant with stems above the ground that do not become woody.

Herbicide. A chemical that is used for killing unwanted plants or to prevent seeds in the ground from sprouting.

Humidity. The amount of moisture in the air.

Humus. Partly or wholly decomposed organic matter.

Hybrid. A new plant variety developed by the cross-pollination of two plants that are genetically different. Hybrids are indicated by x, as in *Begonia x tuberhybrida*.

Insecticide. A chemical for killing insects.

Invasive. Describing plants that spread out of control.

Island. A flower bed surrounded by lawn or water.

Leaflet. A portion of a compound leaf with no bud in its axil.

Loam. Soil that is rich in humus.

Mature plant. A plant that is old enough to produce blooms and seeds.

Mulch. A protective covering for the soil. Spread around plants it helps to control temperature, check evaporation, and protect against extreme winter temperatures. Organic mulches enrich the soil as they rot.

Named variety. Another term for cultivar.

Naturalized. Describing plants that are well established in a natural setting. In a planting, those that have been set to appear natural.

Neutral soil. Soil that is neither acid or alkaline, having a pH of 7.

Offset or **Offshoot.** A small plant growing from the main stem of a perennial, just under the ground. Often these can be severed from the parent and grown into new plants.

Ovary. The base of the pistil (female portion of a flower) where the seeds are produced.

Peat moss. Sphagnum moss that is partially

decomposed.

Peat pellets. Small pellets of peat that swell up when watered. They are often used for rooting cuttings or starting seeds.

Pendulous. Flowers that hang loosely on the stem.

Perennial. A plant that lives for more than two years. Commonly refers to herbaceous flowering plants that may or may not be winter hardy.

Perianth. The collective term for the calyx, corolla, and corona.

pH. A symbol indicating the concentration of hydrogen ions in soil that represents the degree of alkalinity or acidity of the soil; the higher numbers indicate increased alkalinity and 7 is neutral. Most garden soils range from 5 to 6½ in pH, and the majority of perennials can grow well within this latitude. Some plants, how ever, demand conditions that are more or less acid.

Petal. One of the series of flower parts arranged outside the stamens and pistil, and inside the sepals; collectively, the corolla.

Picotee. A flower with an outer margin of a different color, as in irises and tuberous begonias.

Pistil. The female reproductive organ in a flower. It consists of an ovary, style, and stigma.

Plicata. Petals of one color with borders of different colors, as in irises.

Pollen. The dustlike particles produced by the male stamens on a flower. They are usually brown or yellow in color, and with most perennials, are spread from flower to flower by bees. With ornamental grasses, pollen is transferred by the wind.

Pollination. The fertilization of the female ova of a plant by the transfer of pollen from the male portion of the same or a different flower, resulting in a seed. In addition to pollination by insects and wind, it also can be done by artificial means, and gardeners often hybridize with a small paint brush or Q-tip.

Propagate. To produce new plants either from seeds or by rooting a part of a plant.

Raceme. A long flower cluster on a central stalk.

Reflexed. Petals that curve backward toward the stem.

Rhizome. The fleshy root of a plant such as iris.

Rock garden. A garden consisting of low-growing, spreading plants growing among rocks, often set on a slope.

Scale. A modified leaf that may cover a bud. In true bulbs the scales are bases of leaves that swell with stored food. The scales on lilies are very pronounced, on tulips they are much tighter. Scales are also small insects that feed on plants. Peel off the loose outer scales of a bulb, and use them to start new plants.

Scape. The leafless stalk on which the flowers of some plants, such as lycoris, are produced.

Selection. The choosing of the best of a group of seedlings or wild plants to propagate or use for breeding.

Sepal. One of the series of flower parts arranged outside the stamens and pistil, and outside the petals; collectively, the calyx.

Shade. A reduced amount of sunlight, preferred by some bulbs. Light shade usually refers to a few hours of morning or late afternoon sun, but considerable skylight all day long. Moderate shade is filtered light as that coming though trees with light foliage, but little or no direct sun at any time. Heavy shade is that under trees with thick foliage, and is suitable for only a few plant species.

Spadix. A floral spike with a fleshy axis, usually enclosed in a spathe.

Spathe. A bract that encloses the flowers in some plants such as calla lilies.

Species. Groups of plants within a genus that have the potential to breed freely with each other but not with plants outside the genus.

Stamen. The male reproductive organ in a flower. It produces pollen.

Standard. An iris petal that usually stands upright.

Stolon. An unthickened rhizome from which

new plants sprout and grow.

Subspecies. A naturally occurring, slight variant of a species.

Systemic. Chemicals that a plant absorbs which then permeate it. Certain insecticides, herbicides, and fungicides are systemic.

Terminal. Describing the bud or spike at the tip of the central stem of a plant.

Tissue culture. The asexual propagation of plants by the rapid increase of cell growth under carefuly controlled conditions of temperature, nutrition, pH, and sanitation in a laboratory.

Transpiration. The process of losing moisture by a plant, usually through its leaves.

Trumpet. A long corona.

Tuber. Fleshy root of a plant in which food is stored. Dahlias grow from tubers.

Tuber-corm. A flat disk-shaped bulbous root resembling a top. Buds emerge from the top and fibrous roots from the base.

Tunic. The thin, paperlike layer that covers some bulbs such as tulips.

Umbel. A cluster of flowers that all come from the same point.

Unisexual flower. A flower that has either stamens or a pistil, but not both.

Variety. A classification of naturally occurring plants that consistently differ slightly from the main species. Formerly it also referred to named cultivated plants, but those are now properly called cultivars. A variety is indicated by var., as in *Hyacinthus orientalis* var. *albulus*.

Vegetative propagation. Propagation other than by seeds.

Viability. The ability of a bulb to grow or a seed to germinate.

Water stress. The condition whereby a plant loses water faster than absorbs it.

Whorl. A group of three or more leaves or shoots all coming from a single node.

Wild garden. A planting purposely planned to appear natural and uncultivated. It may consist completely of native plants, or include natural-looking exotics as well.

Index

Italic page numbers indicate illustrations.

B

Ballhead onion. *See Allium sphaerocephalum*
Basket flower. *See Hymenocallis*
Batalin tulip. *See Tulipa batalinii*
Bearded iris. *See Iris* x *germanica*
Beds and borders, bulbs for, 10
Beetles, 47
Begonia (tuberous), 10, 21, *152*
    culture, 139
    description of, 138–40
    pruning and disbudding, 139
    storing, 139–40, *140*
Bloom care, after, 41, *41*
Blooming problems, 40, 41
Blooming times
    for spring bulbs, 20
    for summer and fall bulbs, 21
Bluebells. *See Endymion hispanicus/Scilla campanulata; Muscari*
Blue globe onion. *See Allium caeruleum/azureum*
Borers, 47, 121
Botrytis, 45, 121
Brazil oxalis. *See Oxalis braziliensis*
Brodiae. See Triteleia
Brown's lily. *See Lilium brownii*
Bud blast, 45
Bugle-lily. *See Watsonia*
Bulbil lily. *See Lilium bulbiferum*
Bulbils, 8, *8*, 131, *179*
Bulblets, 6, *6*, 8, 130, 177–78
Bulbocodium vernum, 12, 20
Bulbs
    botanical versus common names for, 7–8
    difference between true bulbs and their relatives, 5–7, *6*, *7*
    displays, 25–26
    height and color of, and planting tips, 15–18
    history of, 4–5
    idiosyncrasies of, 12, 14–15
    selecting, 27–31
    use of the term, 5
Buttercup. *See Ranunculus*
Buying bulbs
    in bloom, 29
    mail-order suppliers, 28, 200–202

C

Caladium, 21, 140–41
Calla lily. *See Zantedeschia*
Camass. *See Camassia*
Camassia, 20, 98–99
    cusickii (Cusick camass), 62, 99
    leichtlinii, 99
    quamash, 99
    scilloides (Wild hyacinth), 99
Canada lily. *See Lilium canadense*
Canna, 10, 21
    aranyalon, *149*
    description of, 141–42
    x *generalis* (Common garden canna), 141
    indica (Indian shot), 141, *149*
Cape cowslip. *See Lachenalia*
Cardiocrinum giganteum, 31
Carolina spring beauty. *See Claytonia caroliniana*
Caucasian lily. *See Lilium monadelphum*
Chilling period, 33, 69
Chionodoxa, 4
    blooming times, 20
    description of, 99
    height of, 23
    luciliae, 62, 99
    for naturalizing, 56, 59, 62
    sardensis, 62, 99
Chives. *See Allium schoenoprasum*
Christmas fern. *See Polystichum acrostichoides*
Claytonia, 99
    caroliniana (Carolina spring beauty), 99
    megarhiza, 99
    virginica, 99
Cliff tulip. *See Tulipa saxatilis*
Clivia, 170
Cloth-of-gold crocus. *See Crocus angustifolius*
Colchicum, 10, 11, 12
    autumnale (Autumn crocus), 160–61
    blooming times, 21
    byzantinum, 161
    cilicicum, 161
    culture, 160
    differences between *Crocus* and, 159
    height of, 23
    luteum, 160
    for naturalizing, 56, 58, 62
    species, 160–61
    speciosum (Showy autumn crocus), 62, 161

E

Easter lily. *See Lilium longiflorum*
Elephant's-ear. *See Caladium; Colocasia*
Endymion
    hispanicus/Scilla campanulata (Spanish bluebells),
        20, 24, 53, 56, 100–101, *107*
    non-scriptus (English bluebells), 101
English bluebells. *See Endymion non-scriptus*
English iris. *See Iris xiphioides*
Eranthis, 20, 56, 101
    cilicica (Winter aconite), 31
    hyemalis (Winter aconite), 31, 63, 101
    x *Tubergenii* (Tubergen winter aconite), 101
Eremurus, 20
Erythronium, 20, 101–2
    americanum, 101–2
    dens-canis (Dog-tooth violet), 102
    revolutum (Mahogany fawn lily), 102
    tuolumnense, *108*
Eucomis, 118

F

Fall bulbs
    for beds and borders, 10
    blooming times for, 21
    for cut flower gardens, 10
    for ground covers, 11
    planting, 33
    for rock gardens, 12
Ferns, 19, 22
Fertilizers, 35–36, 37, 40, 61
    for forcing bulbs, 68
Flame anemone. *See Anemone x fulgens*
Florentine tulip. *See Tulipa sylvestris*
Forcing bulbs, 43
    chilling, 69
    containers for, 67, *67*, 68
    cultivars for, 74
    hyacinths, 73–74
    Narcissus tazetta (paper-white), 72–73
    planting methods, 67–69, *68*
    preparing for blooming, 69–71
    soil for, 67–68
    staking, 70–71, *70*
    tender bulbs, 72
    transplanting and saving, 71–72
    in water, 72, 73
    watering, 68–69
Formosa lily. *See Lilium formosanum*
Foster tulip. *See Tulipa fosteriana*
Foxtail lily. *See Eremurus*
Freesia, 72, 172
Fritillaria, 102
    imperialis (Crown imperial) 20, 23, 102
    meleagris (Guinea-hen flower), 20
    persica (Persian fritillary), 102
    pudica (Yellow bell), 102
Fritillary. *See Fritillaria*
Fungal diseases, 44–45, 120–21

G

Galanthus, 3, 11, 31
    blooming times, 20
    in containers, 24
    description of, 102–3
    elwesii (Giant snowdrop), 63, 103
    height of, 23
    for naturalizing, 56, 59, 63
    nivalis (Common snowdrop), 11, 31, 56, 63, 103
Galtonia, 145, *149*
Garlic. *See Allium*
Giant allium. *See Allium giganteum*
Giant snowdrop. *See Galanthus elwesii*
Gladiolus, 19, *112*
    blooming times, 21
    choosing, 146–47
    cultivars and species, 151
    description of, 146–52
    diseases and insects affecting, 46
    grandiflorus, *147*
    overwintering the corms, 149–50
    planting and culture, 147–49
    tubergenii 'Charm', *147*
Gladiolus, Abyssinian. *See Acidanthera*
Gloriosa
    description of, 153–54
    rothschildiana (Rothschild gloriosa-lily), 21, 154
    superba (Malabar gloriosa-lily), 154
Glory-of-the-snow. *See Chionodoxa*
Gloxinia. *See Sinningia*
Gold-banded lily. *See Lilium auratum*
Golden calla. *See Zantedeschia elliottiana*
Golden garlic. *See Allium moly*

Golden lycoris. *See Lycoris africana/aurea*
Grape hyacinth. *See Muscari*
Grass nut. *See Tritelia laxa*
Gray mold, 45
Gray's lily. *See Lilium grayi*
Greig tulip. *See Tulipa greigii*
Ground covers, bulbs for, 10–11
Guinea-hen flower. *See Fritillaria meleagris*

H

Hager tulip. *See Tulipa hageri*
Hardiness, 28–29, 30
Height
    bulbs classified by, 23
    planting tips, 15–18
Hermodactylus/Iris tuberosa, 31, 103
Heterosporium leaf spots, 121
Hippeastrum, 172–73
Humboldt lily. *See Lilium humboldtii*
Hyacinthus, 10
    blooming times, 20
    candicans (summer hyacinth), 145
    cultivars for forcing, 74
    culture, 79
    description of, 78–79
    forcing, 70, 73–74, 79
    orientalis, 78, 80
    propagation, 79–80, 79
    varieties and cultivars, 80
Hybridizing, 187
    choosing parent bulbs, 187
    cross-pollination, 188–90
    handling seedlings, 190
    registering new cultivars, 191
    storing pollen, 190
Hymenocallis, 21, 118–19, *154*
    caribaea, 155
    caroliniana (Inland spider-lily), 119
    narcissiflora (Peruvian daffodil), 119
    speciosa (Winter spice spider-lily), 155
Hypoxis, 119

I

Indian shot. *See Canna indica*
Indoor growing, 167
    containers for, 168

flowering bulbs for, 170–75
    increasing humidity, 168
    potting, 169–70
    problems for, 168–69
    soil recipe, 169
Inland spider-lily. *See Hymenocallis caroliniana*
Insects, 46, 47–49
Ipheion, 103–4
Iris, 10
    acutiloba, 31
    blooming times, 20
    classification of, 119–20
    cristata (Dwarf crested iris), 59, 63, 121
    culture, 120
    danfordiae (Miniature iris), 24, 104
    description of, 104, 119–24
    diseases and insects affecting, 46, 120–21
    ensata/kaempferi (Japanese iris), 121–22
    × *germanica* (Bearded iris), *111*, 122–23
    histrioides, 104
    paradoxa, 31
    persica, 31
    popular species, 121–24
    pseudacorus (Yellow flag), 123
    pumila (Dwarf bearded iris), *111*, 123
    reblooming, 124
    sibirica (Siberian iris), *57*, 123
    terms, 120
    xiphioides (English iris), 123–24
Iris reticulata (Dwarf iris), 11, 12
    blooming times, 20
    in containers, 24
    description of, 104
    for naturalizing, 56, 63
Iris tuberosa. *See Hermodactylus*
Italian arum. *See Arum*
Italian crocus. *See Crocus imperati*
Ixia, *114*, 124

J

Jack-in-the-pulpit. *See Arisaema triphyllum*
Jacobean lily. *See Sprekelia*
Japanese iris. *See Iris ensata/kaempferi*
Japanese Turk's-cap lily. *See Lilium hansonii*
Jekyll, Gertrude, 17–18
Jonquil. *See Narcissus jonquilla*

Petticoat narcissus. *See Narcissus bulbocodium*
pH, 36, 40
Phlox, *12*
Pineapple lily. *See Eucomis*
Planting
 container growing, 22–25
 depth, 37–38, *38*
 fall bulbs, 33
 height and color, selection and, 15–18, 23
 late, 34
 marking bulb location, 18–19, 42, *42*
 mulching, 39–40
 site, 34
 soil preparation, 34–36
 spring bulbs, 32–33
 summer bulbs, 33
 techniques, 37–39, *37, 39*
 tools, 36–37, *36*
Poet's narcissus. *See Narcissus poeticus*
Polianthes, 21, 155
Polystichum acrostichoides, 19
Poppy anemone. *See Anemone coronaria*
Powdery mildew, 45
Propagation
 of dahlias, 145
 of hyacinths, 79–80, *79*
 of liles, 130–31
 methods, 177–85
Purple trillium. *See Trillium erectum*
Puschkinia scilloides/libanotica (Striped Squill), 20, 24, 54, 59, 64, 106

R

Ramps. *See Allium tricoccum*
Ranunculus, *154*
 amplexicaulis, 12
 asiaticus (Persian buttercup), 21, 156
 description of, 155–56
Recordkeeping, 42
Red lily leaf beetle (*Lilliocerus lilii*), 47
Red spider lily. *See Lycoris radiata*
Regal lily. *See Lilium regale*
Repellents, natural, 49
Reproduction, 177
Rhizomes, 6, *6*, 181
Rock gardens, bulbs for, 11–12
Rodents, 37, 50

Rosenbach onion. *See Allium rosenbachianum*
Rosy onion. *See Allium roseum*
Rothschild gloriosa-lily. *See Gloriosa rothschildiana*
Rots, 46, 121
Row covers, 43, *43*
Royal fern. *See Osmunda regalis*
Rubellum lily. *See Lilium rubellum*

S

Saffron crocus. *See Crocus sativus*
Scales, 5, 8, 130–31
Scarborough lily. *See Vallota*
Scilla
 bifolia (Twin-leaf squill), 64, 106
 description of, 106–7
 litardierei/pratensis (Meadow squill), 64, 106
 mitschtschenkoana/tubergeniana, 20, 107
Scilla campanulata. *See Endymion hispanicus*
Scilla siberica
 blooming times, 20
 in containers, 24
 description of, 106
 for naturalizing, 64
 white, 4
Scorch, 121
Scotch crocus. *See Crocus biflorus*
Sea onion. *See Urginea maritima*
Seed, growing bulbs from, 183–85
Showy autumn crocus. *See Colchicum speciosum*
Showy/Japanese lily. *See Lilium speciosum*
Siberian iris. *See Iris sibirica*
Siberian squill. *See Scilla siberica*
Sicily cyclamen. *See Cyclamen cilicium*
Sierra lily. *See Lilium parvum*
Sinningia, 174–75
Slimleaf tulip. *See Tulipa linifolia*
Slugs, 48
Snails, 48
Snake's-head iris. *See Hermodactylus*
Snow crocus. *See Crocus chrysanthus*
Snowdrops. *See Galanthus*
Snowflake. *See Leucojum*
Soil
 for forcing bulbs, 67–68
 preparation, 34–36
 recipe for indoor growing, 169
Spanish bluebells. *See Endymion hispanicus*